E X P L O R I N G

Beyond Yellowstone

*Hiking, Camping, and Vacationing in
the National Forests surrounding
Yellowstone and Grand Teton*

Ron Adkison

WILDERNESS PRESS
BERKELEY

FIRST EDITION AUGUST 1996

Copyright © 1996 by Ron Adkison

Photos and maps by the author except as noted
Book design by Margaret Copeland
Cover design by Larry Van Dyke
Cover photo © 1996 by George Wuerthner
Back cover photo © 1996 by Sean Arbabi

Library of Congress Card Catalog Number 96-9265
International Standard Book Number 0-89997-180-6

Manufactured in the United States of America

Published by   Wilderness Press
               2440 Bancroft Way
               Berkeley, CA 94704
               (800) 443-7227
               Fax (510) 548-1355

               Write, call or fax for free catalog.

Front cover photo: **Looking toward Hell Roaring Plateau at head of Rock Creek.
Custer National Forest, Montana.**

Back cover photo: **Moose *(Alces alces).***

Frontispiece photo: **Brooks Lake and the Pinnacle Buttes.**

Library of Congress Cataloging-in-Publication Data

Adkison, Ron
    Exploring beyond Yellowstone: hiking, camping, and vacationing in the national forests
surrounding Yellowstone and Grand Teton / Ron Adkison. — 1st ed.
        p.   cm.
    Includes bibliographical references (p.   ) and index.
    ISBN 0-89997-180-6
    1. Outdoor recreation—Yellowstone National Park Region—Guidebooks. 2. Hiking—Yellowstone
National Park Region—Guidebooks. 3. Camping—Yellowstone National Park Region—Guidebooks.
4. Outdoor recreation—Wyoming—Grand Teton National Park Region—Guidebooks. 5. Hiking—
Wyoming—Grand Teton National Park Region—Guidebooks. 6. Camping—Wyoming—Grand Teton
National Park Region—Guidebooks. 7. Grand Teton National Park Region (Wyo.)—Guidebooks.
8. Yellowstone National Park Region—Guidebooks. I. Title
GV191.42.Y44A35   1996
917.87'52—dc20
                                                                          96-9265
                                                                          CIP

Acknowledgments

My family and I have lived in, hiked, camped, and explored the Greater Yellowstone area for several years, so when Wilderness Press agreed to publish this book, I thought I had already accomplished enough research to quickly produce a comprehensive guidebook to dayhikes and campgrounds in the region. I was wrong.

As I explored Greater Yellowstone during two summers, and digested many books—50 in all—I began to realize there is much more to this fascinating region than I had ever imagined.

Among the many people who helped me gain knowledge of Greater Yellowstone, I owe the greatest debt to the employees of the Forest Service at the Shoshone, Custer, Gallatin, Bridger-Teton, and Targhee national forests. Without them, this book would never have been completed.

My wife, Lynette, deserves great credit not only for the original idea for the book, but also for shouldering the burden of all the domestic responsibilities during my lengthy absences. Without the support and understanding of my wife and two children, this book would still be an unfulfilled dream.

I also wish to extend special thanks to those who offered their welcome company to Kelly (my border collie) and me on the trail: Jim Wood, Jason Van Hook, David Descombs, Chris Guyot, and Chafiq Itrib.

Ron Adkison
Dry Creek, Highland Mountains, Montana
May 1996

Hiking in the backcountry entails unavoidable risk that every hiker assumes and must be aware of and respect. The fact that a trail is described in this book is not a representation that it will be safe for you. Trails vary greatly in difficulty and in the degree of conditioning and agility one needs to enjoy them safely. On some hikes routes may have changed or conditions may have deteriorated since the descriptions were written. Also trail conditions can change even from day to day, owing to weather and other factors. A trail that is safe on a dry day or for a highly conditioned, agile, properly equipped hiker may be completely unsafe for someone else or unsafe under adverse weather conditions.

You can minimize your risks on the trail by being knowledgeable, prepared and alert. There is not space in this book for a general treatise on safety in the mountains, but there are a number of good books and public courses on the subject and you should take advantage of them to increase your knowledge. Just as important, you should always be aware of your own limitations and of conditions existing when and where you are hiking. If conditions are dangerous, or if you're not prepared to deal with them safely, choose a different hike! It's better to have wasted a drive than to be the subject of a mountain rescue.

These warnings are not intended to scare you off the trails. Millions of people have safe and enjoyable hikes every year. However, one element of the beauty, freedom and excitement of the wilderness is the presence of risks that do not confront us at home. When you hike you assume those risks. They can be met safely, but only if you exercise your own independent judgement and common sense.

TABLE OF CONTENTS

Campgrounds in This Book

Max. TL=maximum trailer length; Tb=tables; Tl=toilets; W=water; F=fire pits and/or grills; B=bear-resistant containers; BL=boat launch; Te=telephones; PR=paved access roads; FA=fishing access

Chapter One—Northwest

Campground	Location	Units	Fee	Dates Open	Max. TL	Facilities
1. Beaver Creek	Gallatin	65	Y	6/15-9/10	32'	Tb, Tl, W, B, F
2. Cabin Creek	Gallatin	15	Y	5/31-9/15	32'	Tb, Tl, W, F
3. Lonesomehurst	Gallatin	26	Y	5/31-9/15	32'	Tb, Tl, W, F, BL, Te, FA
4. Cherry Creek	Gallatin	6	N	5/31-10/15	N	Tb, Tl
5. Spring Creek	Gallatin	10	N	5/31-10/15	N	Tb, Tl, FA
6. Red Cliff	Gallatin	72	Y	5/31-9/10	25'	Tb, Tl, W, F, B, FA
7. Moose Flat	Gallatin	14	Y	5/31-9/10	25'	Tb, Tl, W, F, FA
8. Swan Creek	Gallatin	13	Y	5/31-9/10	25'	Tb, Tl, W, F, PR
9. Greek Creek	Gallatin	14	Y	5/31-9/10	25'	Tb, Tl, W, F, Te, FA
10. Spire Rock	Gallatin	18	N	5/31-9/10	N	Tb, Tl, F
11. Riverside	Targhee	57	Y	5/31-9/10	30'	Tb, Tl, W, F, B, PR, FA
12. Box Canyon	Targhee	19	Y	5/31-9/10	25'	Tb, Tl, W, F, FA
13. Buffalo	Targhee	127	Y	5/31-9/10	32'	Tb, Tl, W, F, B, PR, FA
14. Upper Coffeepot	Targhee	15	Y	5/31-9/10	25'	Tb, Tl, W, F, B, FA
15. Flat Rock	Targhee	40	Y	5/31-9/10	25'-35'	Tb, Tl, W, F, B, FA
16. Upper Lake	Red Rock Lks. NWR	12	N	5/31-10/1	N	Tb, Tl, W, F, FA

Chapter Two—Southwest

Campground	Location	Units	Fee	Dates Open	Max. TL	Facilities
17. Mike Harris	Targhee	12	Y	5/31-9/15	20'	Tb, Tl, W, F
18. Trail Creek	Targhee	11	Y	5/31-9/15	20'	Tb, Tl, W, F
19. Palisades Creek	Targhee	7	Y	5/31-9/15	30'	Tb, Tl, W, F
20. Alpine	Targhee	42	Y	5/31-9/15	24'-35'	Tb, Tl, W, F

Chapter Three—Southeast

Campground	Location	Units	Fee	Dates Open	Max. TL	Facilities
21. Atherton Creek	Bridger-Teton	19	Y	6/5-10/30	25'	Tb, Tl, W, F, PR, FA, BL
22. Red Hills	Bridger-Teton	5	Y	6/5-10/30	N	Tb, Tl, W, F, FA
23. Crystal Creek	Bridger-Teton	6	Y	6/5-10/30	20'	Tb, Tl, W, F, FA
24. Curtis Canyon	Bridger-Teton	12	Y	6/5-9/10	20'	Tb, Tl, W, F
25. Hoback	Bridger-Teton	14	Y	6/5-9/10	25'	Tb, Tl, W, F, PR, FA
26. Granite Creek	Bridger-Teton	52	Y	6/25-9/10	25'	Tb, Tl, W, F, FA
27. Kozy	Bridger-Teton	8	Y	6/5-9/10	18'	Tb, Tl, W, F, PR, FA
28. Sheffield Creek	Bridger-Teton	4	N	6/5-11/15	N	Tb, Tl, F, B
29. Turpin Meadow	Bridger-Teton	18	Y	6/1-10/31	25'	Tb, Tl, W, F, B, FA
30. Hatchet	Bridger-Teton	9	Y	6/25-9/10	25'	Tb, Tl, W, F, B
31. Falls	Shoshone	45	Y	6/1-10/30	32'	Tb, Tl, W, F, B
32. Pinnacle	Shoshone	21	Y	6/20-9/10	22'	Tb, Tl, W, F, B, FA
33. Brooks Lake	Shoshone	14	Y	6/20-9/30	22'	Tb, Tl, W, F, B, FA, BL

Chapter Four—North

Campground	Location	Units	Fee	Dates Open	Max. TL	Facilities
34. Tom Miner	Gallatin	16	Y	6/1-10/30	20'	Tb, Tl, W, F
35. Soda Butte	Gallatin	21	Y	6/15-9/15	20'	Tb, Tl, W, F, B
36. Colter	Gallatin	23	Y	6/15-9/15	20'	Tb, Tl, W, F, B
37. Chief Joseph	Gallatin	7	Y	6/15-9/15	15'	Tb, Tl, W, F, B
38. Fox Creek	Shoshone	27	Y	6/1-9/30	32'	Tb, Tl, W, F, B, FA
39. Crazy Creek	Shoshone	15	Y	6/1-10/20	32'	Tb, Tl, W, F, B, FA
40. Lake Creek	Shoshone	6	Y	7/1-9/7	22'	Tb, Tl, W, F, B
41. Hunter Peak	Shoshone	9	Y	6/1-11/30	32'	Tb, Tl, W, F, B, FA
42. Beartooth Lake	Shoshone	21	Y	7/1-9/7	32'	Tb, Tl, W, F, B, BL, FA
43. Island Lake	Shoshone	20	Y	7/1-9/7	32'	Tb, Tl, W, F, B, BL, FA
44. Parkside	Custer	25	Y	5/22-9/6	30'	Tb, Tl, W, F, B, PR, FA
45. Greenough Lake	Custer	18	Y	5/22-9/6	30'	Tb, Tl, W, F, B, PR, FA
46. Limber Pine	Custer	15	Y	5/22-9/6	30'	Tb, Tl, W, F, B, PR, FA
47. M-K	Custer	11	N	5/22-9/6	20'	Tb, Tl, F, FA
48. Basin	Custer	30	Y	5/22-9/6	25'	Tb, Tl, W, F, B, PR, FA
49. Cascade	Custer	30	Y	5/22-9/6	25'	Tb, Tl, W, F, B, FA

Chapter Five—East

Campground	Location	Units	Fee	Dates Open	Max. TL	Facilities
50. Big Game	Shoshone	17	Y	6/1-9/30	32'	Tb, Tl, W, F, B, PR, FA
51. Wapiti	Shoshone	41	Y	6/1-9/30	32'	Tb, Tl, W, F, B, PR, FA
52. Elk Fork	Shoshone	13	Y	6/1-9/30	22'	Tb, Tl, W, F, B, PR
53. Clearwater	Shoshone	7	Y	6/1-9/30	N	Tb, Tl, W, F, B, FA
54. Rex Hale	Shoshone	8	Y	6/1-9/30	16'	Tb, Tl, W, F, B, PR, FA
55. Newton Creek	Shoshone	31	Y	6/1-9/30	22'	Tb, Tl, W, F, B, FA
56. Eagle Creek	Shoshone	20	Y	6/1-9/30	22'	Tb, Tl, W, F, B, FA
57. Sleeping Giant	Shoshone	6	Y	6/15-9/30	22'	Tb, Tl, W, F, B, FA
58. Three Mile	Shoshone	20	Y	6/15-9/30	22'	Tb, Tl, W, F, FA
59. Pahaska	Shoshone	24	Y	6/15-9/30	22'	Tb, Tl, W, F

Trips in This Book

Chapter One—Northwest

Trip	Location	Distance	Difficulty	Use	Wildlife Viewing	Bear Danger	Back-pack	Mtn. Bike	Map/ Trailhd
1. Sheep Lake	Gallatin	13.0	Mod. stren.	Low	Good	Low	Y	N	1/1
2. Blue Danube & Avalanche Lakes	Gallatin	11.3-12.7	Mod. stren.	Low	Good	Low	Y	N	2/2
3. Red Canyon	Gallatin	1.0	Easy	Low	Good	Mod.	N	N	3/3
4. Tepee Creek	Gallatin	6.0	Mod.	Mod.	Good	Mod.	N	N	4/4
5. Golden Trout Lks.	Gallatin	5.0	Mod.	Low	Good	Low	Y	N	5/5
6. Lava Lake	Gallatin	5.8	Mod.	Mod.	Fair	Low	Y	N	6/6
7. Garnet Mtn. Look.	Gallatin	8.0	Stren.	Mod.	Good	Low	N	Y	6/7
8. Gallatin Rvrsid. Tr.	Gallatin	6.0	Easy	Mod.	Fair	Low	N	N	6/7
9. Coffin Lake	Gallatin	10.4	Mod.	Mod.	Good	Low	Y	N	7/8
10. Rock Creek Basin	Targhee	8.8	Mod. easy	Mod.	Fair	Low	N	Y	8/9
11. Hell Roaring Ck.	BLM-Dillon R.A.	6.4	Mod. easy	Low	Good	Low	N	N	9/10
12. Cliff Lake	Beaverhead	8.0	Mod. easy	Low	Good	Low	N	Y	10/11

Chapter Two—Southwest

Trip	Location	Distance	Difficulty	Use	Wildlife Viewing	Bear Danger	Back-pack	Mtn. Bike	Map/ Trailhd
13. Ski Lake	Bridger-Teton	4.8	Mod. easy	Heavy	Fair	Low	N	N	11/12
14. Coal Creek Mdws.	Targhee	4.8	Mod.	Mod.	Good	Low	Y	N	11/13
15. Oliver Peak	Targhee	8.6	Mod.	Low	Good	Low	N	Y	12/14
16. Wind & Ice Caves	Targhee	5.6 to 6.6	Mod.	Mod.	Good	Low	N	N	13/15
17. Lwr. Palisades Lk.	Targhee	8.5	Mod. easy	Mod.	Fair	Low	Y	N	14/16
18. Blowout Canyon	Targhee	2.4	Mod.	Low	Fair	Low	N	N	15/17

Chapter Three—Southeast

Trip	Location	Distance	Difficulty	Use	Wildlife Viewing	Bear Danger	Back-pack	Mtn. Bike	Map/ Trailhd
19. Red Hills	Bridger-Teton	3.0 to 3.8	Mod.	Low	Fair	Low	N	N	16/18
20. Grizzly Lake	Bridger-Teton	9.0	Mod.	Mod.	Good	Low	Y	N	16/19
21. Goodwin Lake	Bridger-Teton	6.0	Mod.	Heavy	Fair	Low	Y	N	17/20
22. Granite High Line	Bridger-Teton	7.5	Mod.	Low	Exc.	Low	N	N	18/21
23. Shoal Falls	Bridger-Teton	12.4	Stren.	Low	Exc.	Low	Y	N	18,19/21
24. Cliff Creek Falls	Bridger-Teton	11.8	Mod.	Low	Good	Low	N	Y	20/22
25. Roosevelt Mdws.	Bridger-Teton	9.0	Mod.	Low	Good	Low	Y	N	21/23
26. Huckleberry Mtn.	Bridger-Teton	11.0	Stren.	Low	Good	High	N	N	22/24
27. Up. Brooks Lk.	Bridger-Teton	7.0	Easy	Mod.	Fair	Mod.	Y	N	23/2
28. Jade Lakes	Bridger-Teton	4.6 to 5.3	Mod. easy	Heavy	Good	Mod.	Y	N	23/25
29. Bonneville Pass	Bridger-Teton	4.6	Easy	Mod.	Good	Mod.	N	N	23/26

Chapter Four—North

Trip	Location	Distance	Difficulty	Use	Wildlife Viewing	Bear Danger	Back-pack	Mtn. Bike	Map/ Trailhd
30. Petrified Forest Trail	Gallatin	2.0	Mod. easy	Mod.	Exc.	Mod.	N	N	24/27
31. Buffalo Horn Pass	Gallatin	4.6	Mod.	Low	Exc.	Mod.	N	Y	24/27
32. Lady of the Lake	Gallatin	4.8	Easy	Mod.	Good	Mod.	Y	N	25/28
33. Rock Island Lake	Gallatin	6.2	Mod. easy	Mod.	Good	Mod.	Y	N	26/29
34. Ivy Lake	Shoshone	8.2	Mod.	Mod.	Good	Mod.	Y	N	27/30
35. Granite Lake	Shoshone	9.6	Mod.	Mod.	Good	Mod.	Y	N	28/31
36. Native Lake	Shoshone	7.6	Mod.	Mod.	Good	Mod.	Y	N	28/32
37. Beauty Lake (from Beartoot Lake)	Shoshone	7.6	Mod.	Mod.	Good	Mod.	Y	N	29/33
38. Beauty Lake (from Island Lake)	Shoshone	6.0	Easy	Heavy	Fair	Mod.	Y	N	29/34
39. Stockade Lake	Shoshone	5.6	Mod. easy	Mod.	Good	Mod.	Y	N	30/35
40. Glacier Lake	Shoshone/Custer	3.2	Stren.	Mod.	Fair	Low	Y	N	31/36
41. Basin Lakes	Custer	7.6	Mod. stren.	Mod.	Fair	Low	Y	N	32/37
42. Timberline Lake	Custer	8.8	Mod. stren.	Mod.	Fair	Low	Y	N	33/38

Chapter Five—East

Trip	Location	Distance	Difficulty	Use	Wildlife Viewing	Bear Danger	Back-pack	Mtn. Bike	Map/ Trailhd
43. Elk Fork	Shoshone	6.2	Easy	Low	Good	Mod.	N	Y	34/39
44. Clearwater Creek	Shoshone	2.2	Easy	Low	Good	Mod.	N	Y	34/40
45. Blackwater Fire Mem.	Shoshone	7.2	Mod.	Mod.	Good	Mod.	N	N	35/41
46. Sam Berry Meadow	Shoshone	7.2	Mod. easy	Low	Good	Mod.	N	N	36/42

Upper Jade Lake

INTRODUCTION

The six national forests that surround Yellowstone and Grand Teton national parks are part of a vast region of magnificent Rocky Mountain landscapes that offer a wealth of diverse recreational opportunities, ranging from fishing and river rafting, to wildlife viewing, camping, scenic driving, sightseeing, mountain climbing, bicycling, and hiking.

At the heart of this region is our nation's oldest national park, Yellowstone. The park's most dominating feature is a vast volcanic plateau with an average elevation of 8,000 feet, and it is world famous for its steaming geysers and abundant wildlife. Sprawling across 2.2 million acres, Yellowstone is the second largest national park in the lower 48 states(only Death Valley is larger), but the park is only a part of a much greater, interconnected landscape.

From the Yellowstone Plateau, 13 mountain ranges and a score of high elevation river valleys radiate in all directions, like so many spokes on a wheel. To the west of the plateau are the Henrys Lake and Centennial mountains; the Madison and Gallatin ranges rise to the northwest. North and east of Yellowstone are the Beartooth and Absaroka ranges; to the southeast are the Gros Ventre, Salt River, Wyoming, and Wind River ranges. And in the south are the Teton, Snake River, and Big Hole mountains. Three major river systems—the Green-Colorado, the Snake-Columbia, and the Yellowstone-Missouri—and their tributaries, gather their waters from these highlands.

This mountainous landscape, located where Idaho, Wyoming, and Montana meet, and where the Middle and Northern Rocky Mountains merge, is called the Greater Yellowstone area. It is regarded as the largest relatively undisturbed ecosystem in the temperate climate zones of the Earth. Greater Yellowstone encompasses roughly 18 million acres, and includes two national parks, six national forests, three national wildlife refuges, and Bureau of Land Management, state, and private holdings.

Although no precise boundaries for Greater Yellowstone have been defined, it is fairly easy to visualize this geographically defined area. Greater Yellowstone encompasses the mountainous landscapes generally above 5,000 feet in elevation that surround Yellowstone and Grand Teton national parks. Bounding these mountainous lands are lower elevation, semi-arid valleys and prairies, covered by a sea of grass and sagebrush.

The Greater Yellowstone region is a land of superlatives. Here you will find the largest aggregation of wilderness lands—some six million acres—in the contiguous U.S., the largest undisturbed geothermal region, the most extensive petrified forests, the largest elk herds on Earth, and one of the world's few remaining free-ranging bison herds. Greater Yellowstone also contains critical habitat for rare and endangered species including grizzly bear, trumpeter swan, peregrine falcon, bald eagle, and the recently reintroduced gray wolf.

Yellowstone and Grand Teton national parks are not ecological islands. Standing alone, the two parks could not sustain the intricate web of life that exists in the Greater Yellowstone region. Just as the great forest fires of 1988 ignored the political boundaries that humans have imposed on this landscape, so do the thousands of bison, elk, deer, bighorn sheep, moose, and a variety of birds in their seasonal migrations. Forests, meadows, rivers, and streams do not simply end at park boundaries, but rather extend into the neighboring national forests where habitats, climate, and landforms are much the same. Geothermal features are not confined to Yellowstone National Park, and the aquifers that sustain them reach well beyond park boundaries.

More than 80% of the annual average of 10 million visitors to the region travel here from outside the tri-state area of Wyoming, Idaho, and Montana that comprises Greater Yellowstone. Grand Teton and Yellowstone national parks alone account for 7 million of those visitors.

Most park visitors are on a tight schedule imposed by a one– or two– week vacation. These visitors usually pass quickly along one of the nine major highways that lead through the surrounding national forests in anticipation of the grand spectacles of nature they expect to see in Yellowstone and Grand Teton. Although the two parks are jewels in the crown of the national park system, some of the best hiking and camping opportunities lie beyond the parks, in the national forests of Greater Yellowstone. Not everyone comes to Yellowstone and Grand Teton to hike, but those who intend to do so may be deterred by the large number of hikers who pound the parks' trails. Moreover, most of Yellowstone's trails pass through dense, nearly viewless, lodgepole-pine forests, and many of Grand Teton's trails require strenuous ascents of up to 4,000 feet through precipitous canyons to reach the alpine high country. Most visitors simply do not have the time or desire to plan an extended trip and hike for several days into some of America's wildest and relatively unknown lands.

This guidebook focuses on the national forest lands of Greater Yellowstone, a wild, grand and mountainous landscape that harbors scenery and wildlife comparable to those in Yellowstone and Grand Teton national parks. The 46 dayhikes included here represent the best short hikes outside the parks. Most of the dayhikes and the 59 national forest campgrounds described in this book are easily accessible, lying alongside or near the region's major highways.

This book fills the needs of visitors who wish to extend their stay in Greater Yellowstone's national forests while dayhiking, camping, or simply basking among some of nature's finest examples of wild and unspoiled mountain scenery.

Black bear and other wildlife are abundant in Greater Yellowstone

USING THIS BOOK

Trail Descriptions

The **Distance** figures show the total distance of a trip. In a round trip, you retrace your outbound route. A loop trip involves no retracing.

Low/High Elevation figures give you an idea of how much you'll climb and descend.

The **Difficulty** rating is based on the average hiker's ability to walk over rugged terrain at high elevations. Hikers in poor physical condition may find a hike rated moderate to be quite strenuous.

The **Use** classification shows the average level of use a trail receives. Low use suggests that you may meet fewer than five other groups on the trail per day; moderate means five to ten groups per day; and heavy means ten or more groups are likely to be seen on the trail each day.

The **Suited For** classification tells whether the trip is 1) a dayhike, 2) a dayhike or backpack (a trail that can be completed in a day, but also offers good backcountry camping and perhaps fishing), or 3) a mountain bike trip. Only trails that are open to mountain bikes and also well-suited for a bicycle trip are suggested for this classification.

Best Season shows the months in which there is the greatest probability of fair weather and snow-free tread. Stream depth levels noted in the trip descriptions indicate the average flow during the *Best Season*.

Wildlife Viewing is rated as fair, good, or excellent. A "fair" rating shows a low probability of seeing wildlife, due to factors including poor habitat and heavy forest cover. A "good" rating indicates a a 50/50 chance of observing wildlife, and an "excellent" rating means you are very likely to see wildlife along the trail.

The **Grizzly Bear Danger** rating gives you an idea of the likelihood of encountering a grizzly on the trail. A low rating means grizzlies are rarely, if ever, seen along the trail. A moderate rating shows it's possible to meet a grizzly, and a high rating means the trail passes through prime grizzly bear habitat and special precautions should be followed. Remember—grizzlies may be encountered anywhere in Greater Yellowstone (see *Hiking in Grizzly Country*, pg. 8).

Map/Trailhead shows the trip's map and trailhead numbers on the book's maps. Large numbers on maps are the trip number, and small numbers are the trailhead number.

Nearest Campgrounds show the national forest campgrounds closest to the trailhead.

Campground descriptions

Under **Location** for each campground is its general location in a mountain range or canyon, and the national forest ranger district that administers the site. Many campgrounds' driving directions are under the "Location" heading, but some are not. For campgrounds located at trailheads or along trailhead access roads, driving directions are given in the *Driving to the Trailhead* section for hiking trips. The number of the hiking trip to see for directions is also listed.

Facilities gives you a general idea of what to expect in campgrounds, such as paved or gravel roads, whether a fee is charged, and the maximum length of a trailer (or motor home) that a campground can accommodate. "Facilities" also includes information on the availability of water, tables, toilets, and fire pits (located on the ground) or fire grills (located on a stand above the ground). Some campground fire pits have removable grills, and are called fire pits with grills in this book.

Dates Usually Open indicates the season for each campground. Dates can vary due to snow conditions and other factors. Visitors planning to use a campground toward either end of the season should contact the appropriate ranger district office before their trip and make sure the site will be open.

The Setting tells about the scenery at a campground, its forest cover (if any), near-by rivers, lakes, and streams, proximity to busy highways, and other facts to help you choose the site that best meets your needs and expectations.

Campsite at Spring Creek Campground, Hebgen Lake

HIKING IN GREATER YELLOWSTONE

Most visitors to Greater Yellowstone spend only a day or two in the national parks, trying to see as much scenery from their cars, from roadside turnouts, and from short nature trails as they can squeeze into their vacations. Unfortunately, few visitors slow down long enough to savor and truly appreciate the unspoiled scenery that surrounds them. Yet no one visiting the region should miss the fabulous natural attractions of either national park. Those who wish to spend some of their time at a slower pace, away from busy park roads, large and noisy campgrounds, and crowded trails, will enjoy the national forests of Greater Yellowstone.

The 46 dayhikes in this guidebook are easily accessible, and the trails are well-defined and easy to follow. They avoid major stream fords and, as much as possible, prime grizzly bear habitat. The dayhikes vary in length from 1 to 13 miles, with scenery ranging from deep canyons to lofty ridges; from cool, peaceful forests to wildflower-rich meadows; and from glacier-gouged basins and timberline lakes to windswept alpine peaks.

These trails penetrate the fringes of both federally designated and de-facto wilderness areas, including the Lee Metcalf Wilderness in Montana, the Absaroka-Beartooth Wilderness in Montana and Wyoming, and the North Absaroka, Washakie, Teton, Gros Ventre, and Jedediah Smith wilderness areas in Wyoming. There are hikes here in most of the major mountain ranges of Greater Yellowstone: the Centennial, Henrys Lake, Madison, Gallatin, Beartooth, Absaroka, Gros Ventre, Wyoming, Snake River, and Teton ranges.

All the dayhikes can be taken by anyone in good physical condition, provided they are acclimated to the region's high elevations. Some hiking trips offer scenic destinations and good camping areas, providing the opportunity for an extended stay for those who come prepared to backpack.

Hiking in Greater Yellowstone is much the same as hiking in other regions of the mountainous West, with one exception: the presence of the grizzly bear. Although the hikes in this book attempt to avoid grizzly-occupied areas, grizzlies range widely in search of food and you could encounter one along some of the region's trails, particularly those near Yellowstone National Park. Some basic knowledge of grizzly bears and how to avoid encounters with them is your best insurance for a safe trip into grizzly country (see *Hiking in Grizzly Country*, pg. 8).

Beyond the roadways of Greater Yellowstone, keep in mind that you are entering wild country. Although hiking here is not inherently dangerous, there is no guarantee of safety. Rockfalls, thunderstorms, snowfields, falling snags, swollen streams, sudden wet and cold weather, and grizzly bears are some of the hazards you could encounter on the trail. Although the risks are minimal, awareness and recognition of hazardous situations will help to insure a safe trip.

Stream Crossings

There are few streams requiring fords—except in early summer—along trails described in this book. Streams that aren't bridged usually require no more than a rock-hop or a log crossing. Keep in mind that logs or rocks when wet are slippery, and may be more dangerous than a ford. There are a few streams that require a ford, but these are typically shallow and are easily waded across.

During early summer, streams will be running high with snowmelt. If you encounter a raging torrent across your trail, your best decision may be to turn around and go back to the trailhead, saving the trail for another day, or choosing an alternate trail to take. In forested areas, particularly in areas hosting Engelmann spruce, you may find a fallen tree

Fallen logs afford dry crossings of many streams

lying across the stream, since these shallow-rooted spruces frequently topple.

If you must ford a stream, search for a place where the stream's waters are wide, slow moving, and shallow. Plan your course before entering the water. Find a stout staff to use as a "third leg" to aid your balance on the slippery stream bed. Don't cross in your boots; wearing wet boots invites painful rubs and blisters. If you expect a major stream ford, pack sandals or lightweight shoes. Turn sideways to minimize your resistance to the current, and proceed with caution and attention to obstacles in the stream bed.

Drinking Water

You should carry water on any trip in this book, rather than drinking from streams and lakes. Even in the pristine backcountry of Greater Yellowstone, various microscopic bacteria and protozoans may be present in surface water supplies, most notably Giardia lamblia, which can cause a miserable intestinal illness. Its symptoms, including nausea, cramps, and diarrhea, usually appear one to three weeks after exposure, and though the illness is treatable, suffering

the symptoms isn't worth the risk of drinking untreated water. One to two quarts per person should be enough for most day-hikes in this book.

Backpackers, however, must rely on purifying backcountry water sources for their drinking and cooking needs. The pump-type water filters that are widely available at backpacking and sporting goods stores are the easiest and best means of treating backcountry water. Select a filter with a pore size of 0.4 micrometers or less, which will insure filtration of Giardia cysts.

Mosquitoes

Mosquitoes are ubiquitous throughout Greater Yellowstone from June through mid-August. During that time an effective insect repellent is a necessity, whether you're on a trail or in a campground. The most effective repellents contain at least 90% of the strong chemical DEET. If you prefer to use a natural product, however, those containing citronella as the main ingredient are most effective.

Dogs

Many visitors to Greater Yellowstone bring the family dog, either by choice or by necessity. Dogs aren't allowed on trails in the national parks, but your dog can join you on trails in the national forests.

If you take your dog on the trail, keep it on a leash at all times to avoid harassing wildlife and other hikers. An uncontrolled dog could provoke an attack by a grizzly bear, but dogs, with their acute sense of smell, can often detect a nearby bear before you can, thereby helping you to avoid a surprise encounter.

Equestrians

Equestrians frequently use the trails of Greater Yellowstone. When you meet pack or saddle stock on the trail, yield the right-of-way. Avoid conflicts with equestrians by stepping well off the trail, on the downhill side if terrain permits. Speak in a normal tone of voice so the animals will know you're there and not become frightened.

Before Setting Out on the Trail

- Allow two or three days to acclimate to Greater Yellowstone's high elevations. The average elevation of Yellowstone National Park is 8,000 feet, and many trails in this book ascend to elevations of up to 10,000 feet.
- Study the maps and descriptions in this guidebook to familiarize yourself with your chosen hiking area.
- Check with the appropriate ranger station for updated weather forecasts, trail conditions, and grizzly bear activity.
- Allow ample time to reach your destination and return to the trailhead before dark. Hiking on steep trails at high elevations may take longer than you expect.
- Be prepared and carry appropriate equipment in your day pack. Wear sturdy hiking boots—not running shoes, and wear a hat and sunglasses to protect yourself from the intense sunshine at high elevations. Carry a first-aid kit, a waterproof parka or poncho, insect repellent, water, sunscreen, a sweater or lightweight parka, a small flashlight, and plenty of food.
- Be sure to purchase the required fishing license for all persons over 12 years of age for the state in which you intend to fish. Licenses are available that allow you to fish for one day, a week, or the entire season. You can purchase a fishing license in most communities surrounding Greater Yellowstone. Obtain a copy of state fishing regulations when you purchase your license.

On the Trail

- Avoid walking out of the trailbed, even if it is muddy, wet, or snow-covered. Leaving the trailbed leads to the creation of multiple paths and destroys vegetation. Restrain the urge to shortcut switchbacks. Shortcuts also destroy trailside vegetation, and their steep paths become runoff channels that erode slopes and undermine trails.

- Don't leave established trails and travel cross-country unless you are an experienced hiker and capable of routefinding with a topographic map and compass.
- Refrain from picking wildflowers; their color and fragrance fade rapidly after picking. Simply enjoy them or photograph them, leaving the flowers for others to enjoy, and so they can complete their blooming cycle and perpetuate the beauty of the area.
- Stay together on the trail; there is safety in numbers in grizzly country.
- Loose rock and narrow trails on steep slopes require constant attention. Use caution when hiking in burned areas. Snags sometimes topple unexpectedly, and can fall even if the wind is light.
- Don't take unnecessary chances in the backcountry. If darkness is approaching, if a thunderstorm threatens, if a swollen stream or snow blocks your way, or if you encounter signs of grizzly activity, wise hikers will return to the trailhead.
- Always pack out your trash, and food scraps that may attract animals. Bears conditioned to human food are a menace to hikers, and usually are destroyed by authorities.

Backpacking

- Study the regulations for the wilderness area in which you plan to travel. A list of wilderness regulations is at the end of each chapter.
- A reliable tent is almost a necessity for protection from unpredictable weather, and from hordes of blood-thirsty mosquitoes until late season. Although a tent is not resistant to bears, it can offer a measure of safety: studies have shown that people sleeping in tents are less likely to be injured by a grizzly bear than people sleeping without shelter. Since bears sometimes bite or claw at a tent, it is a good idea to have a roomy one that allows some space between you and the tent's walls.
- Use a backpack stove. Watching the alpenglow engulf the high peaks in

vivid color or star gazing after dark is far more rewarding than staring into the flames of a campfire. If you must build a fire, do so only if dead and down wood is abundant, and use existing fire rings instead of building new ones. Build fires on bare mineral soil, not in meadows. Extinguish your fire with water and be sure the ashes are cold before breaking camp.

• Choose a campsite at least 200 feet from trails, lakes, streams, and other campers. Select a durable site, in a forested or sandy area. Avoid camping on delicate meadow vegetation.

• Bring a large jug or water bag to reduce the number of trips you make to the water source. Lakeshore and streamside vegetation is fragile and is easily damaged.

• Wash dishes and yourself at least 200 feet from lakes and streams. Avoid using soap; even biodegradable soaps can pollute water sources. Sand and gravel are quite effective for cleaning cookware.

• Bury human waste in a hole 6-8 inches deep, and at least 200 feet from your campsite, trails, and water sources or potential watercourses. A small plastic garden trowel works well for this purpose.

Hiking in Grizzly Country

The great grizzly bear is synonymous with wild, unspoiled country, and some 200 grizzlies inhabit the wilds of Greater Yellowstone. The bulk of this population is centered in Yellowstone National Park and in the Teton Wilderness, the Absaroka Range, and the southern reaches of the Absaroka-Beartooth Wilderness.

However, grizzlies require vast stretches of wilderness in which to survive, and they range widely from about April until November in search of food. Although the hiking trips in this guidebook attempt to avoid prime grizzly habitat, on some hikes there remains a chance that you may encounter a bear. A "Grizzly Bear Danger" rating is given for each hike, based on the probability of grizzlies being in the area.

All visitors to Greater Yellowstone should heed the warnings of Yellowstone National Park officials that wild animals are potentially dangerous, and should not be approached closely. Nevertheless, too many visitors disregard those warnings, and each year some people are seriously injured or killed by wild animals, particularly by bison in Yellowstone.

Statistically, you stand a greater chance of being injured on the region's highways than by a grizzly. From 1900 to 1979, grizzly bears inflicted injuries on only 56 people in Yellowstone National Park, an average of less than one injury per year.

Black bears also inhabit Greater Yellowstone, and they should be treated with respect, though they are far less likely than grizzlies to attack hikers. Grizzlies are well known for aggressive behavior, but they don't typically seek out hikers and attack them.

Just like people, individual grizzly bears vary widely in their behavior. Some are more aggressive than others, but all bears are unpredictable. Grizzlies may behave aggressively or attack if you approach too closely and they perceive you to be a threat.

Before setting out on any hike in Greater Yellowstone, telephone or visit the appropriate ranger district office to ask about recent bear activity along your route. If grizzlies have recently been seen along your trail, choose another trail instead of taking the risk of an encounter.

Hikers are safer when traveling in groups of four or more. Grizzlies find large numbers of people intimidating, and are less likely to act aggressively toward groups. People who hike alone in grizzly country are assuming the greatest risk of injury if they encounter an aggressive bear.

To avoid a surprise encounter with a grizzly, you should announce your presence, particularly in places of heavy forest cover and on winding trails, where visibility is limited to only a short distance ahead. Some hikers attach bells to their packs, but the constant jingling of a bell can be very irritating, and the sound doesn't carry very far. Instead, use a bell only when approaching blind

Black bear tracks. Notice the wedge-shaped indentation on the instep of the hind foot (left), and the short claw prints.

spots in the trail, or briefly engage in louder-than-normal conversation, or even singing. Although excessive noise is out of character with the wilderness experience, it is preferable to the alternative of a surprise meeting with a grizzly.

Be alert while on the trail. Don't hike after dark, when grizzlies are most active. Watch for signs of grizzly activity during your hike. Both black and grizzly bears turn over rocks and tear apart logs and stumps in search of insects, but only grizzlies dig for roots and bulbs, and for small animals in their burrows.

The shape of the tracks is the surest way to determine what species of bear left them. The toe prints of a black bear form a pronounced arc, and the individual toes are noticeably separate. A grizzly bear's toes

form a straighter line, and the toe prints are joined. Grizzly bears have long front claws, rarely less than 1.75 inches long, whereas the claws of black bears seldom exceed 1.5 inches, so the distance between the toe prints and the imprint of the claws is greater in a grizzly track. The back foot of a grizzly has a triangle shape, with a pointed heel. Black bears have a prominent wedge in the instep of their back feet.

Some people carry firearms into grizzly country for protection. A gun, however, can give you a false sense of security, and unless you are an expert capable of shooting

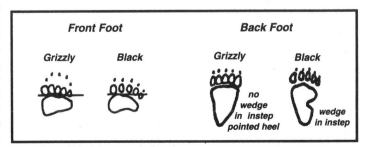

Grizzly and black bear track shapes

to kill a charging grizzly moving at speeds of up to 30 miles per hour, leave your gun at home. A wounded grizzly will become enraged and will vigorously attack you. Moreover, grizzlies are protected under the Endangered Species Act, and it is unlawful to shoot them.

An alternate form of protection is a cap-saicin-based bear repellent spray, and veteran bear country hikers never leave the trailhead without it. This spray is available in canisters with a holster that attaches to your belt. You can find it in most sporting goods stores in the gateway communities of Greater Yellowstone. The spray contains a strong irritant derived from cayenne peppers, and in recent years its use has stopped several charging grizzlies in their tracks. The results of using this repellent may vary, and its range is limited to about 15 feet, so it should be used only as a last resort; don't bet your life on its effectiveness.

If you spot a grizzly from the trail, try to remain calm. If the bear is not aware of you, leave the area quietly, detour widely around it or, better still, terminate your hike and return to the trailhead. If a grizzly detects your presence at a distance, it may either ignore you, stand on its hind legs and try to decide what you are (grizzlies have limited eyesight but a strong sense of smell), or run away.

In the unlikely event that you are confronted with a grizzly at close range, your actions, based on what the bear does, may influence the outcome of the encounter. Try to restrain the urge to run from a bear. Running will trigger the predatory instincts of the bear, and you can't outrun a bear that can travel faster than 40 feet per second. Look for climbable trees nearby, but you will need time to find a suitable tree and then climb well out of reach of the bear.

Sometimes grizzlies will charge. Occasionally these are "bluff" charges, in which the bear breaks off the charge, stops suddenly, or runs past you. A bear may charge repeatedly but never make contact with you. If confronted with a charging bear, you can stand your ground, move

slowly away, or use your repellent spray. Stay quiet or talk calmly, and try to remain unthreatening to the bear.

If a bear attacks you, as a last resort you must play dead. Drop to the ground and curl into a ball, with your hands locked together behind your neck, and your knees tucked tightly against your chest. Your pack will offer some protection for your back. Many people survive bear attacks by playing dead, but it takes hidden reserves of courage you may not realize you have.

A grizzly may bite or claw at you, and despite the pain and terror, it is important to remain as quiet and still as possible. When the bear feels that you are no longer a threat, it will probably wander off. Don't move until you are sure the bear is gone, or it may return and attack you again.

Although the above information may frighten some people away from hiking in Greater Yellowstone, the chances of seeing a grizzly are remote. But if you ever encounter one of the great bears on a trail, these guidelines could help save your life. If you intend to do any extensive hiking in grizzly country, read Stephen Herero's excellent book on bear attacks, listed in the *Suggested Reading* at the end of this book.

Backpackers must take additional precautions against bears while in camp. Although it's black bears that more commonly raid backcountry campsites for food, food odors can attract a grizzly as well. Your cooking area should be at least 100 yards from your tent. Better still, consider cooking your evening meal on the trail, then hiking another mile or two to a campsite. Keep food odors away from your tent and sleeping bag, and change out of your "cooking clothes" before retiring to your tent.

Hang all of your food, cooking utensils, cooking clothes, and any other odorous items, in a tree by bearbagging them. Use the counterbalance method rather than tying off one end of your rope to a tree. To properly bearbag your food, you will need one or two stuffsacks, and about 50 feet of nylon parachute cord. Tie one end of the cord to a rock and throw it over a tree limb at least 16 feet off the ground and 6 feet away from the trunk. Remove the rock and tie the heavier stuffsack onto that end of the cord. Hoist that stuffsack up to the tree limb, then tie a rock or another full stuffsack to the cord you are holding, as high up as you can reach. Tie a loop in the cord and stuff the excess cord into the second stuffsack. Then, with a long stick, push the second stuffsack up until both are suspended at least 10 feet off the ground. To retrieve your food, use the stick to reach the loop you tied in the cord and pull it down.

Weather and Hiking Seasons

From November through May, much of the Greater Yellowstone landscape is blanketed by several feet of snow, rendering its wilderness areas inaccessible to all but the cross-country skier or snowshoer. But by June, most low to mid-elevations are free of snow, and rivers and streams are running full with meltwater from the high mountains. Deep snow lingers in the high country, particularly in cirque basins, and on north- and east-facing slopes, until mid-July. As early as September in some years, but more typically by October, snow again begins to accumulate in the high mountains, making trails in the higher elevations impassable.

The hiking season in Greater Yellowstone is limited, ranging from about four months of snow-free hiking on low elevation trails, to only six weeks to two months on the highest trails in the Beartooth Mountains. Each hiking trip in this guidebook suggests the optimum season for that trail, with the highest probability of fair weather and snow-free tread.

Most visitors come to Greater Yellowstone between mid-June and mid-September, with peak visitation occurring from the last week of July until the third week of August. Summers in the region are mild, with daytime highs averaging from 70-80 degrees F., and nighttime lows averaging around 40. Frost can occur at times during summer, usually after a cold front. At high elevations in the backcountry, frost can be expected overnight any time during the summer.

Precipitation in Greater Yellowstone is highly variable, and its distribution is influenced by the region's mountainous topography. Most storm systems enter the region from the west or northwest, so west-facing slopes and higher elevations capture most of the available moisture from passing storms. The east slopes lie in a rain shadow created by the mountains, and remain relatively dry. For example, Gardiner, Montana, at an elevation of 5,280 feet in the rain shadow east of the Gallatin Range, receives an annual average of only 12 inches of precipitation. By contrast, the southwest corner of Yellowstone National Park, in the Bechler River region, forms the first major mountain mass east of the Snake River Plain in Idaho. When storms cross the plain and reach the edge of the Yellowstone Plateau in the Bechler River region, the clouds rise, the air cools, and large quantities of moisture fall, amounting to an annual average of 70 inches, most of it as winter snow.

During July and August, afternoon thunderstorms are common. Moist, subtropical air masses from the south and southwest, combined with rising thermal air currents from hot lowland valleys, lead to the development of cumulus clouds that can build up very rapidly and can become thunderstorms. Thunderstorms are frequently accompanied by heavy—but usually isolated—rain showers, hail, and possibly snow, strong winds, and lightning. Thunderstorms are typically short, and usually end before midnight, though lingering showers sometimes persist through the night.

Most trails remain open through September, and in some years, until about mid-October. After Labor Day, you're likely to meet few other hikers in the backcountry, and some national forest campgrounds will be closed. Be prepared for periods of snow and cold temperatures during September. These cold spells are usually short-lived, and are often followed by warm, sunny days, and clear, cold nights.

CAMPING IN GREATER YELLOWSTONE

The 59 national forest campgrounds described in this guidebook are either at or near the trailheads for the 46 hiking trips. All the campgrounds are in scenic locations. They range from undeveloped sites where you can camp free of charge, to developed sites with drinking water, tables, fire grills, toilets, and garbage containers, where a fee is charged, ranging from $5 to $8 per night. An additional fee is required for more than one vehicle in most campground sites. Some larger campgrounds can accommodate small trailers and motor homes, but many smaller campgrounds can't. There are no electrical hookups or dumping facilities for RV's in national forest campgrounds.

Visitors are also free to camp in informal, undeveloped campsites throughout the national forests of Greater Yellowstone, except in areas posted for no camping or for day use only. Most of these informal sites are along short spur roads that branch off forest roads and highways. Some may be merely parking places, with only enough room to park your vehicle. If using such a site, be sure to carry out your trash, and use extra caution with your campfires.

Don't expect to find firewood in the national forest campgrounds; years of use have depleted supplies. Some forest roads leading to trailheads offer opportunities to collect dead and down wood for your campfire.

Since Greater Yellowstone has both black and grizzly bears, campers must protect their food supply when away from camp and at night. Much of Greater Yellowstone in Montana and Wyoming lies within the Grizzly Bear Recovery Area, where protecting your food supply is a legal requirement. A list of regulations pertaining to food storage is posted at campgrounds lying within the recovery area.

Some campgrounds located in areas frequented by grizzlies offer bear resistant food storage boxes, and you should use them. If food storage containers are not present, store your food, cookware, and ice chest in the trunk of your car. If you store your food in the cabin of your vehicle, be sure the windows and doors are tightly closed, and cover it with a tablecloth or blanket to keep it out of sight. Bears are intelligent creatures, and those conditioned to camp fare know what an ice chest is, and that dinner is likely to be inside.

Be a good neighbor when staying in a campground. Don't be noisy, and respect the privacy of other campers. Observe the "quiet hours" from 10 P.M. to 6 A.M.—a rule enforced by campground hosts. Dogs must be leashed at all times.

Yellowstone and Grand Teton have many campgrounds, but they do not have enough space to accommodate all the park visitors who wish to use them in July and August. Then park campgrounds fill early each day, and as disappointed campers leave the parks, they seek out the national forest campgrounds close to the parks. Consequently, campgrounds located between the east entrance to Yellowstone and Cody, those located along the Beartooth Highway beyond the northeast entrance of the Park, and campgrounds near West Yellowstone are the most popular in the region and usually fill by late afternoon or evening each day during peak season.

Campsites at several campgrounds listed in this book can be reserved several months in advance. Each chapter tells you which campgrounds have reservation sites, and gives a toll-free telephone number for reservations.

THE WILDLIFE OF GREATER YELLOWSTONE

The Greater Yellowstone region is known throughout the world as a premier wildlife sanctuary, and here you will find the finest wildlife viewing in the lower 48 states. With the exception of the black-footed ferret, Greater Yellowstone contains its complete historical array of vertebrate species.

More than 12 species of reptiles and amphibians, 94 species of mammals, and some 300 species of birds inhabit the region at least part of the year. Many birds and large mammals, however, migrate beyond Greater Yellowstone during the winter.

Humans first entered the region about 10,000 years ago, and it was the abundance of wildlife that lured them here. Today the region is still rich with wildlife that visitors expect to see. For many, wildlife viewing is the primary objective of their trip to Greater Yellowstone. Most animals, however, are hidden from view in the folds of canyons, in the forests, and high among the mountain peaks. The large, open valleys and meadows of Yellowstone Park and adjacent areas offer the best opportunities for roadside wildlife viewing. May and June are the best months for viewing a variety of large mammals and birds from the region's highways. Hikers in the backcountry stand a better chance of observing wildlife, including moose, mule deer, elk, coyote, and possibly bears, among other creatures.

Many visitors to Yellowstone are likely to experience a "wildlife traffic jam." The typical scenario begins when some visitors spot any large animal near a roadside. They quickly stop their cars and abandon them in the roadway, as do others who soon follow. Then, with video cameras whirring and shutters clicking, with shouts and loud voices, a crowd of people begins to converge on the confused and frightened animal. Not only do situations like this put unnecessary stress on the animal; people are putting themselves in danger. No matter how docile wild animals may seem, they are still wild, and they will defend themselves if they feel threatened. Nearly every year some people are seriously injured or killed by wild animals in Greater Yellowstone.

Treat wildlife with respect. Maintain a reasonable distance, and avoid loud noises and sudden movements. For wildlife photography, remain still and hidden, and use a telephoto lens instead of approaching closely.

Ungulates

Bison are symbolic of the wide open spaces of the West, and they once ranged across the Great Plains by the millions. Many Native American tribes depended on the bison for food, clothing, and raw materials. Today only a remnant of the once vast bison population survives in Greater Yellowstone—some of the world's few remaining free-roaming bison herds. Some 2,500 bison inhabit Yellowstone, and about 125 make their home in Grand Teton National Park. Few roam beyond the park's boundaries, except during winter when some of the Yellowstone herds migrate to their winter ranges near West Yellowstone and Gardiner, Montana.

All the other large mammals present in Greater Yellowstone can be found both inside and outside the national parks, excepting the mountain goat, a nonnative species introduced into suitable habitats to the north and south of the parks. Some 90,000 elk live in Greater Yellowstone, but during summer they dwell in the meadows and basins high in the mountains, and are not frequently observed along area highways. The largest member of the deer family, the Shira's moose, is one of the most commonly observed large mammals, both alongside roadways and from backcountry trails. They frequent marshy ponds and willow thickets.

Visitors traveling through Wyoming are likely to see hundreds of pronghorn antelope, but their range in Greater Yellowstone is restricted to the grassy foothills and valleys that border the region. Mule deer are widely distributed throughout Greater Yellowstone, and with an estimated population of some 88,000 they are second only to elk in numbers. Mule deer can be observed throughout the region, from grassy foothills to the highest mountains.

Mountain goats, with their long, white, shaggy coats, and dagger-like horns, are denizens of lofty alpine heights. Goats were introduced into the region and now thrive in the Madison Range, the Absaroka-Beartooth Wilderness, and the Snake River Range. Rocky Mountain bighorn sheep are reclusive inhabitants of alpine ridges and plateaus, where cliffs and outcrops allow them to retreat from danger. Primarily grazers of alpine vegetation in summer, they winter in lower elevations on south-facing exposures that provide both food and safety. Bighorns occupy parts of all the mountain ranges of Greater Yellowstone except the Centennial Mountains and the Snake River Range.

Predators

The grizzly bear, like the bison, epitomizes the vast wilderness that was once the American West. Respected and feared by ancient peoples and modern visitors alike, the great bear is the most dangerous wild mammal in the lower 48 states. Once widespread throughout western North America, from the eastern edge of the Great Plains to the Pacific Ocean, and from the Arctic to Mexico, grizzlies have been reduced to a remnant population of only about 1,000 animals in the contiguous U.S. An estimated 200 grizzlies occupy Greater Yellowstone.

Grizzled means grayish, and the grizzly's fur is often tipped with flecks of gray or white—hence the name "silvertip." Grizzlies typically weigh 300-600 pounds, though much larger individuals have been reported, and when standing they can reach a height of up to 8 feet. These bears are only occasionally sighted in Greater Yellowstone. They are omnivorous, eating both plants and animals. Black bears also range through-

out the region, typically in forested areas, but they tend to avoid areas occupied by grizzlies.

Coyotes are common in Greater Yellowstone, from the sagebrush-clad valleys to alpine heights. They are occasionally seen beside roadways and along backcountry trails. Other predators are present in Greater Yellowstone but are seldom observed. These include the mountain lion, bobcat, lynx, wolverine, pine marten, badger, striped skunk, river otter, mink, short-tailed and long-tailed weasels, raccoon, and red fox. The gray wolf, reintroduced into Yellowstone in 1995, may be seen or heard on occasion, in the future, if they are successful in repopulating the region.

Rodents

Visitors often overlook the rodents of Greater Yellowstone in favor of the large mammals and the abundant birds. But most campers and hikers are likely to have numerous encounters with rodents during their visit to the region. From the shrill whistle of the yellow-bellied marmot to the echoing screech of the pika in alpine environs; from the sudden chatter of the red squirrel to the muffled hiss of a startled porcupine in the forest; and from the rustling of mice in your backpack at night to the food-begging antics of the golden-mantled ground squirrel and least chipmunk at your campsite, rodents will likely be your most frequent wild companions both on the trail and in the campground.

The golden mantled ground squirrel is a frequent companion in camp

Beavers, the largest rodents in the West, were the focus of the Rocky Mountain fur trade during the early part of the 19th Century. Nearly trapped to extinction, beavers have made a comeback in Greater Yellowstone. Although they are seldom seen, their dams, ponds, and other results of their handiwork can often be observed along streams bordered by willows, aspens, and cottonwoods.

Reptiles and Amphibians

Reptiles and amphibians are uncommon in Greater Yellowstone, due in part to the cold climate. The spotted frog and boreal toad are the most common amphibians. The boreal toad is an inhabitant of subalpine areas up to timberline. The wandering garter snake is seen in moist areas near streambanks and lakeshores. This aquatic snake feeds on frogs, tadpoles, fish, and insects. The only poisonous snake in the region is the prairie rattlesnake, but it is seldom seen above the low elevation fringes of Greater Yellowstone.

Fish

Fish are widely distributed throughout Greater Yellowstone's abundant waters. Of the 22 species of fish present in the region, 15 of them are native. Fish are not only an important food source for animals such as the white pelican, bald eagle, osprey, river otter, mink, and grizzly bear; they are important to people as well, and they provide outstanding recreational opportunities throughout the region. Greater Yellowstone contains the highest concentration of blue-ribbon trout streams in the lower 48 states, and many other lakes and streams are classified as hosting "outstanding" or "substantial" fisheries.

Visitors travel to Greater Yellowstone from across the nation and abroad to test their angling skills against cutthroat, rainbow, brook, brown, lake, and golden trout, arctic grayling, and mountain whitefish. Many of the mountain lakes described in this guidebook offer excellent angling.

Birds

Greater Yellowstone's lakes, rivers, meadows, and forests offer many fine opportunities for bird-watching. The region hosts more than 300 avian species, some of which are year-round residents. The greatest numbers of birds are found in the region from mid-July through mid-September.

Some birds, such as the golden eagle, common raven, red-tailed hawk, and American robin, are found in all habitats of Greater Yellowstone, while others have specific habitat requirements. In forested areas, common birds include Clark's nutcracker, Steller's jay, gray jay, Williamson's sapsucker, mountain chickadee, red crossbill, pine siskin, pine grosbeak, hairy woodpecker, ruffed and blue grouse, brown creeper, and dark-eyed junco. In the waters of mid-elevation lakes and rivers you will find the American white pelican, green-winged teal, common merganser, Mallard duck, Canada goose, osprey, bald eagle, great blue heron, spotted sandpiper, belted kingfisher, California gull, killdeer, dipper, yellow warbler, and trumpeter swan. Open areas, including low-elevation grasslands, meadow-covered slopes, and alpine meadows, host such species as western meadowlark, rock wren, cliff swallow, mountain bluebird, black-billed magpie, common nighthawk, and vesper and savannah sparrows.

Raptors range widely throughout Greater Yellowstone. Red-tailed, Cooper's, Swainson's, and sharp-shinned hawks, northern goshawk, and golden eagle are often observed soaring on thermal air currents and cruising in wide, lazy circles overhead. Other raptors present in Greater Yellowstone include the bald eagle and peregrine falcon (both of which are listed as endangered species), osprey, American kestrel, prairie falcon, and the great horned, great gray, and northern pygmy owls.

VEGETATION OF GREATER YELLOWSTONE

More than 1,700 plant species are found in the Greater Yellowstone region, ranging from the sparse grasses and shrubs in the semi-arid lowland valleys and foothills, to alpine cushion plants in the highest reaches of the mountains. In Greater Yellowstone, the combination of a cool and moderately moist climate, rather nutrient-poor soil types, the region's latitude—about halfway between the equator and the north pole—and the high-elevation, mountainous topography, is responsible for the development of the distinct plant associations that prevail here today.

Wildflowers are the most spectacular components of Greater Yellowstone's flora, adding their vivid colors and fragrance to the landscape, from the foothills to the alpine regions. Although each trail description lists common wildflowers at particular places along trails, the use of a good field guide (see *Suggested Reading*) will aid in identification and enhance your enjoyment of wildflowers, shrubs, and trees.

As you travel upward from valley bottoms into the mountains, the vegetation, most notably the forest, changes with elevation. Vegetation patterns exist in belts called life zones, which are determined by climate, topography, and elevation. Four life zones are in Greater Yellowstone: the Foothills (or Transition) Zone; the Montane (or Canadian) Zone; the Subalpine (or Hudsonian) Zone; and the Alpine (or Arctic) Zone. Local variations in climate, due to the mountainous topography, can cause a life zone to extend above or below its typical elevational limits. For each life zone there are typically several associations of plants, called plant communities, that are found within the life zone's range.

The Foothills Zone occurs at the lowest elevations of Greater Yellowstone. This zone occupies valleys and lower mountain slopes, and the vegetation is dominated by grasslands and sagebrush. Although grasslands are found throughout all life zones of the region, the grasslands of the Foothills Zone occur in areas of low precipitation below the lower timberline of the mountains.

Areas dominated by sagebrush may appear to the casual observer to be barren and nearly lifeless, but these shrublands host a rich diversity of early season wildflowers and abundant wildlife. Big sagebrush (Artemisia tridentata) is the dominant sagebrush species in the Foothills Zone, but in favorable locations, such as on hot, dry, south-facing slopes, this plant grows well up into the mountains to an elevation of about 9,000 feet. Other shrubs in the Foothills zone include rabbitbrush and, on saline sites, greasewood.

In the upper limits of the Foothills Zone, where average annual precipitation is 16-18 inches, limber pine, Rocky Mountain juniper, and occasionally Douglas-fir begin to dot the grasslands. Narrowleaf cottonwood, willows and, infrequently, quaking aspen, are found along the moist streambanks of this zone. Few of the hiking trips described in this book lie within the Foothills Zone. Trips 43 and 44 pass through it, Trip 1 to Sheep Lake begins along the fringes of this zone, and Trip 19 to Red Hills, despite its relatively high elevation, also passes through this zone.

The Montane Zone occupies the lower elevations of the region's mountain ranges, generally up to 7,000-7,500 feet, where 16-20 inches of precipitation fall in an average year. Douglas-fir is the dominant conifer in this zone, and scattered groves of quaking aspen are common, particularly south of Yellowstone. Open areas, called parks, are common in this zone, and are either dominated by sagebrush or are rich with grasses and wildflowers.

Understory shrubs are abundant in the Montane Zone, especially in canyons where more moisture is available than on neighboring slopes. Rocky Mountain maple, curlleaf mountain mahogany, mallow-leaved ninebark, red-osier dogwood, blue elderberry, and mountain ash are typical shrubs in this zone. Most campgrounds listed in Chapters 1and 2 lie within the Montane Zone, and most of the hiking trips in those chapters begin in this zone.

The Subalpine Zone is the most widespread of all the life zones in Greater Yellowstone. Lodgepole pine is not only the dominant tree in this zone, it is the most widespread forest tree in the region. The largest continuous forest of lodgepole pine in the U.S. is found on the Yellowstone Plateau, extending west to Island Park in Idaho and south into Grand Teton National Park. Lodgepole pine forms 60% of the forest cover in the region, occupying areas that average about 20-40 inches of annual precipitation. Several factors account for the lodgepole's dominance in Greater Yellowstone, but fire is probably the single most important. Each lodgepole pine bears a number of closed (serotinous) cones, which can open to release seeds only when subjected to the high heat provided by fire. Before the advent of modern firefighting, forest fires were common in the region.

Lodgepoles thrive in sunny openings and have the ability to grow on poor soils, and they are the first conifers to colonize a disturbed site. Look for young lodgepoles on landslide debris, in avalanche chutes, and along roadcuts as you travel through Greater Yellowstone.

Shrubs and wildflowers are sparse in the typically shady lodgepole forests. The most common shrub is the low-growing grouse whortleberry, often forming extensive mats of green foliage. Their tart but small, red berries are a delicious treat when they ripen in late summer. At about 8,000 to 8,500 feet, where annual precipitation increases to 40-60 inches, lodgepole pine is supplanted by forests of Engelmann spruce and subalpine fir. Higher yet, near timberline, whitebark pine joins the forest.

The slender, spire-shaped subalpine fir is common in high precipitation zones, especially in the northern and western

reaches of Greater Yellowstone. Farther east and south, the mountains are somewhat drier, and spruce dominates the forest, subalpine fir occurring in only the coolest and wettest microclimates. Approaching timberline, the forest becomes discontinuous, growing in scattered groves among boulder fields and wildflower-speckled meadows, where whitebark pine is the dominant tree. Near the upper limit of tree growth, trees become stunted and grow in "tree islands", most typically in high meadows and snowy basins, where the tree islands are confined to hummocks. The ground on these hummocks is drier and the snowpack remains relatively shallow. Also, snowmelt occurs earlier, enhanced by the warming "black body effect" of the tree groves, allowing for a longer growing season.

Higher still, trees become more scattered, growing in shrubby, ground-hugging mats called "krummholz" (German for "crooked wood"). The mat-like trees are protected in winter by the snowpack, but stems that extend above the snow are battered by strong winds and the sandblasting effect of blowing ice and snow. Consequently exposed foliage—and sometimes even bark—are abraded

Shooting star

from the windward side of the tree. The remaining foliage on the leeward side of the tree gives it a wind-flagged appearance.

The elevation of timberline in Greater Yellowstone varies from north to south, just as it does everywhere there are high trees. For example, in northern New Mexico, timberline is at 12,500 feet, while in Glacier National Park, near the Canadian border in Montana, timberline occurs at about 7,500 feet. In the southern reaches of Greater Yellowstone, you will find timberline at about 10,000 feet. In the north, in the Beartooth and Madison ranges, for example, timberline is at about 9,600 feet.

The direction a slope faces (the aspect) affects the elevation of timberline. Southern exposures are warmer, windswept, and typically have a thin snowpack, so timberline can extend farther above the expected elevation on those slopes. Conversely, on cold northern exposures where snow lies deep for much of the year, timberline may occur at much lower elevations.

Timberline marks the boundary between the Subalpine Zone and the Alpine Zone. Glaciers retreated from the Alpine Zone of Greater Yellowstone less than 10,000 years ago; hence soils in this zone have had little time to develop and are thin, and bedrock dominates the landscape.

Much like a desert landscape with its stark beauty, the alpine areas of Greater Yellowstone are very alluring, with their serrated peaks, lofty crests, and glacier-carved basins. Vast expanses of tundra are covered in a mat of grasses, sedges, and an array of wildflowers more colorful and fragrant than those found in other life zones. The best place to see Greater Yellowstone's tundra is in the Beartooth Mountains, which contain the largest continuous expanse of alpine tundra in the Rocky Mountains between Colorado and Canada.

The Alpine Zone is a harsh environment dessicated by nearly constant winds and intense sunlight. Frosts and snow can occur at any time in this zone. Plants here grow low to the ground in mats, or cushions, only a few inches high. The growing season is extremely short, ranging from four to six weeks. In moist areas in this zone are found sedge bogs and thickets of dwarf willows. Drier sites host grassy meadows and turf dominated by a wide variety of wildflowers. Most plants bloom more or less simultaneously in mid-summer, with a dramatic display of wildflowers that paint the landscape in shades of red, blue, and yellow. In the highest elevations, boulders may be covered with colorful lichen, but the rest of the landscape is dominated by rock and snow.

Alpine plants have evolved ways to reduce moisture loss caused by winds and sunlight. Most of the plants' energy is directed toward the flowers, so their vegetative parts are small. Leaves are either hairy or covered with a waxy coating, and they may be light gray to reflect sunlight or fleshy to retain moisture.

 **Chapter One**

THE NORTHWEST CORNER
OF GREATER YELLOWSTONE

Introduction

North and west of West Yellowstone, Montana, the rolling, densely forested Yellowstone volcanic plateaus of Yellowstone National Park merges with four lofty mountain ranges, each separated by high, intermountain valleys bisected by world-famous trout streams. The mountain ranges—the Gallatin, Madison, Henrys Lake, and Centennial mountains—are crowned by 10-11,000' peaks that rise above timberline and form an exciting backdrop from area highways. Views of these rugged mountains are especially refreshing to visitors who have spent time on the mostly featureless plateaus of Yellowstone National Park.

Area highways offer good access to the three major rivers of the region: the Madison and the Gallatin in Montana, and the Henrys Fork of the Snake in Idaho. Anglers and floaters from across the nation and abroad flock to these scenic waters each summer to enjoy some of the finest rafting and trout fishing in the U.S. But there is more than dramatic mountains and trout-filled rivers that draws visitors to this northwest corner of Greater Yellowstone. Here there is a strong feeling of remoteness, a sense of wild and unspoiled Western landscapes. Highways are noticeably less busy in this region than elsewhere in Greater Yellowstone, and on the mountain trails you will enjoy greater solitude.

The areas covered in this chapter include Gallatin Canyon, the Madison Range, the Henrys Lake Mountains, and the eastern end of the Centennial Mountains. Gallatin Canyon, a major highway corridor linking Bozeman and West Yellowstone, Montana, is one of the premier scenic attractions of the Greater Yellowstone area. For 70 miles, from the northwest corner of Yellowstone

National Park to the canyon's mouth near Bozeman, travelers are enveloped in a scenic mountain landscape of broad meadows, vast forests, towering ridges with a backdrop of lofty alpine peaks, and the tumultuous Gallatin River, which the highway closely follows.

Dozens of backcountry trails begin either in the canyon or a short distance up a tributary. Five national forest campgrounds are also located in the canyon. The Gallatin River, a famous blue-ribbon trout fishery, is accessible from numerous fishing-access sites.

Rising west of Gallatin Canyon, and bounded on the south by Hebgen Lake, on the north by Gallatin Valley, and on the west by the broad grasslands of Madison Valley, is the lofty Madison Range, the most majestic and unspoiled mountain landscape in this part of Greater Yellowstone. Within this 50-by-20 mile mountain range are many glacier-carved alpine peaks exceeding 11,000 feet, composed of resistant metamorphic rocks—mostly schist and gneiss, dozens of timberline lakes, large wildflower-rich meadows, and vast forests of Douglas-fir, lodgepole pine, subalpine fir, Engelmann spruce, and whitebark pine. Much of the range is protected within the boundaries of the 254,944-acre Lee Metcalf Wilderness and the 35,752-acre Cabin Creek Recreation and Wildlife Management Area.

The Henrys Lake Mountains form a prominent, 25-mile-long horseshoe-shaped ridge along the Continental Divide from Red Rock Pass in the west to Reas Pass in the east. The central part of the range, between Raynolds Pass and Targhee Pass, contains an aggregate of 10,000-foot peaks composed of soft limestones and outcrops of erosion-resistant schist and gneiss. At the top of the horseshoe, where the crest of the range curves southeast, the range projects a series of 10,000-foot ridges about seven miles north into Montana. In this area lies a tract of about 50,000 roadless acres that have been proposed for wilderness designation. This part of the range is characterized by rich forests, open meadows, lofty ridges and peaks, deep canyons, and glacier-carved cirque basins.

The Centennial Mountains, also located along the Continental Divide, are the westernmost mountains of the Greater Yellowstone area covered in this book. From Interstate 15 at Monida Pass in the west to Sawtell Peak near Henrys Lake in the east, the Centennials stretch for 50 miles along the border between Montana and Idaho. On the Idaho side of the range, the Centennials slope gently upward to a crest of 9,000-foot peaks, and then plunge abruptly down a 3,000-foot escarpment into Montana. One of the most notable features of the Centennials is the range's east-west alignment, contrary to the north-south-oriented ranges of the Rocky Mountains. Only two other major ranges in the Rockies are aligned east-west: the Uinta Mountains in Utah, and the Brooks Range in Alaska.

Thick forests of pine, spruce, and fir blanket the south and east slopes of the Centennials, but only a narrow band of forest on the northern escarpment in Montana separates high cirque basins from the broad grasslands of Centennial Valley. Spreading alpine meadows and stunted groves of timberline trees clothe the gentle slopes along the crest of the range. The highest and most prominent peaks are clustered at the eastern end of the range, near Red Rock Pass. But few timberline lakes are found here, due to the soft, erodible nature of the limestones and dolomites that dominate the rocks of the range.

Separating the Henrys Lake and Centennial mountains is the broad, lodgepole-pine-covered basin of Island Park in Idaho. Despite its flat, mostly featureless expanse, Island Park is notable for its geologic history. The nearly circular Island Park basin, about 13 miles across, is a caldera, or collapsed volcano. It was created approximately 1.3 million years ago when a large volcano collapsed during a final catastrophic eruption. South and west of Island Park, the caldera rim can be seen as a low, forested ridge. The eastern rim of the caldera has been buried in more recent lava flows from Yellowstone National Park.

Points of Interest

MADISON RIVER CANYON

The Madison River Canyon Earthquake Area, located along Highway 287 northwest of West Yellowstone, Montana, is a 38,000-acre geological preserve managed by Gallatin National Forest. Around midnight on August 17, 1959, sudden movement along a series of faults bounding the southern edge of the Madison Range triggered a strong 7.1 earthquake. The subsequent damage to the Madison River canyon was dramatic. The highway was buckled and broken, leaving travelers stranded. Several fault scarps were created, each with a vertical displacement of up to 20 feet. The north shore of Hebgen Lake subsided eight feet, destroying and submerging homes. And a massive landslide was triggered near the west end of the canyon.

Thirty seven million cubic yards of broken rock slid from a half-mile-long slope of mountain, filling the canyon floor with over 200 feet of rocky debris that extended 300 feet up the opposite slope of the canyon. The Madison Slide buried a campground, killing 27 people, and dammed the Madison River, forming what is called Earthquake Lake.

Vivid evidence of that earthquake can be seen by visitors in the canyon. The Earthquake Lake visitor center is the starting point for an auto tour of the area. The visitor center is located on Highway 287, 19 miles west of Highway 191 and three miles east of Highway 87. Books, maps, slide programs, and information are available at the visitor center. A pamphlet, keyed to 10 stops along Highway

287, is available at the visitor center and also from a roadside dispenser at the east entrance to the earthquake area, a short distance west of Highway 191.

RED ROCK LAKES NATIONAL WILDLIFE REFUGE

Red Rock Lakes National Wildlife Refuge, located in the remote Centennial Valley in Montana, is a 32,350-acre wetland preserve accessible via the Red Rock Pass Road (see driving directions for Trips 11 and 12).

In 1932, trumpeter swans were on the brink of extinction. Only 69 swans survived at that time in the lower 48 states, all of them in the Greater Yellowstone area, and two-thirds of that number were located at the Red Rock Lakes. By 1935, with the establishment of the Red Rock Lakes National Wildlife Refuge, this vital swan habitat was protected, and their numbers have increased. These beautiful, large, white birds, resembling an oversized goose, are often seen on rivers, lakes, and ponds in Greater Yellowstone. But the Red Rock Lakes area remains the best viewing location. The refuge also harbors 232 other species of birds, and visitors here are likely to see moose, pronghorn antelope, mule deer, elk, and coyotes.

Access and Services

Highways that access campgrounds and trails covered in this chapter all converge at West Yellowstone, Montana, at the West Entrance to Yellowstone National Park.

U.S. 20 leads 52 miles from Ashton, Idaho, to West Yellowstone, via Island Park and Targhee Pass. This busy highway is the principal travel route for Park visitors heading to and from the Park's West Entrance. U.S. 191 is the premier scenic drive in the region. This highway leads 90 miles from Interstate 90 in Bozeman, Montana, to West Yellowstone via Gallatin Canyon. U.S. 287 is the least traveled roadway in this region. This highway leads 71 miles from Ennis, Montana, to West Yellowstone, via the Madison Valley. Montana/Idaho 87 offers an 18-mile shortcut from Highway 20 in

Island Park, Idaho, to Highway 287 in the Madison Valley, via Raynolds Pass and the Continental Divide.

West Yellowstone, Montana (6,660'), is a small, service-oriented town on the western edge of Yellowstone National Park. The town has a full complement of services, including motels, restaurants, gas stations, auto and RV repair, car rentals, groceries, hiking, camping, and fishing supplies, and a medical clinic. The Yellowstone Airport is one mile north of town, with daily commuter connections from larger regional airports. Car rental is also available at the airport.

Island Park, Idaho, is not really a town in the traditional sense. This community consists of a series of small settlements strung out along a 33-mile stretch of Highway 20 in the Island Park basin. Every few miles along this stretch of highway visitors will find a variety of services, including gas stations, motels, groceries, private campgrounds, RV parks, and restaurants. Auto repair is available at Kilgore Junction.

Bozeman, Montana (4,795'), with a population of nearly 30,000, is the cultural and economic hub of the entire Greater Yellowstone area. All services are available in Bozeman, including gas stations, auto repair, car rental, hiking, camping, and fishing supplies, motels, restaurants, groceries, a large hospital, and an airport.

Big Sky, Montana (6,000'), is a year-round resort community located in Gallatin Canyon. Services include gas, towing, restaurants, limited groceries, lodging, fishing supplies, and a medical clinic.

Ennis, Montana (4,944'), located in the rural Madison Valley, serves not only a local ranching community, but a growing tourist trade as well. This small town offers five motels, groceries, restaurants, fuel, auto repair, towing, and a medical clinic.

Ashton, Idaho (5,260'), a town that is the hub of the world's largest seed potato producing area, is a full-service community on the fringes of Greater Yellowstone. Gas, auto and RV repair, towing, groceries, a restaurant, two motels, and a hospital are available in Ashton.

For further information on accommodations and services, contact the chambers of commerce listed below:

West Yellowstone Chamber of Commerce
30 Yellowstone Avenue
P.O. Box 458
West Yellowstone, MT 59758
(406) 646-7701

Bozeman Chamber of Commerce
1205 East Main
Bozeman, MT 59715
(406) 586-5421

Ennis Chamber of Commerce
P.O. Box 291
Ennis, MT 59729
(406) 682-4388

Big Sky Chamber of Commerce
P.O. Box 160100
Big Sky, MT 59716
(406) 995-2511

Ashton Chamber of Commerce
604 Main
P.O. Box 11
Ashton, ID 83420
(208) 652-3987

Campgrounds

1 • BEAVER CREEK (6,595')

Location. In the Madison River Canyon Earthquake Area; 0.6 mile south of Highway 287; 7.0 miles east of the U.S. 287/Montana 87 junction (41 miles south of Ennis, Montana, and 60 miles north of Ashton, Idaho), or 12.5 miles west of the U.S. 287/Montana 191 junction (8.0 miles north of West Yellowstone, and 80 miles south of Bozeman, Montana); Gallatin National Forest, Hebgen Lake Ranger District.
Facilities. 65 camping units, tables, fire pits and grills, water, toilets, bear-resistant garbage containers; maximum trailer length of 32 feet; a fee is charged.

Dates Usually Open. June 15, through Sept. 10.
The Setting. This spacious campground, divided into three separate camping areas—loops A, B, and C—lies on a low ridge above and north of Madison River canyon and the upper end of Earthquake Lake. The canyon here is deep and shadowed, with ridges of the Henrys Lake Mountains to the south, and the Madison Range to the north, looming 3,000 feet above the campground.

Loop A, with 27 camping units, lies in an open, grass-floored forest of lodgepole pine.

Loop B, with 15 camping units, lies above the other two loops on the ridgetop. The first six units lie beneath a shady canopy of lodgepole pine, while the remainder are more open, lying among widely scattered lodgepoles and aspens. Campsites in this loop offer the most expansive views in the campground.

Loop C, with 23 camping units, lies in a shady, predominantly lodgepole-pine forest. The aspen-clad crest of the ridge just south of the loop offers fine views down to Earthquake Lake.

2 • CABIN CREEK (6,470')

Location. In the Madison River Canyon Earthquake Area; on U.S. 287, 8.6 miles east of the U.S. 287/Montana 87 junction, and 10.0 miles west of the U.S. 287/Montana 191 junction; Gallatin National Forest, Hebgen Lake Ranger District.
Facilities. 15 camping units, tables, fire pits with grills, water, toilets, bear-resistant garbage containers; maximum trailer length of 32 feet; a fee is charged.
Dates Usually Open. May 31 through September 15.
The Setting. This small campground lies just north of U.S. 287 in a shady forest of Douglas-fir, beside the wide, rushing waters of Cabin Creek. From the campground, visitors can cross the bridge over the creek and follow a short, paved trail that leads to a large interpretive display explaining the events of the 1959 Madison earthquake. The Cabin Creek fault scarp, resembling a roadcut, rises behind the display.

MAP CORRECTION

Shows the correct southern boundary of Grand Teton National Park from below the word "PARK" eastward to the town of Kelly.

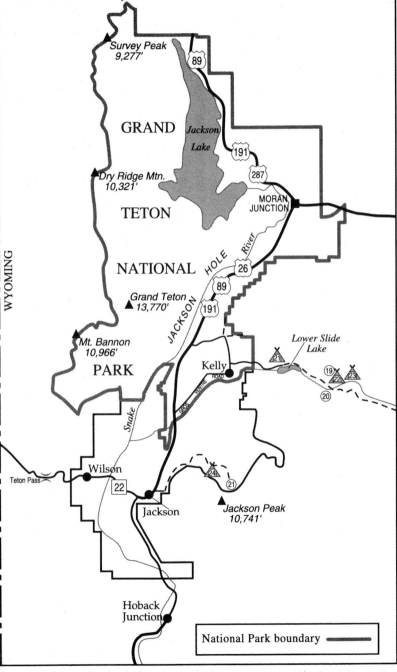

National Park boundary

The Campfire Lodge and Resort lies 50 yards west of the Cabin Creek Campground entrance. The lodge offers cabins, RV hookups, a store, and a cafe.

3 • LONESOMEHURST (6,540')

Location. On the west shore of Hebgen Lake, west of West Yellowstone, Montana; Gallatin National Forest, Hebgen Lake Ranger District; (see driving directions for Trip 9 for exact location).
Facilities. 26 camping units, tables, fire pits, water, toilets, bear-resistant garbage containers, boat launch, pay telephone; maximum trailer length of 32 feet; a fee is charged.
Dates Usually Open. May 31 through September 15.
The Setting. This scenic campground lies in an open forest of small lodgepole pines on the South Fork Arm of Hebgen Lake. There are gravel beaches along the lakeshore. Views stretch northward across the lake to the alpine peaks of the southern Madison Range. A variety of waterfowl are likely to be seen on the lake, in addition to white pelicans, gulls, great blue herons, and osprey.

4 • CHERRY CREEK (6,540')

Location. One mile north of Hebgen Lake Road, on the west shore of Hebgen Lake; Gallatin National Forest, Hebgen Lake Ranger District; (see driving directions for Trip 9 for exact location).
Facilities. Cherry Creek is a small, undeveloped camping area, and can accommodate only about six vehicles. There are some tables, and toilets; no fee.
Dates Usually Open. May 31 through Oct. 15.
The Setting. This camping area lies just above the swampy shore of Hebgen Lake in a forest of lodgepole pine. There are good views eastward across the lake to the Yellowstone Plateau and the southern peaks of the Gallatin Range, in Yellowstone National Park.

5 • SPRING CREEK (6,540')

Location. On the west shore of Hebgen Lake, 0.5 mile north of Hebgen Lake Road; Gallatin National Forest, Hebgen Lake Ranger District; (see driving directions for Trip 9 for exact location).
Facilities. This is an undeveloped camping area, with about 10 campsites. There are toilets and some tables; no fee.
Dates Usually Open. May 31 through Oct. 15.
The Setting. This scenic camping area lies along the grassy west shore of Hebgen Lake in an open forest of lodgepole pine. A few narrow, sandy beaches allow access to the lake from the camping area. A variety of water-dependent birds are likely to be seen here, and possibly moose, mule deer, and elk.

Views are expansive, stretching eastward across the lake to the grassy, aspen-dotted ridge of Horse Butte Peninsula, and beyond to the peaks of the southern Gallatin Range, covered by a forest of gray snags, trees that were consumed in the Madison Fire during the summer of 1988. Southeast of the camping area, you can see across the flat, lodgepole-forested upper Madison Valley to the equally flat, but higher, Yellowstone Plateau.

6 • RED CLIFF (6,300')

Location. In Gallatin Canyon, 0.2 mile east of U.S. 191, 41.0 miles north of West Yellowstone, 47.5 miles south of Bozeman, and 9.7 miles south of Big Sky, Montana; Gallatin National Forest, Bozeman Ranger District.
Facilities. 72 camping units, tables, fire pits and grills, water, toilets, bear-resistant garbage containers; maximum trailer length of 25 feet; a fee is charged.
Dates Usually Open. May 31 through September 10.
The Setting. This is the most spacious and pleasant campground in Gallatin Canyon. The camping units lie along a north loop, and a south loop, on a spruce-shaded bench just east of Gallatin River. There is good access to the river from the campground.

7 • MOOSE FLAT (5,700')

Location. In Gallatin Canyon, just west of U.S. 191, 56.0 miles north of West Yellowstone, 32.0 miles south of Bozeman, and 8.3 miles north of Big Sky, Montana; Gallatin National Forest, Bozeman Ranger District.

Facilities. 14 camping units, tables, fire grills, water, toilets, garbage containers; maximum trailer length of 25 feet; a fee is charged.

Dates Usually Open. May 31 through Sept. 10.

The Setting. This small campground lies on an open, grassy bench next to the Gallatin River. Busy Highway 191 lies just above. The camping units are close to one another, and are screened off from the river by a dense grove of Engelmann spruce. There are good views of the canyon's broken cliffs, talus slopes, and scattered stands of dense forest that rise to skyline ridges, 1,000 to 2,000 feet above the campground.

8 • SWAN CREEK (5,750')

Location. In Swan Creek canyon, 0.5 to 1.0 mile east of Gallatin Canyon and U.S. 191; 57.1 miles north of West Yellowstone, 7.2 miles north of Big Sky, and 30.9 miles south of Bozeman, Montana; Gallatin National Forest, Bozeman Ranger District.

Facilities. 13 camping units, tables, fire pits with grills, water, toilets, garbage containers; paved campground access road; maximum trailer length of 25 feet; a fee is charged.

Dates Usually Open. May 31 through Sept. 10.

The Setting. This campground is separated into two areas; sites 1-6 lie 0.5 mile east of U.S. 191 on gravel Swan Creek Road, and sites 7-13 lie one half mile farther east on Swan Creek Road. The campground lies in deep, densely forested Swan Creek canyon. Campsites are shaded by an open forest of lodgepole pine and Engelmann spruce, a few yards north of wide and shallow Swan Creek.

9 • GREEK CREEK (5,620')

Location. In Gallatin Canyon, on U.S. 191, 58.0 miles north of West Yellowstone, 8.3 miles north of Big Sky, and 30.0 miles south of Bozeman, Montana; Gallatin National Forest, Bozeman Ranger District.

Facilities. 14 camping units, tables, fire grills, water, toilets, garbage containers;

pay telephone; maximum trailer length of 25 feet; a fee is charged.

Dates Usually Open. May 31 through Sept. 10.

The Setting. This small but pleasant campground is divided into two loops lying on either side of the highway. The south loop lies alongside the Gallatin River in a forest of Engelmann spruce, with good access to the river. The north loop lies in a shady grove of spruce and Douglas-fir, with thickets of red-osier dogwood and Wood's rose nearby. The pay telephone is located midway through this loop.

10 • SPIRE ROCK (5,600')

Location. In Squaw Creek canyon, 0.9 mile east of Trailhead 7 (see driving directions for Trip 7 and 8), and 2.7 miles east of U.S. 191 in Gallatin Canyon; Gallatin National Forest, Bozeman Ranger District.

Facilities. 18 camping units, tables, fire pits with grills, toilets; no drinking water; no fee.

Dates Usually Open. May 31 through September 10.

The Setting. This shady campground lies in spruce forest along the south banks of wide and shallow Squaw Creek, in the damp, narrow confines of Squaw Creek canyon. The widely spaced campsites lie along a one-mile spur road south of Squaw Creek Road. Good views stretch from the campground to the north wall of the canyon, where broken limestone cliffs, buttresses, and pinnacles rise from the canyon bottom to the skyline.

11 • RIVERSIDE (6,150')

Location. In Island Park, 0.8 mile southeast of U.S. 20, via a paved road, 15.0 miles north of Ashton, Idaho, and 26.6 miles south of the Idaho 87/U.S. 20 junction; Targhee National Forest, Ashton Ranger District.

Facilities. 57 camping units, tables, fire grills, fire pits, water, toilets, bear-resistant garbage containers; paved access road and paved pull-through campsite spurs; maximum trailer length of 30 feet; a fee is charged.

Dates Usually Open. May 31 through September 10.

The Setting. This pleasant, spacious campground lies in an open lodgepole-pine forest, next to the west bank of the tumultuous Henrys Fork. Low gray cliffs and blocky volcanic slopes rise eastward beyond the river.

Loop A, with 21 camping units, lies along the banks of the river. Loop B, also with 21 units, lies west of Loop A, on a forested slope above the river. This loop is accessed via a gravel road, and parking spaces are also graveled. Loop C, with 15 units, lies above the river in forest, and above the access road through the loop; parking spaces are paved.

12 • Box Canyon (6,320')

Location. In Island Park, 1.5 miles southwest of U.S. Highway 20, via a gravel road, 25.3 miles north of Ashton, Idaho, and 16.2 miles south of the Idaho 87/U.S. 20 junction; Targhee National Forest, Island Park Ranger District.
Facilities. 19 camping units, tables, fire grills, fire pits, water, toilets, garbage containers; maximum trailer length of 25 feet; a fee is charged.
Dates Usually Open. May 31 through Sept. 10.
The Setting. This pleasant, open campground lies in a grass-carpeted forest of small lodgepole pine, Douglas-fir, and subalpine fir, just east of the rim of Box Canyon. From the day-use parking area at the campground entrance, a trail leads west for 150 yards to the volcanic rim of Box Canyon, where the Henrys Fork flows 100 feet below. Trails lead steeply down to the river from the rim, and another trail follows the rim south for 2 miles.

13 • Buffalo (6,300')

Location. In Island Park, 0.5 mile east of U.S. 20, 26.5 miles north of Ashton, Idaho, and 0.4 mile north of the highway bridge spanning Buffalo River, or 15 miles south of the U.S. 20/Idaho 87 junction (the campground access road branches east from Highway 20 opposite the signed turnoff to Island Park Dam); Targhee National Forest, Island Park District.

Facilities. 127 camping units, tables, fire grills, water, toilets, bear-resistant garbage containers, paved access road and campsite spurs; maximum trailer length of 32 feet; a fee is charged.
Dates Usually Open. May 31 through Sept. 10.
The Setting. This large campground, with seven loop roads leading to campsites, lies in an open forest of young lodgepole pines along the banks of the broad, placid waters of the Buffalo River, a major Henrys Fork tributary. The Buffalo River originates from several large springs issuing from the western edge of the Yellowstone Plateau, 6 miles upstream from the campground.

14 • Upper Coffeepot (6,305')

Location. In Island Park, 1.7 miles southwest of U.S. 20 (a national forest sign says it is 2.5 miles to the campground), 31.5 miles north of Ashton, Idaho, and 10.0 miles south of the Idaho 87/U.S. 20 junction; Targhee National Forest, Island Park Ranger District.
Facilities. 15 camping units, tables, fire pits, water, toilets, bear-resistant garbage containers; maximum trailer length of 25 feet; a fee is charged.
Dates Usually Open. May 31 through September 10.
The Setting. This scenic campground lies in an open forest of young lodgepole pines, just above the grassy east banks of the slow-moving Henrys Fork of the Snake River. There is excellent river access from the campground, and fishing for trout, whitefish, and kokanee salmon. The Coffeepot Rapids Trail follows the east bank of the river downstream 2.3 miles through lodgepole forest to Coffeepot Rapids, a turbulent stretch of the Henrys Fork.

15 • Flat Rock (6,400')

Location. In Island Park, 0.1 mile west of U.S. 20, via a gravel road, 31.75 miles north of Ashton, Idaho, and 9.75 miles south of the Idaho 87/U.S. 20 junction (the turnoff lies 0.2 mile south of Macks Inn); Targhee National Forest, Island Park Ranger District.
Facilities. 40 camping units, tables, fire pits and grills, water, toilets, bear-resistant

garbage containers; maximum trailer length in Loop A is 25 feet, in Loop B, 35 feet—paved access road; Loop B also has paved campsite spurs; a fee is charged.
Dates Usually Open. May 31 through September 10.
The Setting. Loop B, signed as the upper campground, has 17 sites and lies in shady lodgepole forest, just west of the highway. Loop A, the lower campground, has 23 sites and lies in an open forest of scattered lodgepole pines on a grassy slope, just above the grassy banks of Henrys Fork of the Snake River.

16 • UPPER LAKE (6,640')

Location. In Centennial Valley, on the southwest shore of Upper Red Rock Lake, in the Red Rock Lakes National Wildlife Refuge, Montana; (see driving directions for Trips 11 and 12 for exact location).
Facilities. 12 camping units, tables, fire grills, piped spring water (potable), toilets; no fee.
Dates Usually Open. May 31 through Oct. 1.
The Setting. This scenic, remote campground is located just above the willow-clad southwest shore of Upper Red Rock Lake in an extensive grove of aspen. A wide variety of water-dependent birds, including trumpeter swans, are likely to be seen here, as well as moose, pronghorn antelope, mule deer, and coyotes. The open setting of the campground allows broad, panoramic vistas. Rolling, grassy hills to the north and east foreground more distant views of the Snowcrest Range to the northwest, the Gravelly Range to the north, and the craggy peaks of the Madison Range to the northeast. The abrupt northern escarpment of the Centennial Mountains juts 3,000 feet skyward just south of the campground.

Reservations

Reservations can be made over the telephone for selected sites in Beaver Creek (#1), Cabin Creek (#2), and Lonesomehurst (#3) campgrounds by dialing 1-800-280-2267.

Reservations for selected sites in Buffalo (#13), and Flat Rock (#15) campgrounds can be made by dialing 1-800-283-2267.

For Further Information

Information regarding Trips 1 and 12:

Beaverhead National Forest
Madison Ranger District
5 Forest Service Road
Ennis, MT 59729
(406) 682-4253

Information regarding Trips 2, 3, 9; Campgrounds 1-5:

Gallatin National Forest
Hebgen Lake Ranger District
P.O. Box 520
West Yellowstone, MT 59758
(406) 646-7369

Information regarding Trips 4-8; Campgrounds 6-10:

Gallatin National Forest
Bozeman Ranger District
3710 Fallon St., Box C
Bozeman, MT 59715
(406) 587-6920

Information regarding Trip 10; Campgrounds 11-15:

Targhee National Forest
Island Park Ranger District
P.O. Box 220
Island Park, ID 83429
(208) 558-7301

Information regarding Trip 11:

Bureau of Land Management
Dillon Resource Area Office
P.O. Box 1048, Ibey Building
Dillon, MT 59725
(406) 683-2337

Information regarding Campground 16:

**Red Rock Lakes National
Wildlife Refuge**
Monida Star Route, Box 15
Lima, MT 59739
(406) 276-3536

Wilderness Regulations

The only wilderness area covered in this chapter is the Lee Metcalf Wilderness, in the Madison Range in Montana. Backpackers should study the regulations below.

1. Camping in one location for more than 14 days is prohibited.
2. Camping and campfires are not permitted within 200 feet of any lake in the Wilderness.
3. Cutting or damaging any tree, timber, or snag is prohibited.
4. The limit people per group is 15.

Trip 1
SHEEP CREEK TO SHEEP LAKE

Distance: 13.0 miles, round trip.
Low/High Elevations: 6,480'/9,071'.
Difficulty: Moderately strenuous.
Use: Low.
Suited For: Dayhike or backpack.
Best Season: July through mid-September.
Wildlife Viewing: Good.
Grizzly Bear Danger: Low.
Map/Trailhead: 1/1.
Nearest Campgrounds: Beaver Creek, 11.0 miles, and Cabin Creek, 12.6 miles from the trailhead.
Driving to the Trailhead: Follow U.S. 287 to the junction with Montana 87, 41.0 miles south of Ennis, and 30.0 miles west of West Yellowstone, Montana, and turn south onto Highway 87, heading toward Raynolds Pass and Idaho. After 1.4 miles south from the junction, turn left (east) onto Sheep Creek Road, indicated by a NATIONAL FOR-EST ACCESS sign. This turnoff is 7.1 miles north of Raynolds Pass, and 58.3 miles north of Ashton, Idaho.

The Sheep Creek Road, a public access road across private property, is a good dirt road, but is rough and rocky in places, and slippery when wet. The road leads eastward across the Missouri Flats, so named because homesteaders from Missouri settled here in the late 1800s. Avoid numerous spur roads leading to summer cabins as you proceed, and enter Beaverhead National Forest after 2.1 miles. You will reach the loop at the roadend and trailhead after another 0.5 mile. Pit toilets and an information sign are here.

Introduction: This long hike at the northern part of the Henrys Lake Mountains leads you from the foot of the range to a scenic timberline lake encircled by imposing 10,000-foot peaks. The good trail maintains a steady, moderate grade throughout its length. Fishing in Sheep Lake is fair for pan-sized cutthroat trout, but the few spartan campsites at the lake are poor.

Description: The trail begins at 6,480 feet, in a grove of small aspens at the south end of the parking area. The trail quickly leads to a bridged crossing of wide and shallow Sheep Creek, beyond which we meander a few yards to a small irrigation ditch, cross a one-plank bridge, then curve east and climb easily into the canyon's mouth.

Soon we reach another, larger irrigation ditch, spanned by a log footbridge. We then ascend gently into the canyon of Sheep Creek where, 0.4 mile from the trailhead, we cross to the north bank of the creek via another log footbridge. Several yards east of the crossing, we pass through a gate (please keep closed) that bars cattle from entering the canyon.

The trail follows the north bank of the creek for the next 1.3 miles, rising gently, but moderately at times, through park-like forests of Douglas-fir or, when alongside the tumbling creek, through shady groves of Engelmann spruce. Steep slopes rise more than 2,000 feet above the narrow confines of the canyon bottom, their forested flanks broken by fields of talus and by cliffs and pinnacles of gray and buff-toned limestone.

Wildflowers and understory shrubs in this peaceful forest are abundant and diverse. They include cow parsnip, yellow columbine, Richardson and sticky geraniums, mountain bog gentian, western coneflower, lupine, meadow rue, yarrow, wild strawberry, Oregon grape, cinquefoil, subalpine daisy, blue elderberry, mountain ash, thimbleberry, buffaloberry, snowberry, common juniper, and Rocky Mountain maple.

At length we step across a small tributary, then reach a third footbridge across Sheep Creek, at 7,160 feet and 1.7 miles. Once across the creek, we are confronted with a 450-foot ascent, and we get underway by ascending switchbacks at a moderate grade upon north-facing slopes. These slopes are clothed in a shady forest of Douglas-fir that obscure views of the canyon. But midway up this ascent we pass briefly through a small, sloping meadow, from which we enjoy well-earned views of the distant, alpine summits of the Gravelly Range, framed by the precipitous canyon walls of Sheep Creek.

Once the switchbacks end, we traverse southeast, reaching Sheep Creek and another bridge at 7,650 feet, 0.7 mile from the previous crossing. Here the canyon, and our vistas, open up. The rocky battlements of 10,321-foot Sheep Mountain, and the lofty pyramid of Peak 10274 rise boldly at the head of the canyon. On the eastern skyline are a series of rounded summits lying just below the 10,000-foot level. This eastern ridge is crowned in the southeast by the broad alpine plateau of 9,971-foot Coffin Mountain, which contrasts its buff-toned limestones with the dark metamorphic schists that compose the peaks on the canyon's opposite side.

Reflecting the increase in elevation are sloping, subalpine meadows, and a change in the forest trees. Lodgepole pine, subalpine fir, Engelmann spruce, and farther up the trail, whitebark pine grow in scattered groves among the meadows. A delight to the senses are myriad wildflowers such as Indian paintbrush, groundsel, cinquefoil, yarrow, mountain dandelion, and subalpine daisy.

Trail to Sheep Lake in Sheep Creek canyon

Beyond the fourth bridge our trail rises gently to moderately, alternating between conifer groves and open meadows. We stay well above and southeast of the creek, which may be dry during late summer. After hiking another 1.5 miles, the canyon rises more steeply ahead of us, and the trail then leads us higher up the canyon's eastern slopes and across fields of talus, steeply-sloping meadows, and over ice-polished rocky knolls.

Outstanding vistas stretch northward from these slopes, reaching into the southern Madison Range. We can see a host of craggy peaks that rise above West Fork Beaver Creek (see Trip 2), but the view is dominated by the stony finger of 11,316-foot Hilgard Peak, the Madison's highest summit.

A few moments before reaching a minor avalanche chute, we may notice a faint trail that branches left, climbing northeast, and ultimately leading to West Fork Watkins Creek, over a divide to the east. Ignoring that trail, we'll find a profusion of yellow columbines as we enter the avalanche chute, just below a grove of snow-flattened subalpine firs.

Soon we curve into the cirque at the head of Sheep Creek, cross a bridge over a minor stream, then bend northwest, ascending moderately on the east slopes of a low, rocky ridge. We climb a short but steep pitch as we round the nose of the ridge and curve into pleasant streamside meadows alongside Sheep Creek, shaded by an open canopy of subalpine fir and whitebark pine. In early summer these narrow meadows are enlivened by the large white blooms of marsh marigold. Cutthroat trout can be seen rising to insects in the meandering waters of Sheep Creek.

An enjoyable stroll of 350 yards leads us to an old stone dam at the outlet of 9,071-foot Sheep Lake, 6.5 miles from the trailhead. The lakeshore is steep and rocky, surrounded by low cliff bands and talus slopes that host a scattering of timberline conifers. The somber metamorphic dome of Peak 10606, the highest summit in the Henrys Lake Mountains, looms over the southwest shore of the lake.

To the northwest, a broken, tree-feathered ridge rises to Peak 10274, much less imposing when viewed from this angle than from farther down-canyon.

The 25-acre lake fills the floor of its cirque, so there is little room to pitch a tent. A few small, poor campsites can be found near the dam, but sites near the meadows just below the lake are the best choice for an overnight stay.

From Sheep Lake, return the way you came.

Trip 2

WEST FORK BEAVER CREEK TO BLUE DANUBE AND AVALANCHE LAKES

Distance: 11.3 miles round trip to Avalanche Lake; 12.7 miles round trip to Blue Danube Lake.
Low/High Elevations: 6,850'/9,020'.
Difficulty: Moderately strenuous.
Use: Low.
Suited For: Dayhike or backpack.
Best Season: July through mid-September.
Wildlife Viewing: Good.
Grizzly Bear Danger: Low.
Map/Trailhead: 2/2.
Nearest Campgrounds: Beaver Creek, 4.0 miles, and Cabin Creek, 4.3 miles from the trailhead.
Driving to the Trailhead: Follow U.S. 287 to the signed Beaver Creek Road, 11.8 miles east of the U.S. 287/Montana 87 junction, 8.0 miles east of the Earthquake Lake visitor center, and 0.7 mile east of the turnoff to Beaver Creek Campground; or 10.8 miles west of the U.S. 287/U.S. 191 junction (8.0 miles north of West Yellowstone, and 80.0 miles south of Bozeman, Montana), and 1.0 mile west of Cabin Creek Campground.

Drive north on good wide, gravel Beaver Creek Road up the deep, forested canyon of Beaver Creek 3.3 miles to a small parking area on the west side of the road, signed for the

West Fork Beaver Creek Trail. There are several undeveloped camping areas in Beaver Creek between the highway and the trailhead. **Introduction:** This long dayhike leads into the most accessible high lake basin in the Madison Range. The good trail is well-defined, and has a smooth tread during the first half of the trip, a rocky tread thereafter. The grade ranges from gentle to moderate.

With a choice of two separate lake basins to visit at the Canyon's end, fishing for pan-sized golden trout, numerous good campsites, and a scenic backdrop of 10,000-foot peaks, this trip is well-suited for an extended stay. Since this trip lies within the Lee Metcalf Wilderness, wilderness regulations apply for overnight backcountry visitors.

Description: From the west side of the parking area at 6,907 feet, we follow three switchbacks downhill through Douglas-fir and Engelmann spruce forest to the sturdy bridge spanning Beaver Creek. Shortly thereafter we pass a sign proclaiming our entry into the Taylor-Hilgard Unit of the Lee Metcalf Wilderness, then we ascend moderately, away from Beaver Creek, through

a shady forest of spruce and lodgepole pine. Tall western coneflower and cow parsnip are the most conspicuous plants in the rich, green ground cover.

As we gain elevation, we begin to angle southwest across a broad, open avalanche swath that allows fine views across half-mile-deep Beaver Creek canyon to the 800-foot-high cliff on the north prow of Boat Mountain, and down-canyon to the soaring ramparts of the Henrys Lake Mountains.

A protracted traverse ensues, leading across steep slopes beneath an open canopy of Douglas-fir. Sunny openings are enlivened by an array of wildflowers, including yarrow, Oregon grape, lupine, arrowleaf balsamroot, valerian, western coneflower, cow parsnip, pearly everlasting, and Indian paintbrush.

Our trail, rising at a steady, moderate grade, soon curves westward as we exchange views of Beaver Creek canyon for views of the creek's West Fork, which now rumbles far below. The slopes ahead are drained by numerous steep gullies, some of which contain rivulets. At 2.2 miles we rockhop a larger stream that cascades down the mountainside from the northwest (a difficult

One of the Triple Lakes

crossing in early summer), draining the remote Ramona Lake basin 1,500 feet above.

The trail ahead inclines moderately steeply and becomes rocky, but increasingly broad vistas will distract us from our labors. The precipitous West Fork canyon frames fine views of Boat Mountain and the broad alpine summit of 10,653-foot Sage Peak, on the eastern skyline. Across the West Fork canyon, to the south, lateral moraines on the flanks of Peak 10077 illustrate the 1,000-foot depth of ice during the canyon's last major glaciation.

Our high traverse finally ends as we reach the cascading West Fork and walk upstream beside it. Douglas-firs have now been supplanted by lodgepole pines and subalpine firs. Views of high peaks to the west lure us onward, and shortly we reach the tumbling waters of Avalanche Lake's outlet stream among tall Engelmann spruces. We can either rockhop the wide but shallow creek at the crossing or cross on a large spruce log just upstream.

The rocky trail ahead winds moderately uphill via switchbacks, through a shady subalpine forest of spruce, fir, and whitebark pine. Huckleberry and grouse whortleberry are common trailside plants on the shady forest floor. When the ascent abates, we stroll west to a one-acre, forest-fringed meadow, where we reach a signed junction next to a small creek at 8,525 feet, 4.4 miles from the trailhead. The right fork is the more frequently used trail, leading to Avalanche Lake in 1.0 mile. The left fork leads to Blue Danube Lake in 1.7 miles, nestled in a much larger basin and with more camping areas than at Avalanche Lake. Elevation gain on both trails is comparable.

If Avalanche Lake is your goal, turn right at the junction, follow the rocky trail, and ascend moderately steeply through subalpine forest. Soon you approach a wide but shallow creek as you enter a small, sloping meadow. Alpine groundsel's yellow flowers bloom in profusion alongside the trail here. Rockhop the creek a few moments later, then climb briefly to a larger meadow, surrounded on three sides by towering alpine peaks, the highest of which is Peak 10828, rising on the northern skyline.

From that meadow it is only 250 yards up the trail to the shores of 9,020-foot Avalanche Lake, a 12-acre timberline gem. This basin is small in size but long on rugged alpine beauty: pyramid-like peaks exceeding 10,000 feet in elevation jut skyward above the lake to the south, west, and north.

A trail follows the lake's north shore, where you can find fair campsites beneath an open canopy of timberline conifers. Golden trout to 12 inches can be seen in the lake's clear, deep waters, but lakeside forest makes flycasting difficult.

To visit Blue Danube Lake, bear left at the aforementioned junction, curve around a minor hill to an emerald-green tarn, then hop across its muddy outlet. The trail ahead climbs moderately through the subalpine forest, first southeast, then south, and finally southwest as we curve into the lower reaches of the lake's basin. Amid a thinning forest of whitebark pine and subalpine fir, we enjoy fine views of the alpine peaks and ridges that enclose the basin.

Our trail levels out after 1.3 miles, next to the largest of the Triple Lakes, skirts the north shore, passes a marshy tarn, and then becomes indistinct. Head southwest for 200 yards to the low, whitebark-clad ridge ahead. On the opposite side of the ridge, Blue Danube Lake spreads out below.

This very scenic 20-acre lake lies just below timberline in a spacious cirque at 9,020 feet. Meadows, forest groves, and rock outcrops circle the lake. Peaks' 10280 and 10260, on the crest of the Madison Range, rise behind the lake to the west and northwest, respectively. On the southern skyline, a cliff-bounded ridge embraces the basin, fringed on its crest with shaggy whitebarks. Just above the southwest shore of the lake there rises an intermediate ridge composed of large angular boulders. That ridge is a terminal moraine, representing the extent of the last minor glaciation in the basin.

There are good campsites in the open, timberline forest on benches above the lake's south, east, and north shores, and the lake's deep, clear waters are full of golden trout to 12 inches.

From these scenic Madison Range lakes, retrace your steps back to the trailhead.

Trip 3

RED CANYON FAULT SCARP

Distance: 1.0 mile round trip.
Low/High Elevations: 7,120'/7,280'.
Difficulty: Easy.
Use: Low.
Suited For: Dayhike.
Best Season: Mid-June through mid-October.
Wildlife Viewing: Good.
Grizzly Bear Danger: Moderate.
Map/Trailhead: 3/3.
Nearest Campgrounds: Beaver Creek, 14.3 miles, and Cabin Creek, 12.0 miles from the trailhead.
Driving to the Trailhead: Follow U.S. 287 for 0.6 mile west of the U.S. 287/U.S. 191 junction (8.0 miles north of West Yellowstone, and 80.0 miles south of Bozeman, Montana), or 22.0 miles east of the U.S. 287/Montana 87 junction and 18.3 miles east of the Earthquake Lake visitor center, to a northbound dirt road signed for RED CANYON and FOREST ROAD 681.

This is a narrow and rocky dirt road, and you drive north from the broad grassy flats north of Hebgen Lake and into the scenic meadows and forests of Red Canyon en route to the trailhead. After driving 2.8 miles from the highway, you reach the roadend and trailhead in an expansive, meadow-floored bowl. Toilets and a destination and mileage sign are located at the trailhead. There are several undeveloped camping areas along the Red Canyon Road and at the trailhead.

Introduction: This short trip into Red Canyon combines a pleasant walk through shady forests and alongside a small stream with a close-up look at the Red Canyon fault scarp,

a break on the slopes of the canyon that was created by the Madison River Canyon Earthquake of 1959.

Description: From parking area at 7,120 feet, walk north up the road for several yards to a vehicle barricade, and follow the trail beyond into the shady canyon. Engelmann spruce and lodgepole pine border small Red Canyon Creek and clothe the slopes above. Bold Kirkwood Ridge rises ahead on the northern skyline, its flanks dotted with conifers and limestone outcrops.

The broad-leaved thimbleberry grows in profusion on shady trailside slopes, and a variety of wildflowers enliven the canyon's floor with their colorful blooms. Look for cow parsnip, sticky geranium, western coneflower, yellow mule's ears, lupine, red Indian paintbrush, birchleaf spirea, and subalpine daisy.

At 0.25 mile, the trail forks. Part of the original trail was destroyed in the 1959 earthquake, but we can follow this trail (the right fork) for 150 yards through a flower-rich meadow to the foot of the fault scarp. Several yards east of the scarp, Red Canyon Creek tumbles over a series of minor ledges, where the streambed was offset by movement along the Red Canyon Fault.

The newer trail, curving left from the fork, leaves the canyon bottom, ascending through a parklike stand of Douglas-fir via two switchbacks. Beyond the second switchback, we follow the trail on a gentle traverse through open forest for 250 yards to the fault scarp.

The scarp is an obvious break in the slope above the trail, looking much like a road cut. We can visually trace the scarp to the west along the south slopes of Kirkwood Ridge. Erosion and vegetation have begun to soften the scarp's profile, but it remains as an obvious feature. During the 1959 earthquake, the slopes along the fault were offset by 15-20 feet. The north side of the fault was uplifted, while the south side slipped down. Uplift from earthquakes over the last 65 million years is responsible for the mountainous terrain of Greater Yellowstone.

The Red Canyon Trail continues steeply uphill from the fault scarp, leading deep into the wild interior of the Madison Range. You may wish to continue ahead for another 150 yards to an area of unusual fin-like projections of limestone, where small Red Canyon Creek has carved a narrow, V-shaped gorge.

After enjoying Red Canyon, return the way you came.

Trip 4

TEPEE CREEK TRAIL TO BUFFALO HORN DIVIDE

Distance: 6.0 miles, round trip.
Low/High Elevations: 6,671'/7,600'.
Difficulty: Moderate.
Use: Moderate.
Suited For: Dayhike.
Best Season: Mid-June through September.
Wildlife Viewing: Good.
Grizzly Bear Danger: Moderate.
Map/Trailhead: 4/4.
Nearest Campgrounds: Red Cliff, 9.1 miles, Moose Flat, 23.8 miles, Swan Creek, 25.2 miles, and Greek Creek, 25.8 miles from the trailhead.
Driving to the Trailhead: The signed Tepee Creek Trail begins at the trailhead parking area, 200 yards northeast of U.S. 191, 31.6 miles north of West Yellowstone, Montana, 23.6 miles north of the U.S. 191/287 junction, and 1.0 mile northwest of the signed Yellowstone National Park boundary. Visitors driving through Gallatin Canyon from the north will find the trailhead 57.4 miles south of Bozeman and 15.5 miles south of Big Sky, Montana.

Introduction: Near the northwest corner of Yellowstone National Park, the gentle slopes of the Gallatin Range shed their mantle of dense conifer forests and open up into broad grassy valleys and tree-fringed ridges. These expansive grasslands are important winter ranges for large elk herds, and hikers here in late spring and in autumn are likely to observe some of these herds.

This trip into Tepee Creek valley, just outside of Yellowstone, is one of the finest mid-elevation meadow walks in Greater Yellowstone. A profusion of wildflowers, and groves of pine and aspen decorate the open valley. Memorable vistas continue to expand throughout the trip, stretching from the Gallatin Range, to the upper Gallatin River valley, and to the bold alpine peaks of the Madison Range. The trail, open to horse and foot traffic only, is easy to follow, with only occasional moderate grades.

Description: From the trailhead at 6,671 feet, our trail leads northeast into the broad, grassy valley of Tepee Creek. Open conifer forests fringe the rolling ridges that embrace the valley, and groves of lodgepole pine reach down the green slopes toward the valley floor. Sagebrush and shrub cinquefoil stud the grasslands, and an assortment of wildflowers add their color and fragrance.

Western foothills of the Gallatin Range from Buffalo Horn Divide

Among the myriad blooms, we will see buckwheat, long-plumed avens, Everts thistle, whorled penstemon, groundsel, and blue-eyed grass.

The trail divides into multiple, parallel paths as we proceed through the meadows, often approaching the banks of trickling Tepee Creek. After 1.1 miles of pleasant, nearly level walking, we reach a signed junction. The eastbound trail, signed for Yellowstone National Park, ascends the ridge on the southeast skyline, en route to Daly Creek in the Park.

We bear left at the junction, signed for Buffalo Horn Divide, and ascend a moderate grade for 0.2 mile, then begin a gentle, undulating traverse. Isolated groves of aspen and lodgepole pine begin to appear alongside the trail as we proceed, and views continue to expand as we follow the meadows north. Crown Butte rises to the southeast of the valley, its flat summit crowned by tall conifers and rimmed by volcanic cliffs. The tree-fringed dome of 8,431-foot Grouse Mountain looms above the trail on the western skyline.

The final 0.3 mile of the trail leading to Buffalo Horn Divide rises at a moderate grade, and after walking 3.0 miles from the trailhead, we crest the divide at a 7,600-foot saddle. Here the meadows of the valley end abruptly, and lodgepole pine forest blankets the north-facing slopes below us. The broad, grassy saddle of the Divide supports a colorful display of wildflowers. In addition to many of the aforementioned blooms, here we will also see American bistort, woods forget-me-not, dandelion, lupine, yarrow, larkspur, and valerian.

From the signed four-way junction at Buffalo Horn Divide, we can follow the right-hand, eastbound fork for 100-200 yards for the best vistas from the ridge just above the saddle. In the foreground, the broad, verdant valley of Tepee Creek frames a fine view of the southern Madison Range, crowned by the bold pyramid of 10,653-foot Sage Peak. Our view also stretches southeast along the foothills of the Gallatin Range,

where volcanic buttes and conifer groves contrast with the velvet spread of vast meadows. On the eastern skyline are the gently rolling, grassy and rocky summits of the Gallatins, lying within the boundaries of Yellowstone.

Eventually, we must retrace our flower-decked trail back to the trailhead.

Trip 5

PORTAL CREEK TO GOLDEN TROUT LAKES

Distance: 5.0 miles, round trip.
Low/High Elevations: 8,000'/9,050'.
Difficulty: Moderate.
Use: Low.
Suited For: Dayhike or backpack.
Best Season: July through September.
Wildlife Viewing: Good.
Grizzly Bear Danger: Low.
Map/Trailhead: 5/5.
Nearest Campgrounds: Moose Flat, 10.8 miles, Swan Creek, 12.4 miles, Greek Creek, 12.8 miles, and Red Cliff, 19.1 miles from the trailhead.
Driving to the Trailhead: From U.S. Highway 191 in Gallatin Canyon, 5.8 miles north of Big Sky, or 36.0 miles south of Bozeman, Montana, and 3.9 miles south of Moose Flat Campground, turn southeast onto signed Portal Creek Road, Forest Road 984.

This good gravel road steadily ascends the deep canyon of Portal Creek. It is a one-lane road in places, with turnouts. After 3.9 miles the road forks: right to the Hidden Lakes Trail, and left to the Windy Pass and Golden Trout Lakes trails. Bear left and proceed south up the canyon, now on a one-lane forest road that is rough and rocky in places.

After another 2.9 miles, a sign indicates the Windy Pass trailhead, but we continue, following a pronounced curve in the road, and reach the roadend and trailhead parking area 0.1 mile farther.

Introduction: This short trip visits one of the few lake basins carved by ancient glaciers into the flanks of the 50-mile-long Gallatin Range. High above Gallatin Canyon, the Golden Trout Lakes lie in a shallow cirque below the broad alpine summit of Eaglehead Mountain. Several good campsites invite hikers to stay the night at the largest lake in the chain, where anglers will find good fishing for golden trout to 10 inches.

Description: The signed trail begins a few yards west of the vehicle barricade at the roadend at 8,000 feet, and leads south. We ascend gently at first, through a shady forest of Engelmann spruce, subalpine fir, and lodgepole pine.

Our southbound trail leads us across gentle terrain, past two shallow ponds, and then along the western margin of a small meadow. Beyond that spread we ascend a moderate grade, and 0.5 mile from the trailhead we cross a long-closed logging road. Three switchbacks ensue after crossing the road, but the grade abates above them, when we reach a signed junction with the westbound Hidden Lakes Cutoff Trail.

Here we bear left and continue south through the forest. Soon the trees scatter into groves, and whitebark pine joins the ranks of fir and spruce. At length we enter a lovely meadow, its sloping spread enlivened by the blooms of spring beauty and glacier lily in early summer, and by lupine and Indian paintbrush later in the season.

After leaving the meadow, we quickly descend to a rockhop crossing of the small creek draining the Golden Trout lakes, then begin ascending steep grades through the shady, north-slope forest. Shortly we hop across the creek to the west bank, then wind through the forest for several yards to a soggy meadow, where we jump across the creek one last time. A steady, moderately steep ascent ensues, leading us over slopes studded with boulders and shaded by the subalpine forest. The grade eventually ends as we reach the east shore of the largest of the Golden Trout Lakes at 9,050 feet, 2.5 miles from the trailhead.

The small lake, about 10 acres, rests in a shallow cirque carved into the north flanks of 9,976-foot Eaglehead Mountain, the broad, rocky alpine summit to the south. Whitebark-fringed ridges extend north from the mountain, and bound the cirque on the east and west. Timberline forest surrounds the lake, and good campsites can be found above the north and east shores. Two smaller lakes lie above this lake to the west, and another can be found in the lower part of the basin, to the east, but they are barren of fish and are seldom visited.

After enjoying this remote lake basin, retrace your steps to the trailhead.

Trip 6
GALLATIN CANYON TO LAVA LAKE

Distance: 5.8 miles, round trip.
Low/High Elevations: 5,495'/7,100'.
Difficulty: Moderate.
Use: Moderate.
Suited For: Dayhike or backpack.
Best Season: Late June through September.
Wildlife Viewing: Fair.
Grizzly Bear Danger: Low.
Map/Trailhead: 6/6.
Nearest Campgrounds: Greek Creek, 3.4 miles, Moose Flat, 5.4 miles, Swan Creek, 4.8 miles, Spire Rock, 6.5 miles, and Red Cliff, 20.3 miles from the trailhead.
Driving to the Trailhead: From U.S. 191 in Gallatin Canyon, 27 miles south of Bozeman and 61 miles north of West Yellowstone, Montana, the unsigned road to your trailhead branches south immediately north of a bridge over the Gallatin River. Southbound drivers should note that the turnoff is just before crossing the second bridge spanning the river. A flashing, 35-mile-per-hour warning sign indicates your approach to the bridge from either direction.

A short row of roadside mailboxes gives the only suggestion of this turnoff. To more easily pinpoint the location of this road, note your odometer reading and drive 3.2

miles north of Greek Creek Campground or 3.8 miles south of signed Squaw Creek Road in Gallatin Canyon.

Follow the trailhead access road south along the west bank of the Gallatin River. Paved at first, the road quickly narrows into a one-lane dirt road. You reach the trailhead parking area after 0.2 mile, located on the south side of the road. A large national forest information sign and a pair of pit toilets are at the trailhead.

Introduction: Anchoring the northern end of the Madison Range is an aggregate of more than one dozen 10,000-foot peaks, over three dozen timberline lakes, long and deep U-shaped glacier-carved valleys, and the most extensive backcountry trail network in the range. This area, the Spanish Peaks Unit of the Lee Metcalf Wilderness, is one of the most breathtaking—and heavily visited—areas in the range.

This scenic dayhike, a favorite of Bozeman-area residents, leads up the heavily forested canyon of Cascade Creek to the largest lake in the Madison Range, 40-acre Lava Lake. Although the round-trip hike can be completed in about three hours, the dramatic setting of this forest-rimmed lake—in a deep cirque surrounded by alpine peaks soaring more than 3,000 feet above—invites hikers to linger for an overnight stay in one of several fair to good campsites. Lee Metcalf Wilderness regulations apply to

Lava Lake in the Spanish Peaks, Madison Range

visitors staying overnight in the backcountry.

Description: Our trail begins at 5,495 feet, just behind an information sign at the south edge of the parking area. Here in the moist, shady confines of Gallatin Canyon we find a forest of Engelmann spruce and a rich, green understory including red-osier dogwood, Rocky Mountain maple, mountain alder, snowberry, thimbleberry, and birchleaf spirea.

We quickly leave all that greenery behind as our rocky, moderately ascending trail leads us into a drier forest of lodgepole pine. We soon traverse briefly above a group of summer cabins, then curve into the steep canyon of Cascade Creek. True to its name, this small but turbulent stream tumbles hurriedly down its steep, bouldery bed.

The trail stays above and northwest of the noisy creek in a mostly viewless forest of lodgepole pine and Douglas-fir, with an understory of birchleaf spirea, dogbane, snowberry, Wood's rose, Oregon grape, grouse whortleberry, and the shade-loving prince's pine.

After passing the sign proclaiming entry into the Spanish Peaks Unit of the Lee Metcalf Wilderness, the canyon becomes even more confined, and the dense forest of spindly lodgepoles casts considerable shade. In this forest it is easy to understand why Native American tribes preferred the straight, slim poles of this tree for their lodges.

After one mile we cross a wide but shallow tributary creek via a pole bridge and, 100 yards beyond, we cross another, smaller creek. At 1.9-miles the character of the canyon changes abruptly as the trail levels off beside a wet, willow-and conifer-dotted meadow. Dense forests and blocky talus slopes rise 2,000 feet above to Peak 9,069, high on the southeast skyline.

At the upper end of the meadow we cross Cascade Creek via a two-log footbridge and wind uphill for 150 yards to the foot of a series of eight switchbacks. We can leave the trail here and venture a few yards west into a thicket of bracken fern, cow parsnip, thimbleberry, and elderberry, to view part of Hoodoo Cascade, a small but pretty high-angle cascade 50 yards up-canyon.

We then follow switchbacks, rising at a steady, moderate grade, in a forest that now includes subalpine fir and spruce. At length we level off north of the lake, pass a few scattered basalt boulders—presumably the lava from which the lake gets its name—and soon reach the northeast shore of 7,100-foot Lava Lake, 2.9 miles from the trailhead.

The main trail continues briefly along the lakeshore before climbing over 2,000 feet to the crest of Asbestos Ridge on the eastern skyline. Several boot-worn trails lead south and west to campsites and rocky promontories on the lakeshore.

The lake lies in a deep glacial trough, from which the U-shaped upper valley of Cascade Creek stretches away to the south for 3 miles. Hanging valleys, cirques, and a host of lofty summits complete the magnificent surroundings. Especially prominent are 9,850-foot Table Mountain to the south, and 10,416-foot Jumbo Mountain to the southwest.

Good campsites are located near the northeast shore, and fair sites lie above the north and northwest shores in pine, spruce, and fir forest. Fishing is good for rainbow trout to 12 inches.

From Lava Lake, retrace your steps to the trailhead.

Trip 7

GARNET MOUNTAIN LOOKOUT

Distance: 8.0 miles, round trip.
Low/High Elevations: 5,400'/8,245'.
Difficulty: Strenuous.
Use: Moderate.
Suited For: Dayhike or mountain bike trip.
Best Season: Late June through Sept.
Wildlife Viewing: Good.
Grizzly Bear Danger: Low.

Map/Trailhead: 6/7.
Nearest Campgrounds: Spire Rock, 0.9 mile, Greek Creek, 7.0 miles, Swan Creek, 8.4 miles, Moose Flat, 8.8 miles, and Red Cliff, 23.5 miles from the trailhead.
Driving to the Trailhead: Follow U.S. Highway 191 in Gallatin Canyon to the signed turnoff for Squaw Creek Road, 24.5 miles south of Bozeman, 17.3 miles north of Big Sky, and 64.8 miles north of West Yellowstone, Montana. Turn north onto Squaw Creek Road, immediately bridge the Gallatin River, then turn right beyond the bridge, following the good gravel road past the Squaw Creek Work Center (USFS) and above the banks of the river.

After 1.6 miles, avoid a right-branching road leading to a church camp, and continue into the lower reaches of Squaw Creek canyon to the small trailhead parking area, indicated by a prominent destination and mileage sign, 1.8 miles from the highway.
Introduction: Fire lookout towers are usually located on isolated mountain peaks that provide unobstructed panoramas of the surrounding country, and the Garnet Mountain lookout is no exception.

Garnet Mountain is a massive, dome-shaped prominence lying at the end of a long ridge extending westward from the crest of the Gallatin Range, high above lower Gallatin Canyon. This rigorous trip, uphill all the way to the lookout, leads to the mountain's 8,245-foot summit, where an inspiring panorama unfolds, encompassing a broad sweep of the mountains and valleys of northwestern Greater Yellowstone.

Hikers who enjoy mountaintop sunrises and sunsets will find fair campsites among isolated groves of timberline trees on the flat summit—if you pack enough water. Less spartan accommodations are available in the lookout tower, which can be rented between December 1 and October 15, by contacting the Bozeman Ranger District (see *For Further Information,* above). A maximum group size of four people can rent the cabin, with a five-day limit on the length of stay. Cost is $20 per night. The cabin has second-floor sleeping quarters, with two bunk beds and mattresses, table, chairs, and a wood stove, but no water. Firewood is available.

Description: From the trailhead at 5,400 feet, the Garnet Mountain and Gallatin Riverside trails begin as one path, and we proceed across the sturdy bridge spanning Squaw Creek. Beyond the bridge, we briefly skirt a narrow meadow, then enter a shady forest of Douglas-fir, ascending southwest at a gentle to moderate grade. At 0.3 mile the trails diverge, and we bear left, continuing our ascent beneath a forest canopy that now includes lodgepole pine.

As we ascend the steep slopes of Garnet Mountain and rise higher above Gallatin Canyon, the forest opens up and Douglas-fir becomes the dominant tree, with a scattering of Rocky Mountain juniper. These slopes are rich with greenery, including the shrubs of mallow-leaved ninebark, huckleberry, buffaloberry, and Utah honeysuckle. Numerous wildflowers dot the slopes, including lupine, penstemon, puccoon, birch-leaf spirea, and yarrow.

The forest trees continue to scatter as we proceed, and aspen eventually begin to appear. The broad dome of Garnet Mountain, its talus slopes clothed in greenery and groves of timberline conifers, looms ever closer as we trudge up the steadily ascending

trail. At 1.3 miles and 6,480 feet, a north-trending switchback leads us almost to the crest of a grassy ridge, where trailside slopes are decorated by an assortment of colorful blooms, now including arrowleaf balsamroot, Indian paintbrush, sticky geranium, and northern sweetvetch.

Instead of cresting the ridge, the trail leads us southeast and away from it. Over-the-shoulder views reach north across the yawning defile of Squaw Creek to the bold limestone crag of Storm Castle, but we soon enter lodgepole-pine forest in a south-trending draw, where the views become obscured.

Beyond the head of the draw, the trail opens in a broad saddle at 7,200 feet, 2.1 miles from the trailhead. Wildflowers are even more diverse on these grassy slopes, and additional blooms include American bistort, wild iris, larkspur, woods forget-me-not, clematis, and cliff anemone. Views from the saddle reach southwest across the shadowed depths of Gallatin Canyon to the Spanish Peaks of the Madison Range, a striking array of 10,000-foot summits.

The grade moderates beyond the saddle, and ahead we traverse the mountain's southwest slopes, crossing flower-studded openings and passing beneath an open canopy of scattered Douglas-firs and whitebark pines. At 3.0 miles and 7,600 feet, we reach an old 4WD road, leading north and southeast. Here we turn left and ascend that road north on moderate to steep grades over open slopes. Shooting star, larkspur, mountain bluebells, and phlox enliven the grassy slopes, and sagebrush appears as we approach the lookout tower.

Crest of the Gallatin Range from Garnet Mountain Lookout

Garnet Mountain Lookout

Soon we gain the crest of Garnet Mountain, and wind among scattered groves of whitebark pine and subalpine fir to the 8,245-foot summit, crowned by the lookout tower. The lookout's second-floor balcony offers a top-of-the world vista of southwest Montana that easily justifies the effort required to enjoy it.

Our view reaches 40 miles west to the alpine peaks of the Tobacco Root Mountains, and to the northwest and north, rolling, grassy hills stretch to the far horizon. To the northeast, beyond the depths of Squaw Creek canyon, lies the crest of the Bridger Range, north of Bozeman, Montana. The volcanic peaks of the Gallatin Range, their flanks hollowed by cirques, fill our view from east to southeast. Since the Gallatins are unprotected by wilderness designation, much of their slopes below the timberline in our view are scarred by logging roads and clearcuts.

The Spanish Peaks, to the southwest, part of the Madison Range, are protected by wilderness designation, and their lower slopes are densely mantled in forests of pine, spruce, and fir. Above the forested slopes, jagged alpine peaks rise to the skyline, dominated by the thumb-shaped crag of 11,015-foot Gallatin Peak. Lava Lake and Hoodoo Cascade (see Trip 6) are visible in the Cascade Creek cirque, on the flanks of the Spanish Peaks to the southwest.

Eventually, we must leave the grand vistas behind and retrace our route to the trailhead.

Trip 8
GALLATIN RIVERSIDE TRAIL

Distance: Up to 6.0 miles, round trip.
Low/High Elevations: 5,400'/5,650'.
Difficulty: Easy.
Use: Moderate.
Suited For: Dayhike.
Best Season: Mid-May through mid-October.
Wildlife Viewing: Fair.
Grizzly Bear Danger: Low.
Map/Trailhead: 6/7.
Nearest Campgrounds: See *Nearest Campgrounds* for Trip 7.
Driving to the Trailhead: See driving directions for Trip 7.
Introduction: Gathering its waters on the flanks of the southern Gallatin Range in Yellowstone National Park, the mighty Gallatin River flows through canyons and valleys for some 80 miles, to the Three Forks of the Missouri River (named by the Lewis and Clark Expedition), northwest of Bozeman, Montana. U.S. 191 follows the river throughout much of its course, but this pleasant trip offers the only trail access to the banks of the river in Gallatin Canyon, passing through peaceful forests of Engelmann spruce and Douglas-fir in the moist confines of the lower canyon. Anglers will enjoy combining this easy hike with the good fishing the river offers for brook, rainbow, and brown trout, and mountain whitefish.

Description: From the trailhead, follow Trip 7 for 0.3 mile, then bear right onto the signed Gallatin Riverside Trail. Our trail continues southwest, traversing slopes clothed in a forest of lodgepole pine and Douglas-fir, with a shrubby understory of mallow-leaved ninebark.

Soon we curve around the shoulder of a minor ridge above Gallatin Canyon, then open up on sunny, west-facing slopes. These slopes support a variety of wildflowers including lupine, Indian paint-brush, western wallflower, yarrow, long-leaf phlox, and woodland star.

We then descend toward the Gallatin River via four switchbacks, reaching level terrain on a grassy bench just above and east of the river. Here we meet an old road coming from the church camp on Squaw Creek after 0.7 mile, and turn left, following the road south. After another 0.3 mile, the road ends at a vehicle barricade, and we continue south, now on the trail. Soon the bench ends, and we follow along steep slopes just above the riverbank.

The trail ahead ranges from the river's edge to the slopes well above it, and the tread is rocky where we cross boulder fields, but smooth where we pass through stands of conifers. Thickets of shrubs clothe the slopes, including wild rose, Rocky Mountain maple, red-osier dogwood, huckleberry, wild rasp-berry, currant, and mallow-leaved ninebark. The delicate blooms of yellow columbine and the fronds of rockbrake fern decorate sheltered recesses alongside the trail.

Several outfitters offer daily float trips on the river, and we are likely to see numerous rafts pass during the course of the hike. Views in the canyon are restricted, but we will have occasional views of densely forested slopes, broken by limestone outcrops, that rise to tall ridges some 2,000 feet above.

The trail continues along the river, through occasional rocky and overgrown stretches, at times dropping to the riverbank to avoid talus slopes or limestone outcrops. During spring snowmelt runoff parts of the trail may be underwater, and there is often no alternate route above. Exercise caution when approaching this large, powerful river; if the trail is submerged, you must return to the trailhead.

The farther we follow the trail, the more overgrown with shrubs it becomes, and after about 2.0 miles, the trail is too overgrown and faint for carefree walking. Many hikers find a scenic spot in the first 1.5 miles, then backtrack to the trailhead. Those who persist on the trail will find that the tread becomes well defined after about 2.5 miles.

The trail ends at Highway 191, just east of a bridge over the river, at a low-speed curve in the highway. This bridge lies just east of the turnoff to Trailhead 6 for Lava Lake (see Trip 6). A large turnout offers ample parking east of the bridge, and can be used as an alternate trailhead. The Gallatin Riverside Trail is unsigned here, but is easy to follow as it leads north alongside the river.

Trip 9
WATKINS CREEK TO COFFIN LAKE

Distance: 10.4 miles round trip.
Low/High Elevations: 6,700'/8,450'.
Difficulty: Moderate.
Use: Moderate.
Suited For: Dayhike or backpack.
Best Season: July through mid-September.
Wildlife Viewing: Good.
Grizzly Bear Danger: Low.
Map/Trailhead: 7/8.
Nearest Campgrounds: Spring Creek, 2.7 miles, Cherry Creek, 6.7 miles, and Lonesomehurst, 8.1 miles from the trailhead.
Driving to the Trailhead: Follow U.S. Highway 20 for 7.2 miles west of West Yellowstone, Montana, or 2.1 miles east of Targhee Pass on the Continental Divide, and turn north onto Forest Road 167 (the Hebgen Lake Road), where a large destination and mileage sign points to a Gallatin National Forest recreation area.

This is a good, wide, gravel road, but due to heavy summer traffic the roadbed develops a severe washboard surface in places. Proceed generally north on this road, passing turnoffs to Lonesomehurst Campground after 3.5 miles, Cherry Creek camping area after 4.9 miles, and Spring Creek camping area after 8.9 miles. From the Spring Creek camping area, continue along the southwest shore of Hebgen Lake for another 2.6 miles to a

Watkins Creek valley in the Henrys Lake Mountains, near Hebgen Lake

southbound spur road signed for Watkins Creek Trail (one-third mile west of the entrance to Firehole Guest Ranch). Turn left here and proceed 0.1 mile to the trailhead parking area, 11.6 miles from Highway 20. A national forest information sign is located at the trailhead.

Introduction: Watkins Creek is the principal drainage on the northeast slope of the Henrys Lake Mountains, gathering its waters on the Montana side of the Continental Divide, and draining into Hebgen Lake, a sprawling impoundment on the Madison River. From the broad meadows and aspen groves of its lower reaches, to the ice-gouged cirques and alpine peaks of its headwaters, the prominent canyon of Watkins Creek attracts the attention of even the most jaded travelers as they drive Highway 287 along the north shore of Hebgen Lake.

This pleasant and memorable hike ascends the canyon of Watkins Creek, leading through flower-filled meadows, aspen groves, and rich forests to a timberline lake brimming with fat cutthroat and rainbow trout.

Description: From the trailhead at 6,700 feet, our trip begins as we pass through a gate in a fenceline that bars cattle from grazing the rich meadows of Watkins Creek. The trail rises gently at first, then moderately, as we amble through tall-grass meadows enlivened by the blooms of harebell, sticky geranium, yarrow, lupine, and in early summer, pasqueflower and arrowleaf balsamroot. The mile-long, cliff-edged alpine mesa of 9,971-foot Coffin Mountain rises prominently on the southwest skyline.

Soon we climb in earnest as we enter an open forest of Douglas-fir and aspen, then curve briefly southeast, heading for Watkins Creek. Once we are within earshot of that small stream, the forest opens up, and a grand view of Watkins Creek valley unfolds.

In the foreground are broad, sagebrush-studded meadows and groves of aspen, flanked on either side by a discontinuous forest. At the valley's head, an inviting, mile-wide alpine cirque spreads out below the limestone cliffs of 10,180-foot Bald Peak. A pleasant, but shadeless, stroll through the meadows ensues on the gently climbing trail. Never out of earshot of the creek, we are seldom close enough to see it.

After 1.6 miles an obscure horse trail branches left (east), and follows the opposite bank of the creek, heading north to the Firehole Guest Ranch. Just beyond that obscure junction is an old barricade of concrete posts. Our trail to this point is on a long-closed jeep road, but the old scars of the road have healed, and now only the single track of our trail is apparent.

We then enter a pine and fir forest and 2.5 miles from the trailhead we reach a signed junction. The left fork continues on up Watkins Creek to the Continental Divide Trail, but we bear right toward Coffin Lake. The sign also indicates that Sheep Lake (see Trip 1) lies 5 miles ahead, but the junction with the obscure, seldom-used trail leading there is very difficult to find.

Our trail angles west, ascending moderately to a rock-hop crossing of shallow, eight-foot-wide West Fork Coffin Creek. Quickly thereafter we jump across another, smaller stream, then begin a moderately steep ascent through predominantly lodgepole forest just north of audible Coffin Creek. En route we splash through two cold, spring-fed streams issuing from the south slopes of Coffin Mountain, which now looms boldly above to the northwest.

Beyond the springs the ascent continues via switchbacks, but the grade finally abates as we approach the log jam at the outlet of Coffin Lake. The tread soon becomes wet and muddy as we negotiate the north shores of the lake in a forest of Engelmann spruce, subalpine fir, and whitebark pine. At 5.2 miles we reach a large, dusty campsite and the apparent end of the trail, next to a cold stream that tumbles down from the south slopes of Coffin Mountain. A boot-worn path continues west, undulating along the bouldery north shore of the lake.

Although the overused campsite at the lake is not very inviting for an overnight stay, the lake itself lies in a scenic timberline setting. Low cliffs and boulder-littered slopes composed of gray metamorphic schist abut the west shore of the lake, and to

the south, gravelly slopes and cliff bands composed of buff-toned limestone rise to the broad summit of Peak 9469. More limestone slopes rise steeply north of the lake to the alpine flanks of Coffin Mountain. On the western skyline, the grassy dome of Peak 10541 rises above a rockbound, ice-scoured landscape of minor cirque basins.

Fishing access is best along the west and northwest shores, where rocky knolls plunge into deep water. Huckleberries and small, red, grouse whortleberries are abundant above the north shore west of the campsite. These wilderness delicacies are an added bonus for hikers visiting the lake in mid-to-late-August.

From the lake, retrace your course to the trailhead.

Trip 10

SAWTELL PEAK TRAILHEAD TO ROCK CREEK BASIN

Distance: 8.8 miles round trip.
Low/High Elevations: 8,800'/9,320'.
Difficulty: Moderately easy.
Use: Moderate.
Suited For: Dayhike or mountain bike trip.
Best Season: July through mid-September.
Wildlife Viewing: Fair.
Grizzly Bear Danger: Low.
Map/Trailhead: 8/9.
Nearest Campgrounds: Flat Rock, 11.8 miles, Upper Coffeepot, 13.7 miles, Buffalo, 16.9 miles, Box Canyon, 20.4 miles, and Riverside, 29.4 miles from the trailhead.
Driving to the Trailhead: From U.S. 20, 33.0 miles north of Ashton, Idaho, and 1.6 miles north of Mack's Inn, or 7.5 miles south of the U.S 20/Idaho 87 junction, and 10.6 miles southwest of Targhee Pass, turn west onto the signed Sawtell Peak Road (Forest Road 024), opposite the Island Park Resort.

This is a well-maintained gravel road, and though it climbs 2,600 feet to the trailhead, it maintains a gentle to moderate grade throughout its length. However, it is not recommended for large RV's.

After driving 10.0 miles up the forested eastern slopes of the Centennial Mountains, you reach the signed Sawtell Peak Trailhead at a switchback in the road. The small parking area has room for about five cars. The F.A.A. radar facility atop Sawtell Peak lies another 1.8 miles up the road, and it affords a sweeping panorama of the Greater Yellowstone area, from the Yellowstone Plateau in the east to the craggy Tetons in the southeast.

Introduction: The Centennial Mountains stretch nearly 50 miles eastward from Monida Pass along the Continental Divide, and then the divide curves abruptly north. From where the divide turns north, a prominent Centennial spur ridge continues east and rises to the bold dome of Sawtell Peak. Sawtell Peak (9,880'), with the tall white F.A.A. radar dome on its summit can be seen for great distances, from the Madison Valley in the north, to the Teton Basin in the south.

This grand dayhike, beginning on the southern flanks of Sawtell Peak, follows a long-closed road along timberline ridges to the wildflower-rich meadows of Rock Creek Basin, a broad cirque on the northeast slopes of the Centennial Mountains in Idaho. In addition to an exciting, and fairly easy walk along timberline ridges, the vistas are unparalleled in Greater Yellowstone, stretching from the Teton Range in the southeast to the Absaroka Range on the eastern edge of Yellowstone National Park.

Rock Creek Basin is a popular rockhounding area, and marine fossils can be found in the limestone cliffs that rise

above. The route is open to mountain bikes but closed to motorized vehicles.

Description: From the ridgetop trailhead at 9,050 feet, we descend west, dropping steeply at first in a timberline forest of subalpine fir and whitebark pine. The grade soon moderates as we reach a minor draw, and then climb easily to merge with an old road after 0.3 mile, where we turn left.

The road was built by the Forest Service in the early 1960s in an attempt to restore the Rock Creek watershed after years of overgrazing by domestic sheep. The Forest Service carved terraces into the alpine grasslands of the basin, hoping to check erosion on the easily erodible limestone slopes, and thus prevent extensive siltation of the valuable Henrys Lake fishery below.

The old road has begun to blend into the rubbly, volcanic slopes (composed of rhyolite), and we follow a single footpath along the narrow roadbed. An easy, undulating, west-trending traverse on south-facing slopes follows, leading past a scattering of picturesque, wind-flagged whitebark pines and subalpine firs.

As we progress, grand vistas expand to the far horizons—a sweeping panorama stretching across fully half of the Greater Yellowstone area. To the east, our view stretches across Island Park basin to the

Mt. Jefferson, highest peak in the Centennial Mountains, rises above the trail to Rock Creek Basin

west slopes of the Yellowstone Plateau. Thousands of acres of gray snags cover the plateau's slopes, the remains of a once-vast lodgepole-pine forest consumed by the North Fork Fire in the summer of 1988. That 504,025-acre blaze was started by woodcutters in the Targhee National Forest, burned into Yellowstone National Park, and nearly destroyed the historic Old Faithful Inn.

Much of the park is concealed behind the plateau's rim, but our view reaches to the high peaks of the Absaroka Range, 80 miles distant on the far eastern boundary of the Park. To the southeast we gaze across 60 miles of forested volcanic plateaus to the jagged profile of the Tetons. South and west of the Tetons are the Snake River Range and the Big Hole Mountains, respectively.

Forest-rimmed Island Park Reservoir lies to the south, beyond which the Snake River Plain, punctuated by volcanic buttes, stretches away into the heat-hazy distance of eastern Idaho. We also have occasional westward views along the crest of the Centennials to the lofty Lima Peaks, 60 miles away near Monida Pass and Interstate 15. We will enjoy all these vistas for the remaining ridgetop segment of our trip. Wildflowers adorning the grassy, dark volcanic trailside slopes include cinquefoil, lupine, American bistort, groundsel, yarrow, cous biscuitroot, and dogtooth violet.

A faint jeep track forks left from our trail at 0.8 mile, and after another 0.8 mile, we cross a shoulder of the Continental Divide and enter Montana, beginning a gradual descent. Ahead of us to the northwest looms the shining limestone pyramid of 10,196-foot Mt. Jefferson, the apex of the Centennials. The grassy bowl of upper Hell Roaring Canyon lies below to the south.

Soon the old road begins to closely follow the divide and becomes narrow and rocky. Views from this crest now extend north past verdant Rock Creek Basin to distant Montana ranges, including the bald peaks of the Snowcrest Range and the elevated plateau of the Gravelly Range.

At 2.4 miles we reach a 9,040-foot saddle on the Continental Divide, where the old road bends north and begins to descend steadily into the basin. The saddle makes a convenient terminus for hikers who would rather not descend into—and climb back out of—Rock Creek Basin.

Those who choose to continue will descend into a shady forest of subalpine fir, whitebark pine, and Engelmann spruce, negotiate a series of short switchbacks, then curve northwest, and soon reach the timberline meadows of the glacier-carved basin. A scattering of stunted trees dot the basin, growing in tree-islands atop hummocks that rise out of the meadows.

The rich meadows of the basin support a profusion of colorful wildflowers such as Indian paintbrush, buttercup, dogtooth violet, shooting star, mountain bluebell, Henderson's spring parsley, and bracted lousewort.

The descent ends at 8,800 feet, 0.5 mile from the saddle. Most hikers will probably end the trip here, stop for lunch, and soak up the alpine splendor that surrounds the basin. Good views extend northeast past the radar-capped dome of Sawtell Peak to Henrys Lake and beyond, to the southern peaks of the Gallatin Range in the northwest corner of Yellowstone Park.

Those who continue will follow the road as it climbs northwest, ascending gently at first between small meadows below and dwarf willows and a ground-hugging mat of krummholz trees, mostly subalpine fir, above. Limestone pinnacles jut from talus slopes at the headwall of the basin just above us to the west.

Soon the grade steepens as you rise to a minor ridge studded with stunted conifers. Once you crest the ridge, you descend into the westernmost reaches of the basin. To the west Mt. Jefferson looms on the skyline, and a host of limestone spires tower above the basin to the south.

Ditch-like terraces soon begin to appear on nearby slopes; ignore them and stay on the roadbed. The descent leads into a grassy draw where a small stream may be flowing in early summer—the first water en route. Continue downhill, heading northeast, finally leveling off on a broad, grassy saddle at 8,950 feet, 4.2 miles from the trailhead.

The old road continues along the open, south-facing slopes ahead, where terraces have been carved from the basin floor nearly to the summit of Peak 9584. Once again you can terminate the trip, or continue ahead for 0.2 mile via a trailless route to tiny Lake Marie, one of only six lakes in the Centennials. To get there, leave the road at the 8950-foot saddle and head northwest across a small meadow to its western edge, where steep, tree-dotted slopes fall away into Lake Marie's basin. A pause here on the rim of the basin allows us to gaze north, far into the remote mountainous landscape of southwestern Montana. The broad expanse of the Gravelly Range stretches to the north. Beyond are the peaks of the Tobacco Root Mountains, and on the far northern horizon, the rolling shoulders of the Big Belt Mountains.

Stay to the right (north) of a steep gully and descend 175 feet to the south shore of the shallow tarn. A minor stream tumbles into the lake from the southwest, draining the cirque carved into the flanks of Mt. Jefferson. The waters of the 8,750-foot lake are too shallow to support a fishery, but the scenic and remote setting makes the visit to the lake worth the effort. Although Lake Marie was created by the action of glacial ice, a landslide of great limestone boulders now dams the outlet.

From the lake, return the way you came.

Trip 11

RED ROCK PASS TO HELL ROARING CREEK

Distance: 6.4 miles round trip.
Low/High Elevations: 7,000'/7,350'.
Difficulty: Moderately easy.
Use: Low.
Suited For: Dayhike.
Best Season: Mid-June through Sept.

Wildlife Viewing: Good.
Grizzly Bear Danger: Low.
Map/Trailhead: 9/10.
Nearest Campground: Upper Lake, 12.8 miles from the trailhead.
Driving to the Trailhead: Northbound drivers on U.S. 20 should proceed 37.0 miles north of Ashton, Idaho, and 5.5 miles north of Mack's Inn, and turn west onto Forest Road 053, where a prominent sign points the way to Lakeview and Red Rock Lakes National Wildlife Refuge. This road, labeled Bootjack Pass Road on national forest maps, is paved for the first 0.6 mile, beyond which it becomes a wide gravel road. After topping out on Bootjack Pass, the road descends to the edge of the broad meadows south of Henrys Lake.

After 4.8 miles from U.S. 20, pass the private Sawtell Shadows Campground, and after another 2.5 miles reach a junction with signed Forest Road 055, branching right toward Idaho 87. Bearing left at the junction, continue for another 4.2 miles to prominently signed Red Rock Pass (7,120') on the Continental Divide., 11.5 miles from Highway 20. Just east of the sign at the pass, a prominent jeep track turns south into the forest. Abundant Continental Divide Trail (CDT) markers on roadside trees show the route. Park in one of the wide spots along this track just south of the Red Rock Pass Road.

Alternately, drivers on Idaho 87, 4.0 miles southeast of Raynolds Pass, and 5.2 miles northwest of the U.S. 20/Idaho 87 junction, should turn west where a large sign points to Red Rock Lakes NWR. Paved for the first 2.7 miles, and wide gravel thereafter, this road, Forest Road 055, follows the north and west shores of Henrys Lake to the aforementioned junction with Forest Road 053, 5.5 miles from Highway 87. From this junction, continue straight ahead, following the directions given above to reach the trailhead.

Visitors wishing to reach Upper Lake Campground in the Red Rock Lakes NWR can continue west on the Red Rock Pass Road for 12.8 miles from the pass.

Introduction: Tracing a part of the Continental Divide Trail along the north slope of the Centennial Mountains, this scenic and seldom-used trail surveys a broad sweep of remote mountain scenery and unpopulated intermountain valleys en route to a precipitous canyon and the turbulent waters of Hell Roaring Creek. Hikers on part of Trip 10 will traverse above the headwaters of this stream—the most remote tributary of the Missouri River—while hikers on this trip will enter the portal of the canyon, where it emerges from the mountains before meandering across a high, grassy valley to join the Red Rock River.

Description: From Red Rock Pass follow the poor spur road (CDT markers on nearby trees lead the way) as it winds south beneath a shady canopy of lodgepole pine. After 250 yards the road ends, and the trail begins behind a sign that declares the route ahead is closed to motorized vehicles.

The portal of Hell Roaring Canyon

The trail climbs southeast to the crest of a low moraine, then winds generally south through a predominantly lodgepole forest, climbing over more low moraines and dipping into minor draws, as we closely follow the Continental Divide. The actual watershed divide is indiscernible at this point.

After about 0.25 mile, we pass through a gate, enter Montana, and continue a circuitous, southwest-bound course over hilly moraines. A dense forest of spindly lodgepoles obscures our view, but trailside huckleberries (when ripe in mid-August) and the creamy white blooms of birchleaf spirea capture our attention on this uneventful stretch of trail.

At length the forest opens up as we gently descend into the scenic, aspen-clad basin of Cole Creek, reaching the small stream 0.8 mile from the trailhead. Cole Creek gathers its waters in the cirque above to the southeast, high on the flanks of 9,512-foot Red Rock Mountain. West of that cirque are more 9,000-foot peaks and hanging cirques, and looming above to the southwest is the knob-like summit of 9,439-foot Nemesis Mountain.

We easily rockhop Cole Creek and then reenter forest. Soon Douglas-fir dominates

the forest as we begin a protracted westbound traverse upon the steep north slopes of Nemesis Mountain. The trail is easy to follow and smooth, but the narrow tread has been damaged by cattle that graze here during summer. Few hikers use this trail, but local wildlife does, including elk, mule deer, coyote, moose, and black bear.

On these slopes we cross five precipitous avalanche chutes, the first of which is a broad boulder field where the trail briefly disappears, but the route across is shown by cairns. As we approach this chute, notice the tall Douglas-firs just below the trail. Their boles have been stripped of large branches for 20-30 feet above the ground, indicating the power of the avalanches that sweep down the chute during winter.

From this chute and others ahead we gain expansive vistas of the broad grasslands of Centennial Valley stretching west. The bald alpine peaks of the remote Snowcrest Range and the gentle, forested plateaus of the Gravelly Range rise in the distance to the northwest and north. The craggy peaks of the Madison Range lie on the far northeastern skyline. Far away to the east, beyond the crest of the Henrys Lake Mountains, are the southernmost summits of the Gallatin Range. The only evidences of human presence in this broad panorama are a few isolated ranches and the Red Rock Pass Road in the valley below.

Eventually, we negotiate four switchbacks, steadily descending into a forest of Douglas-fir, then we resume the traverse. Soon the trail curves southwest toward the portal of Hell Roaring Canyon. As its name suggests, the large creek thunders through the narrow declivity ahead, even in late summer when the water level is usually low.

Switchbacks soon lead out of the forest, and the rugged portal opens up ahead. West of the canyon, buff-toned limestone cliffs soar 600 feet up, and the exceedingly steep, broken slopes of Nemesis Mountain jut 2,000 feet above in the east. These rugged cliffs frame a distant view of the gentle, meadow-and-forest-covered slopes at the crest of the Centennials to the south.

The now-rocky trail descends to the banks of Hell Roaring Creek in the narrow gorge, and proceeds south upstream. The canyon becomes increasingly narrow, and at one point you are funneled between cliffs barely 30 feet apart. Willows border the creek, and occasional Douglas-fir, Engelmann spruce, and limber pine—trees usually separated by thousands of feet of elevation—dot the canyon floor.

At 3.2 miles we reach a two-log footbridge spanning the creek at 7,050 feet. The trail continues up-canyon, forking after 0.25 mile into branches that lead southeast to Lillian Lake and south to Blair Lake. Those trails are both about another 4 miles long, and gain considerable elevation, so most of us will terminate our trip at the footbridge.

From Hell Roaring Canyon, retrace your route to the trailhead.

Trip 12
HIDDEN LAKE TO CLIFF LAKE

Distance: 8.0 miles round trip.
Low/High Elevations: 6,315'/6,800'.
Difficulty: Moderately easy.
Use: Low.
Suited For: Dayhike or mountain bike trip.
Best Season: Mid-June through mid-Oct.
Wildlife Viewing: Good.
Grizzly Bear Danger: Low.
Map/Trailhead: 10/11.
Nearest Campground: Upper Lake, 15.0 miles from the trailhead.
Driving to the Trailhead: Follow the driving directions for Trip 11 to Red Rock Pass, and continue west on the good, wide, gravel road, descending into Alaska Basin, the easternmost extension of Centennial Valley. After driving 6.0 miles from the pass, enter Red Rock Lakes National Wildlife Refuge, and 1.1 miles farther the signed Elk Lake Road branches west, straight ahead, and the main road curves south, leading to Upper Lake Campground in 5.7 miles, and ultimately to Interstate 15 at Monida Pass, 35 miles west.

Follow the Elk Lake Road north across Centennial Valley, avoiding signed turnoffs to Widgeon Pond after 2.4 miles and to Landon Camp at 2.8 miles. Enter Beaverhead National Forest 3.9 miles from the main road, at which point our road becomes rougher and rutted in places.

Soon we drive along the west shore of long Elk Lake, passing the cabins of Elk Lake Camp (featuring a restaurant, cabin and boat rentals, and a bar) before climbing into the grassy hills above the lake. The road ahead is much narrower and rutted with a few steep stretches, but can be negotiated by carefully driven passenger cars.

The road descends steeply to the north end of Elk Lake, proceeds north up a grassy valley, and passes an undeveloped camping area among lodgepole pines, 8.6 miles

Cliff Lake

from the main road. We reach the road-end 0.7 mile farther on, at another undeveloped and forested camping area. Pit toilets and a national forest information sign are located here.

Introduction: At the western front of the Henrys Lake Mountains, a series of gently sloping ridges composed of the volcanic rock rhyolite (the same material that covers much of Yellowstone Park), marches northwest to merge with the southern reaches of Montana's Gravelly Range. A prominent but narrow canyon called Lost Mine Canyon slices through these ridges from southwest to northeast.

One-half dozen landslide-dammed, spring-fed lakes form a chain in this 12-mile-long valley. The two northernmost lakes—Cliff and Wade—and the southernmost—Elk Lake—are accessible by road and are popular camping, fishing, and boating areas.

The middle lakes are accessible only by trail, and they offer a scenic and remote hiking destination. The trail in Lost Mine Canyon is well defined and the hiking is easy, the relatively low elevations offer early season access, and the fishing is good for large rainbow and cutthroat trout.

Description: From the lodgepole-pine-shaded trailhead, the highest point of our trip, we immediately descend into a draw where another trail diverges to the right, leading down the draw for one-third mile to Hidden Lake, where Elk Lake Camp maintains a boat dock and offers row boats for rent (inquire at Elk Lake Camp en route to the trailhead).

Bearing left at that junction, we then ascend to a low, pine-covered ridge where we are treated to our first glimpse of the emerald-green waters of Hidden Lake. The smooth trail then leads us downhill and away from views of the lake. The draw and our descent end at the west shore of Hidden Lake. Following the irregular shoreline north, we proceed either through mixed conifer forest or across grassy slopes that host numerous colorful blooms, such as sticky geranium, lupine, Canada goldenrod, yarrow, harebell, and cow parsnip.

At 1.5 miles we reach a signed junction next to a large campsite, at the northwest corner of the lake. Bearing right, we then skirt the lake's north shore, where good views stretch across the lake to the boulder-scarred west slopes of Hidden Lake Bench, which rise 800 feet from the lake to the rim above.

Soon the trail leaves the lakeshore, and we proceed northeast through an old landslide—a maze of rhyolite boulders, small draws, and low ridges. The trail gently descends through the debris beneath an open forest canopy, which allows occasional glimpses of bold Madison Range to the northeast.

At 1.9 miles we level off next to shallow, 10-acre Goose Lake (6,600'). Although shallow, both Goose and Otter lakes are spring-fed, and hence do not freeze in winter sustaining populations of large trout. From Goose Lake meander through open forest, descending 80 feet in 0.25 mile to a low ridge above and east of the clear waters of Otter Lake, also about 10 acres in size.

Although these pleasant, forest-rimmed lakes are the destination of most of the few hikers who come to the canyon, the following 1.25 miles of trail to the Horn Arm of Cliff Lake are a delightful stroll.

The jumbled landslide debris that chokes the canyon is left behind at Otter Lake, and the trail descends from the lake and into the increasingly broad canyon. Tall forested ridges now embrace the canyon, instead of the broken, rocky slopes that surround the lakes.

A short distance below Otter Lake, a small spring-fed stream emerges next to the trail, and we follow its course to a log crossing where the stream banks are enlivened by the yellow blooms of common monkeyflower. The easy stroll continues through meadows along the east banks of the stream, and at length we reach the narrow, shallow, Horn Arm of Cliff Lake at 6,315 feet, 4.0 miles from the trailhead.

Slopes clad in sagebrush and dotted with Douglas-fir rise north of the lake, and to the east rhyolite buttresses and dense forest rise to the rim of Hidden Lake Bench. The trail continues along the lakeshore for 0.6 mile, then climbs steeply to the bench above, ultimately leading to the private property of Selby's Resort on another arm of sprawling Cliff Lake.

From the lake, retrace your route to the trailhead.

Chapter Two

THE SOUTHWESTERN REACHES OF GREATER YELLOWSTONE

Introduction

In the southwestern corner of Greater Yellowstone, the semi-arid volcanic lowlands of the Snake River Plain in Idaho with their rectangular potato fields give way to an abruptly rising wall of magnificent, verdant mountains. Approaches to this region follow valley bottoms, from the broad grasslands of Teton Basin to the deep and winding valley of the South Fork Snake River, but looming mountains are always close by.

Teton Basin is one of the most idyllic mountain valleys in the Rockies. Bounded on the west by the Big Hole Mountains, on the south by the Snake River Range, and on the east by the fabulous Teton Range, the 10-mile-wide, 6,000-foot-high valley lies in a setting of mountain grandeur that rivals Jackson Hole. This area receives some of the highest precipitation in Greater Yellowstone, so the nearby mountains are mantled in rich forests of tall spruces, firs, and pines. Meadow openings between forest groves host a vast array of wildflowers and greenery.

Nineteenth-century fur trappers—the fabled mountain men—bestowed the name "Pierre's Hole" on what is now called Teton Basin. Pierre was an Iroquois in the employ of the Hudson's Bay Company, the British monopoly that controlled the fur trade in the Northwest during the early 19th Century. Teton Basin was the site of the Rocky Mountain fur trade rendezvous in the summer of 1832. Modern highways, including the highway up Trail Creek and over Teton Pass, and the highway over Pine Creek Pass between the Teton Basin and Swan Valley, follow ancient routes used by Indians, and later by the mountain men of the fur trade.

The valley of the Snake River, between Swan Valley, Idaho, and Alpine Junction, Wyoming, is much more confined than Teton Basin. Tall mountains—the Snake River Range and the Caribou Mountains— rise abruptly from the river's banks to summits exceeding 9,000 feet, and with a vertical relief of 4,000 feet. The north slopes of the Caribous are densely mantled in conifer forest, but the southwest slopes of the Snake River Range are more open, providing a stunning backdrop of sweeping, grassy slopes, groves of conifers and aspen, and towering limestone peaks jutting above timberline.

Hikers who enjoy a variety of rich wildflower gardens, hushed, cathedralesque forests, and far-ranging vistas will find the short trips in this chapter much to their liking.

The Snake River Range, commonly known as The Palisades, is one of six mountain ranges in Greater Yellowstone not yet protected under federal wilderness designation. The proposed Palisades Wilderness, which would encompass some 200,000 acres, is strongly opposed by off-road vehicle groups, and the petroleum industry, which believes that the range holds large reserves of oil and natural gas.

This vast roadless area offers backcountry recreation comparable to the best hiking areas in Greater Yellowstone, but it is often overlooked by hikers, who tend to flock to better known hiking areas in the region. Hence much of the range's trails are seldom trod by hikers. Hunters use the range in autumn, cross-country skiers enjoy the broad, open slopes around Teton Pass in winter, but in summer, mountain bikers usually outnumber hikers on the trails.

The Snake River Range offers two distinct faces: one of towering ridges and rugged defiles (see Trips 17-18), and one of vast, meadow-clad slopes, gently contoured ridges, ice-gouged cirques, and alpine summits (see Trip 15). Heavy winter snows and the high water-holding capacity of the soils here support some of the richest meadows and wildflower gardens in Greater Yellowstone.

The serrated profile of the Teton Range is an unforgettable and overwhelming presence in Greater Yellowstone. These towering, 12,000- to 13,000-foot mountains offer the kind of scenery one expects to find in the Rocky Mountains, but few ranges in the Rockies rival the Tetons for sheer magnificence. The range is the youngest in the Rockies, having uplifted along a fault zone at its eastern base only about nine million years ago, compared to the 50-to 65-million year age of most of Greater Yellowstone's mountain ranges. But the rocks exposed in the range are some of the oldest in Greater Yellowstone. Two-billion-year-old granitic rocks compose the range's famous Matterhorn-like peaks. The inexorable forces of erosion have yet to subdue the Teton's jagged profile, so typical of relatively youthful mountains.

Unlike the abruptly rising, 7,000-foot eastern escarpment of the Tetons, the west slope of the range, which is covered in this chapter, is comparatively gentle but no less spectacular. The blocky limestone crags forming the crest of the range rise above emerald-green slopes carpeted in rich vegetation, long and deep, U-shaped, glacier-carved valleys, and broad cirque basins embraced by ice-chiseled bedrock. Rising boldly beyond the crest on the eastern skyline are the landmark peaks of Greater Yellowstone—Mt. Moran, Mt. Owen, Grand Teton, Middle Teton, and South Teton—peaks that due to their prominence and isolation can be seen for great distances.

The west slopes of the Tetons, much like the Snake River Range farther south, lie in a high precipitation zone. There is abundant exposed bedrock here, but where soils have collected—in basins, in canyon bottoms, and on some of the gentler, lower elevation slopes—the wildflower gardens are rich and spectacular.

Although the bulk of the range lies within Wyoming, trailheads on the west slope are accessed via Teton Basin in Idaho. Much of the west slope lies within the boundaries of the 116,535-acre Jedediah Smith Wilderness. Trails are gentler here than those in Grand Teton National Park on the east slope, and much less crowded.

Access and Services

U.S. 26 in Idaho and Idaho 33/Wyoming 22 are the primary roadways that offer access to trails and campgrounds covered in this chapter.

Major east-west highways include: U.S. 26, which follows the South Fork Snake River for 70 miles from Idaho Falls, Idaho, to Hoback Junction, Wyoming; and Idaho 33/Wyoming 22, which leads 77 miles from U.S. Highway 20 at Rexburg, Idaho, through scenic Teton Basin, over one of the steepest mountain passes in the Rockies—Teton Pass—and down to Jackson, Wyoming.

Travelers from the south can access the region via U.S. 89, for a distance of 150 miles from Logan, Utah, to Alpine Junction, Wyoming. From the north, Idaho 32—part of the Teton Scenic Highway—leads 29 miles from Ashton to Idaho 33 near Tetonia, Idaho. From the southeast, U.S. 189 leads 190 miles from Evanston, Wyoming, to Hoback Junction; and U.S. 191 leads 165 miles from Rock Springs, Wyoming, to Hoback Junction.

Towns are small in this region, but most offer a variety of services. They include Swan Valley, Irwin, Victor, Driggs, and Tetonia, Idaho, and Jackson, Wyoming (see Chapter 3 for information regarding Jackson).

In addition to the towns listed below, services are available on Highway 26 at Alpine Junction and Hoback Junction in Wyoming. At Alpine Junction there are three large motels, gas stations, an RV park, and a restaurant. Hoback Junction has an RV park, two gas stations, two general stores, raft trips on the Snake River for hire, and rental cabins at Hoback River Resort.

The small hamlet of Swan Valley, Idaho (5,277'), on U.S. 26, has gas, two motels, restaurants, a general store, an RV park, and towing and auto repair. Irwin, Idaho (5,380'), eight miles east of Swan Valley on U.S. 26, offers gas, a general store, and an RV park. In Teton Basin along Idaho 33, Victor, Idaho (6,207'), offers gas, a restaurant, groceries, a motel, and auto repair.

Driggs, Idaho (6,098'), is the economic hub of Teton Basin, and the town offers a wide variety of services including gas, car repair and towing, three motels (including large Best Western and Super 8 motels), groceries, restaurants, and a medical clinic. Hiking and backpacking equipment is also available.

Tetonia, Idaho (6,093'), at the north end of Teton Basin, has a gas/convenience store, a restaurant, and a large motel—the Teton Mountain View Inn.

For further information on accommodations and services, contact the chamber of commerce:

Teton Valley Chamber of Commerce
P.O. Box 250
Driggs, ID 83422
(208) 354-2500

Campgrounds

17 • MIKE HARRIS (6,550')

Location. In the Snake River Range; 0.4 mile south of Idaho 33, 4.0 miles from Victor, Idaho (see Trip 15 driving directions for exact location); Targhee National Forest, Teton Basin Ranger District.
Facilities. 12 camping units, tables, fire pits with grills, water, toilets, garbage containers; maximum trailer length of 20 feet; a fee is charged.
Dates Usually Open. May 31 through Sept. 15.
The Setting. This peaceful campground lies in a shady forest of lodgepole pine and subalpine fir, on a low hill just south of Trail Creek and Idaho 33. The thick forest blocks views of the busy highway and dampens traffic noise.

18 • TRAIL CREEK (6,680')

Location. In Trail Creek canyon, between the Snake River Range and the Teton Mountains;

just south of Wyoming Highway 22 (the Teton Pass highway), 1.8 miles east of Mike Harris Campground and 5.8 miles east of Victor, Idaho, or 6.7 miles west of Teton Pass; Targhee National Forest, Teton Basin Ranger District.
Facilities. 11 camping units, tables, fire pits with grills, water, toilets, garbage containers; maximum trailer length of 20 feet; a fee is charged.
Dates Usually Open. May 31 through September 15.
The Setting. This pleasant campground is located alongside the clear, cold waters of Trail Creek, a 15-foot-wide, gravel-bottomed stream. Campsites lie beneath a canopy of subalpine fir, Engelmann spruce, and aspen. Some sites are next to the creek, others in the forest. Traffic noise is high due to the proximity of the Teton Pass highway.

19 • PALISADES CREEK (5,550')

Location. In Palisades Creek canyon, in the Snake River Range; 7.2 miles east of Swan Valley, Idaho, and 18.9 miles west of Alpine Junction, Wyoming (see Trip 17 driving directions for exact location); Targhee National Forest, Palisades Ranger District.
Facilities. 7 camping units, tables, fire grills, water, toilets, garbage containers; maximum trailer length of 30 feet; a fee is charged.
Dates Usually Open. May 31 through September 15.
The Setting. Located alongside the ebullient waters of Palisades Creek, this fine campground offers some campsites shaded by Douglas-fir and large, spreading narrowleaf cottonwoods, and others that lie in an open setting among a scattering of Rocky Mountain junipers. Forested slopes soar more than 1,000 feet above to the south, grassy slopes rise to the north, and there are limited views northeast up the rugged defile of Palisades Creek canyon.

20 • ALPINE (5,750')

Location. Above the south shore of Palisades Reservoir and just south of U.S. 26, 2.1 miles west of Alpine Junction, Wyoming, and

26.7 miles east of Swan Valley, Idaho; Targhee National Forest, Palisades Ranger District.

Facilities. 42 camping units, tables, fire pits with grills, water, toilets, garbage containers; maximum trailer length of 24 feet in pull-in units, 35 feet in pull-through units; a fee is charged.

Dates Usually Open. May 31 through September 15.

The Setting. This convenient campground lies a short distance south of U.S. 26, in an open forest of small lodgepole pines, on a bench 150 feet above broad Palisades Reservoir. Peaks of the Snake River Range are visible in the north, and the grassy, partly forested slopes of the Caribou Mountains rise to the south. White pelicans, California gulls, great blue herons, osprey, and other waterfowl are likely to be observed.

Reservations for sites in Alpine Campground can be made by phoning 1-800-283-2267.

Between Alpine and Hoback junctions, in Wyoming, five national forest campgrounds not covered in this guidebook lie along U.S. 26 in the Grand Canyon of the Snake River. From west to east the campgrounds are: Little Cottonwood Creek (5 sites), Station Creek (15 sites), East Table Creek (18 sites), Elbow (9 sites), and Cabin Creek (10 sites). All are open from about early June through mid-September, and have facilities comparable to campgrounds described in this chapter. Reservations can be made for sites in Cabin Creek Campground by phoning 1-800-342-2267.

Other campgrounds in this region that are not covered in this guidebook include the Blowout Boat Ramp/ Campground, and Big Elk Creek Campground.

The Blowout site is located 10.8 miles west of Alpine Junction, and 17.0 miles east of Swan Valley, on the shores of Palisades Reservoir (the campground turnoff is 0.3 mile north of the Blowout Canyon Road; see Trip 18). The 18-site RV campground is located on the edge of the boat ramp parking lot, offering fire pits, toilets, water, and

garbage containers, and a fee is charged. There are some undeveloped camping areas in lodgepole-pine forest just off the highway along the boat ramp access road.

Big Elk Creek Campground is located 1.5 miles east of U.S. 26, on the Big Elk Creek Arm of Palisades Reservoir, 13.5 miles west of Alpine Junction and 14.3 miles east of Swan Valley. The fee campground has 17 camping units, and lies next to the Big Elk Creek trailhead.

For Further Information

For information regarding Trips 14-16; Campgrounds 17-18:

Targhee National Forest
Teton Basin Ranger District
P.O. Box 777
Driggs, ID 83422
(208) 354-2312

For information regarding Trips 17-18; Campgrounds 19-20:

Targhee National Forest
Palisades Ranger District
3659 E. Ririe Highway
Idaho Falls, ID 83401
(208) 523-1412

For information regarding Trip 13:

Bridger-Teton National Forest
Jackson Ranger District
P.O. Box 1689
Jackson, WY 83001
(307) 739-5400

Wilderness Regulations

The only wilderness area covered in this chapter is the Jedediah Smith Wilderness, located along the western slopes of the Teton Mountains. Backpackers should observe the regulations below.

• Maximum group size is 20 people.
• Maximum length of stay at any campsite is 16 consecutive days.

- All campsites must be located at least 200 feet from lakeshores, and 50 feet from stream banks.
- All nonburnable garbage must be packed out. No garbage may be buried.
- Shortcutting switchbacks is prohibited.
- Possession or use of motorized or mechanized vehicles, including bicycles, is prohibited.
- All campfires must be extinguished before leaving camp.
- Detergent use is prohibited in or near surface water.
- Human waste must be buried at least 200 feet from surface water.
- Cutting or defacing live trees or other natural features is prohibited.

Trip 13

TETON PASS HIGHWAY TO SKI LAKE

Distance: 4.8 miles round trip.
Low/High Elevations: 7,750'/8,650'.
Difficulty: Moderately easy.
Use: Heavy.
Suited For: Dayhike.
Best Season: Late June through Sept.
Wildlife Viewing: Fair.
Grizzly Bear Danger: Low.
Map/Trailhead: 11/12.
Nearest Campgrounds: Trail Creek, 7.8 miles, and Mike Harris, 10.1 miles from the trailhead.
Driving to the Trailhead: The trailhead lies alongside Wyoming 22 (the Teton Pass Highway), 10.7 miles west of Jackson, Wyoming, or 1.7 miles east of Teton Pass, and 13.6 miles east of Victor, Idaho.

Park in the large, unsigned, and often congested parking area east of and below the highway just southeast of a prominent low-speed curve in the road, about 25 yards northeast of the signed Phillips Canyon Road.
Introduction: The southern reaches of the Teton Mountains near Teton Pass offer a

delightful contrast to the rugged crags and precipitous canyons usually associated with the Tetons. Here the range is lower in elevation and the contours are gentler, but ridges and peaks still jut above timberline to alpine heights. Prominent cirques have been gouged out of the mountains by ancient glaciers, but there are few lakes on the easily erodible limestone flanks of the southern Tetons.

One exception is the timberline gem of Ski Lake, a half-day hike popular with Jackson residents. This short but scenic walk offers travelers on the steep Teton Pass highway an opportunity to stop for a few hours, stretch their legs, and allow their cars' engines and brakes to cool. The trail visits some of the richest natural flower gardens in all of Greater Yellowstone.
Description: From the large roadside parking area, carefully cross the busy highway and walk a few yards southwest to a steep, northbound dirt road signed PHILLIPS CANYON. Some hikers park on this road, and others attempt to drive it, but the roadbed is exceedingly rough, rocky, and narrow.

The roadway leads first northwest, then northeast, on a gentle-to-moderate ascent beneath a cool, shady canopy of Douglas-fir and subalpine fir. Roadside slopes are mantled with rich green foliage and colorful wildflowers that include Richardson geranium, lupine, bracted lousewort, and arrowleaf balsamroot.

After 0.4 mile and 150 feet of ascent, we bear left onto an eroded old road where a sign points to the Phillips Canyon Trail and lists distances to Ski Lake and Phillips Pass. We now climb moderately up the rocky roadbed, bearing left again after another 150 yards onto true trail.

The trail ahead traverses southeast-facing slopes, following the same direction as the dirt road below, but on a higher contour. Abundant sunlight filters through the open canopy of large Douglas-firs, nurturing a vast array of colorful, fragrant wildflowers, such as Richardson and sticky geraniums, larkspur, arrowleaf balsamroot, valerian, forget-me-not, lupine, Indian paintbrush, silky phacelia, western wall-flower, scarlet gilia, leopard lily, and heartleaf arnica.

After a pleasant half-mile stroll, a very steep, long-closed jeep trail joins our foot trail on the right (from the southeast), beyond which we ascend moderately but briefly up the rocky trail to an 8,200-foot saddle shaded by a stand of subalpine fir. Descending gently from the saddle through shady forest, we soon reach the southern margin of a small, exceedingly flat meadow, probably the silt-buried expanse of an ancient glacial tarn.

An old trail, barricaded with logs, cuts north across the meadow, but our newer trail skirts the meadow's south and west margins, soon meeting the signed Phillips Pass Trail, which branches right, 0.3 mile from the saddle. Backpackers frequently use that trail for its quick access to the Jedediah Smith Wilderness and the scenic Teton Crest Trail via Phillips Pass.

Bearing left at that junction, we ascend moderately through fir forest and flower-rich meadows. After 0.4 mile from the last junction, we jump across a small creek, its banks enlivened by the nodding blooms of mountain bluebells. We then continue the moderate ascent, soon mounting a minor ridge and then curving into the lower reaches of the Ski Lake cirque. A breath-catching pause along this stretch of trail reveals a broad panorama of the southern reaches of Greater Yellowstone. The Gros Ventre Range rises on the eastern horizon, and part of Snake River downstream from Jackson and the serrated crest of the Wyoming Range are visible to the southeast. The rolling green ridges of the Snake River Range dominate the southern view.

Resuming the moderate ascent, we soon reach the usually dry outlet of Ski Lake, which we briefly follow west to the lake's east shore. Set in a deep cirque, this emerald-green lake is surrounded on three sides by verdant slopes, limestone cliff bands, and rounded ridges exceeding 9,000 feet, feathered on their crests with scattered timberline trees.

An open forest of Engelmann spruce, whitebark pine, subalpine fir, and Douglas-fir offers shade along the lake's east and south shores. A few poor campsites lie near the outlet, and others can be found above the east shore in the forest.

From Ski Lake, retrace your route to the trailhead.

Ski Lake

Trip 14

TETON PASS HIGHWAY TO COAL CREEK MEADOWS

Distance: 4.8 miles round trip.
Low/High Elevations: 7,240'/9,000'.
Difficulty: Moderate.
Use: Moderate.
Suited For: Dayhike or backpack.
Best Season: July through mid-September.
Wildlife Viewing: Good.
Grizzly Bear Danger: Low.
Map/Trailhead: 11/13.
Nearest Campgrounds: Trail Creek, 3.4 miles, and Mike Harris, 5.7 miles from the trailhead.
Driving to the Trailhead: The trailhead, just north of Wyoming 22 (the Teton Pass Highway), is indicated by a Coal Creek sign, 2.7 miles west of Teton Pass, and 15.1 miles west of Jackson, Wyoming, or 9.2 miles east of Victor, Idaho. A large Jedediah Smith Wilderness information sign and toilets are at the trailhead.
Introduction: This scenic and memorable hike leads up the southern slopes of the Teton Mountains via Coal Creek canyon. Surrounded by broad alpine mountains, rather than the alplike crags typical of the Tetons, the three lovely and contrasting Coal Creek Meadows offer scenic destinations for dayhikes of various lengths, or fine destinations for an overnight stay.

Adventurous hikers will enjoy the side trip to the crest of Taylor Mountain for far-ranging vistas encompassing a vast sweep of Greater Yellowstone landscapes.

Jedediah Smith Wilderness regulations apply to hikers staying overnight on the trail.
Description: Beginning in the shadow of Taylor Mountain, which looms 3,000 feet above, we pass a wilderness information sign and follow the trail north, up-canyon, passing through wildflower-rich meadows and a forest of scattered subalpine fir. Silky phacelia and sticky geranium are particularly common in the trailside grasslands.

As the canyon begins to curve northeast, ignore a left-branching trail leading to a horse ford of Coal Creek, and continue along the east bank, soon reaching a double-log bridge spanning the creek's noisy whitewater. Just beyond the bridge, the horse trail joins our trail on the left, and we then curve eastward, soon entering the signed Jedediah Smith Wilderness.

The grade ahead is typically gentle, with moderate ascents at times. Our trail often follows the cascading creek closely, but at other times we traverse well above it, alternating between shady subalpine fir forest and meadow openings awash with colorful blooms.

One-half mile from the start we reach a second crossing of Coal Creek, where log bridges span the two creek branches. A shady jaunt on the gradually rising, flower-decked trail leads to a third crossing, not quite one half mile from the last. No bridge is here, but an easy rockhop of the shallow, 10-foot-wide stream affords passage.

Beyond that ford, we quickly enter the first of Coal Creek's meadows, where a broad, verdant bowl opens up. Aspen groves cling

View north from Taylor Mountain. Grand Teton at left.

Coal Creek Meadows

to the east slopes of the bowl, and the soaring limestone battlements of Taylor Mountain sweep skyward to the west.

After crossing an often-dry streambed, we follow switchbacks on a steady, moderate ascent of the bowl's eastern slopes, passing through an extensive grove of aspen enroute. Fine views stretch southward to the meadow-draped slopes and ridges of the Snake River Range.

At 1.8 miles, we enter a second meadow, a sloping spread dotted with conifers and a variety of wildflowers. The moderate ascent continues along the meadow's fringes, passing scattered groves of subalpine fir and whitebark pine. A short but steep stretch of trail leads us to the third, upper meadow of Coal Creek.

This timberline grassland is a scenic delight. Islands of subalpine trees crest the low hummocks that stud the meadow. Slopes of talus and timberline forest sweep upward to the east, and the rugged, cliff-banded flanks of Taylor Mountain rise 1,300 feet up to the west. A cold, voluminous spring issues from the foot of a talus slope

near the northeast edge of the spread, and a good campsite lies in the spruce-fir grove just below it.

At the upper, northern edge of the meadow, at 2.4 miles and 9,000 feet, you reach a signed junction and ponder your options. You can either 1) return the way you came; or 2) follow the steep trail north for 0.2 mile to 9,197-foot Mesquite Creek Divide for a fine view reaching deep into the rugged interior of the Tetons; or 3) take the Taylor Mountain Trail to the west, a short but steep, rocky trail leading to one of the best viewpoints accessible by trail in Greater Yellowstone, a trail that ascends 1,000 feet in one mile.

Those with the energy remaining to tackle the Taylor Mountain Trail will bear left at that junction, following the trail as it ascends southwest above the meadow and curves into a timberline cirque. Look for fossil shells imbedded in some trailside limestone boulders.

Reaching the head of the cirque, our trail climbs northeast into an open stand of whitebark pine and subalpine fir, leading to the shoulder of a steep ridge. One switchback takes us first northwest, then southwest along a narrow limestone ledge at the 10,000-foot contour to a small saddle on Taylor Mountain's crest.

Views are restricted by nearby stunted conifers, but a short and easy scramble northeast along the crest leads to Peak 10068 and a dramatic panorama. But for the finest views, follow the rocky crest southwest for 0.3 mile to the central summit of the mountain at 10,250 feet. The vistas that unfold from that summit easily justify the effort required.

To the north, the ranks of blocky limestone peaks and jagged granitic horns of the Tetons, dominated by 13,770-foot Grand Teton, stretch as far north as Mt. Moran in Grand Teton National Park. On the far northeastern horizon are the Continental Divide summits of the Absaroka Range, on the eastern edge of the Teton Wilderness.

The rugged peaks of the Gros Ventre Range rise on the distant eastern skyline, beyond views of the Snake River, Jackson Hole, and the town of Jackson. Beyond the Gros Ventres and far to the southeast are the northernmost peaks of the Wind River Range.

Closer at hand in our southeast view are two narrow, linear ranges in extreme western Wyoming—the Salt River and Wyoming ranges. South are the lofty peaks, broad cirques, and meadow-clad ridges of the Snake River Range.

West, the slopes of the Teton Mountains fall away into broad Teton Basin, where rectangular farmlands, scattered ranch buildings, and two small towns contrast with this panorama of mostly unspoiled mountain wilderness.

Bounding Teton Basin to the west are the grassy slopes of the Big Hole Mountains, and on the northwest horizon are the Centennial and Henrys Lake mountains, and the western edge of the vast, heavily forested Yellowstone volcanic plateau.

From Taylor Mountain, return the way you came.

Trip 15

MIKESELL CANYON TO OLIVER PEAK

Distance: 8.6 miles round trip.
Low/High Elevations: 6,720'/9,004'.
Difficulty: Moderate.
Use: Low.
Suited For: Dayhike or mountain bike trip.
Best Season: Late June through Sept.
Wildlife Viewing: Good.
Grizzly Bear Danger: Low.
Map/Trailhead: 12/14.
Nearest Campgrounds: Mike Harris, 0.6 mile, and Trail Creek, 2.7 miles from the trailhead.
Driving to the Trailhead: From the junction of Idaho 31 and 33 in Victor, Idaho, go east on Idaho 33, signed for Jackson, Wyoming. After driving 3.9 miles from Victor, turn right (south) onto Forest Road 330, where a prominent Targhee National Forest sign points to Mike Harris Campground.

The good gravel road shortly bridges Trail Creek, and then we turn left where another sign points to the campground and to the Mike Harris Trailhead. The road that continues straight ahead from this junction leads 0.6 mile alongside Mike Harris Creek, where there are six pleasant, but heavily used, undeveloped campsites.

After 0.3 mile from the highway, you reach another junction; right to the campground (in 0.1 mile), left to the Mike Harris Trail. Hikers with low-clearance vehicles are advised to go no farther; but park in the large clearing just south of the Trail Creek bridge, and walk 0.8 mile to the trailhead.

Drivers of high-clearance vehicles will turn left at that junction and follow the poor road, which is narrow and rutted, with potholes and high centers, for 0.5 mile to an unmarked junction. Park at this junction in a wide spot in the road. The southbound road leads 0.1 mile to the beginning of the trail.
Introduction: This fine dayhike ascends the north slopes of the Snake River Range

to its crest, where islands of timberline forests and flower-rich, meadow-draped slopes are more reminiscent of a scene from the Alps than that of an obscure mountain range in eastern Idaho.

Hikers can continue along the crest beyond the 3-mile point and scale 9,004-foot Oliver Peak, an easy off-trail scramble, where grand vistas unfold, revealing the wild interior of the range to the south, and the magnificent Tetons to the north. The trail is open to and frequently used by mountain bikers, but few hikers have discovered this scenic trail.

Description: From the fork in the road at 6,720 feet, we ascend the poor road southwest into the mouth of Mikesell Canyon, reaching the roadend and the beginning of the trail after 200 yards. Occasionally rocky, our trail leads up the narrow, verdant draw of the canyon beneath a canopy of lodgepole pine and a scattering of subalpine fir, Douglas-fir, Engelmann spruce, and aspen. Wildflowers include sticky geranium, valerian, Colorado columbine, and forget-me-not.

After about 1/2 mile of gentle climbing, we leave the canyon floor and ascend easily northward through a Douglas-fir and aspen forest, soon curving southwest near a minor ridge and then entering a forest of pine and fir. The trail ahead ascends moderately to moderately steeply on southeast-facing slopes. Sunny openings in the Douglas-fir forest host a variety of shrubs, such as sagebrush, pachystima, snowberry, tobacco brush, and curl-leaf mountain mahogany, and the colorful blooms of arrowleaf balsamroot, mountain penstemon, scarlet gilia, Oregon grape, puccoon, and sticky geranium. By contrast, the cool north-facing slopes on the opposite side of the canyon support a dense forest of subalpine fir.

The open slopes our trail is ascending also offer the first views thus far, stretching northeast to the massive southern peaks of the Tetons, and south to the high meadows and timberline forest on the range at the head of Mikesell Canyon. Oliver Peak is the conical timberline summit on the south-

east skyline. At length we curve south just below the crest of a ridge, enter a shady forest of Douglas-fir, and then ascend a steep grade. But the grade soon slackens in beautiful timberline wildflower gardens amid scattered groves of tall, spire-topped subalpine firs.

After bending southeast just below the ridge crest, we reach a fork in the trail just west of three destination and mileage signs at 2.9 miles and 8,400 feet. Vistas from this point are dramatic, but they are even better if we follow the right-branching trail (signed for Palisades Forks) a few yards to the crest above.

From here the broad, cultivated expanse of Teton Basin sprawls out to the northwest, flanked on the west by the Big Hole Mountains and on the east by the gentle west slopes of the Teton Range. On the far northwest and northern horizons are the Centennial and Henrys Lake mountains, and the western reaches of the Yellowstone volcanic plateau. The preeminent spire of Grand Teton captures the attention of even the most jaded mountain traveler, as it rises far above lesser Teton summits in the north.

Views from the crest also reach deep into the unspoiled interior of the range, a landscape of beautiful peaks approaching 10,000 feet. Pacific winter storms dump copious amounts of snow on this range, and this combined with the high water-holding capacity of the range's limestone soils causes timberlines to be lower here than elsewhere in Greater Yellowstone.

Our view to the south includes a host of tall summits, some of them rocky, but most are shaded by the green cast of rich summer meadows. Small hanging cirques have been carved by ancient glaciers, and below the peaks are broad mountain valleys, deeply green with vast meadows, aspen groves, and a discontinuous cover of conifer forest.

Some will be satisfied by the grand vistas from this point, and will now return to the trailhead. But if you enjoy strolling among wildflower gardens and the sense of accomplishment gained from scaling a mountain peak, bear left at the ridgetop junction and proceed southeast along the crest of the range.

The trail ahead passes among scattered patches of subalpine-fir forest and leads through high, open meadows, where wild-flowers and rich grasses reach nearly to shoulder height by mid summer. Sticky geranium, lupine, valerian, yampah, sulphur buckwheat, and forget-me-not lend their fra-grance and color to trailside meadows.

After a delightful 0.7-mile stroll from the junction, the crest of the range rises abruptly ahead to Oliver Peak, 0.3 mile and 400 feet above us. To get there, leave the trail just before it begins to contour around the southwest slopes of the peak. Follow the steep ridge east, ascending through sub-alpine-fir forest and brushy openings clad in sagebrush and snowberry.

Atop the 9,004-foot summit, 4.3 miles from the trailhead, vistas are much the same as they were below, but more panoramic. In addition to the aforementioned landmarks, we can now see through the notch of Teton Pass to the high western peaks of the Gros Ventre Range, and on the distant south-east horizon we can see the 10,000-foot summits at the northern end of the Wyoming Range.

From Oliver Peak, retrace your steps to the trailhead.

Trip 16

DARBY CANYON TO WIND CAVE AND ICE CAVE

Distance: 5.6 miles round trip to Wind Cave; 6.6 miles round trip to Ice Cave.
Low/High Elevations: 7,030'/9,200'.
Difficulty: Moderate.
Use: Moderate.
Suited For: Dayhike.
Best Season: July through mid-Sept.
Wildlife Viewing: Good.
Grizzly Bear Danger: Low.

Map/Trailhead: 13/15.
Nearest Campgrounds: Mike Harris, 11.8 miles, and Trail Creek, 13.6 miles from the trailhead.
Driving to the Trailhead: The easy-to-miss turnoff to the trailhead access road, signed for FOREST ROAD 012, DARBY CANYON, and DARBY GIRLS CAMP, lies on the east side of Idaho 33 in Teton Basin, 5.2 miles north of Victor, and 2.6 miles south of Driggs, Idaho. (The landmark Spud Drive-in Theater lies 0.7 mile north of the turnoff.)

Once you locate the turnoff, follow the paved county road east across the valley of Teton Basin toward the foot of the Tetons. At 2.7 miles, the pavement ends and the road becomes narrow with a gravel surface. Turn right (south) at a T-intersection 3.2 miles from the highway. Soon thereafter the road curves east, and begins ascending into Darby Canyon.

At 5.3 miles you reach the spur road to Darby Girls Camp and bear left; the sign points to DARBY TRAILHEAD. The road ends at the small trailhead parking area, next to Darby Creek, 7.8 miles from the highway. There are several undeveloped campsites along the Darby Canyon Road, but no camping is available at the trailhead.

Introduction: This unusual and rewarding trip, on the west slope of the Tetons in the Jedediah Smith Wilderness, leads from the depths of a forested canyon to a broad timberline bowl ringed by bold limestone cliffs and blocky sum-mits. Two aptly named caves penetrate the cliffs on the western flanks of the bowl, and this trail leads to their portals.

(*WARNING:* Do not attempt to explore the caves unless you have ample caving experience, and even then, never do so alone. Before entering either cave, be pre-pared with two flashlights (using the extra one for a spare) with fresh batteries, a hel-met, gloves, and warm clothing. The floor of Ice Cave, as its name suggests, is coated with ice, so instep crampons, an ice axe, a rope, and rock and ice-climbing skills are essential to explore that cave.)

Description: From the trailhead at 7,030 feet, forested slopes and limestone cliff bands soar in the north and the south. Up the canyon to the northeast, bold alpine crags pierce the sky, including flat-topped Peak 10600, and the aptly-named Wedge, rising to 10,360 feet.

These landmarks quickly fade from view as we follow the trail alongside Darby Creek for 100 yards to the footbridge spanning the creek. Beyond the bridge the trail carves through a meadow decked with the colorful blooms of sticky geranium, groundsel, subalpine daisy, yampah, and western coneflower.

Soon we enter an open forest of Engelmann spruce, where a diversity of understory shrubs grow in dense thickets, reflecting the cool microclimate in the canyon and the abundant moisture available on the west slopes of the Tetons, one of the wettest areas of Greater Yellowstone. Here we find red-osier dogwood, mountain ash, Utah honeysuckle, Rocky Mountain maple, serviceberry, thimbleberry, birch-leaf spirea, and gooseberry. Leafy branches arching over the trail insure that hikers will quickly become soaked following recent rainfall.

After 0.4 mile, we cross the usually-dry bed of South Fork Darby Creek, then curve south, entering the Jedediah Smith Wilderness. The trail leads into the mouth of the South Fork's canyon, but large boulders and a limestone cliff band divert the trail onto the slopes above. Here we begin to ascend, via switchbacks, above the canyon's lower gorge. The smooth, gently graded trail leads through a dense forest of Douglas-fir, subalpine fir, and Engelmann spruce.

At 1.7 miles and 7,800 feet we break out of the forest and reach an expansive bowl rimmed by a low band of cliffs. A fine display of wildflowers decorate the trailside slopes, including buckwheat, blue harebell, yampah, yarrow, Engelmann aster, Indian paintbrush, western coneflower, and subalpine daisy.

The trail soon curves northeast, finds a break in the cliffs, and then proceeds southeast, ascending the verdant, flower-decked slopes of the bowl. Wind Cave comes into view from this stretch of the trail. Its dark,

keyhole-shaped portal is visible in the cliff bounding the southwest side of the bowl.

At 2.3 miles the trail curves southwest, and then crosses the dry, bedrock bed of the South Fork, and shortly thereafter enter a forest of subalpine fir. Emerging from that forest, you head southwest across a meadow, and soon reach an unsigned junction at 8,400 feet, 2.6 miles from the trailhead.

To reach Wind Cave, bear right and follow steep switchbacks through the fir forest. Part way up the grade, avoid a path that leads northwest (right) past the foot of a waterfall. The switchbacks and the trail end after 0.2 mile, 30 yards below the cave's entrance. Exercise extreme caution here: an overhanging cliff and a 40-foot waterfall lie just below.

A small stream issues from the mouth of the cave, and we can choose among the paths that follow the rocky stream banks steeply up to the 100-foot-high portal. We enter the cave via slippery, wet, mossy rocks where the stream emerges. But the stream sinks underground a short distance inside the cave, and we can continue, with flashlights, into the cave over the rock-strewn floor. The cave quickly narrows and the ceiling lowers, but you can continue for about 300 yards, occasionally crawling through narrow openings that funnel a cold breeze.

To reach Ice Cave, bear left (southeast) at the unsigned junction below Wind Cave, and ascend a moderate grade through flower-rich meadows and among isolated groves of subalpine fir. Fossil Mountain (10,916 feet), and an array of bold summits rise above this lovely timberline basin at the head of the South Fork.

The wildflower display here is among the finest in Greater Yellowstone. Here we will see the blooms of western coneflower, mountain bluebells, sticky geranium, lupine, beautiful paintbrush, Indian paintbrush, yellow columbine, palish larkspur, Engelmann aster, subalpine daisy, and blue flax.

On the cliff face above the trail to the southwest are two alcoves that could be mistaken for Ice Cave, but that cave's portal is blocked by boulders and is not visible from the trail. After 0.6 mile from the junction, the trail leads across a small stream, beyond which we curve southwest and begin a very steep, 300-foot ascent on unstable scree slopes. The grade ends at the portal of Ice Cave, and a boulder scramble is necessary to enter the cave.

The cave maintains a subfreezing temperature even during summer, and its depths are a welcome refuge on a hot day. A sign just inside the cave warns that climbing gear is required to explore this cave. Those outfitted with crampons, ice axe, a rope, and flashlights, can enter the icy depths of the cave.

After enjoying Darby Canyon's unusual caves, retrace your steps to the trailhead.

Trip 17

PALISADES CREEK CAMPGROUND TO LOWER PALISADES LAKE

Distance: 8.5 miles round trip.
Low/High Elevations: 5,550'/6,131'.
Difficulty: Moderately easy.
Use: Moderate.
Suited For: Dayhike or backpack.
Best Season: June through mid-October.
Wildlife Viewing: Fair.
Grizzly Bear Danger: Low.
Map/Trailhead: 14/16.
Nearest Campgrounds: Palisades Creek, located at the trailhead.
Driving to the Trailhead: From U.S. 26 along the South Fork Snake River in Idaho, 7.2 miles southeast of the town of Swan Valley, and 20.6 miles northwest of Alpine Junction, Wyoming, turn north onto a gravel road where a sign points to Palisades Campground. This turnoff is 200 yards west of the highway bridge over signed Palisades Creek, and is just west of The Lodge at Palisades.

This good gravel road leads 2.1 miles to a bridge over Palisades Creek at the camp-

Palisades Creek

ground entrance. A hiker's parking area is on the left side of the road just before the bridge.
Introduction: The southwest front of the Snake River Range, or The Palisades, is an abruptly rising mountain wall that reaches nearly 5,000 feet skyward from the South Fork Snake River (in a lateral distance of only three to five miles), to the 9,000-foot limestone peaks in the interior of the range. Four prominent canyons deeply incised into this mountain front offer access to the network of trails that cross the Palisades backcountry.

The mountain streams of the range, fed throughout summer by vigorous springs issuing from the porous limestone soils, run wide and deep, but there are few lakes in the range. Glaciers have carved and shaped the canyons and the peaks, but few glacial lakes are found in ranges composed of limestone, such as the Palisades. However, two large lakes lie in the forested middle reaches of Palisades Creek canyon, lakes not created by glaciation, but by large landslides that impounded the creek.

This fine hike lies at a lower elevation than any other in this guidebook, and consequently the hiking season here is longer. Despite the minimal net elevation gain (about 600 feet) and modest distance, the trail to Lower Palisades Lake has minor ups and downs that are not apparent on the map, and the tread is often rocky, and it can be quite muddy in early summer and after rainfall. **Description:** The trail begins at the upper, northeast end of the campground, and rises gently at first, following the southeast banks of large, cascading Palisades Creek, beneath a shady canopy of Douglas-fir and tall narrowleaf cottonwood, and passing a trail register and information sign after 0.25 mile.

The steep, shady slopes above the trail support dense forest and a verdant understory, but the sun-drenched slopes on the opposite canyon wall, broken by limestone cliff bands, hosts only shrubs such as curlleaf mountain mahogany and Rocky Mountain maple. Understory shrubs on trailside slopes also include maple, and red-osier dogwood and mallow-leaved ninebark. Common wildflowers on the canyon floor include sticky geranium, arrowleaf balsamroot, mountain penstemon, scarlet gilia, false Solomon's seal, silky phacelia, and Canada violet.

At 1.1 miles we bridge the creek and continue up-canyon above the northwest banks. These sunny slopes are clothed in a woodland of maple, mountain mahogany, and a scattering of Douglas-fir and Rocky

Lower Palisades Lake

Mountain juniper. Views from these slopes reach more than 2,000 feet above to towering ridges and into precipitous side canyons.

Often the trail is at the creekside, where access to fishing holes and stretches of calm water may entice anglers to test their skill against the cutthroat trout that inhabit the cold, 20-foot-wide creek. At other times the undulating trail leads us 100-200 feet above the creek, from where views both up and down the deep canyon are better.

At 3.3 miles we bridge the creek a second time then enter a narrow defile confined between low limestone cliffs. After another 0.2 mile, we bridge the creek for a third time, returning to the northwest banks. Within one third mile we cross a final bridge just below a turbulent cascade.

Beyond that bridge we leave Palisades Creek, and ascend a minor draw via rocky switchbacks, soon leveling off on a grassy, flower-speckled bench, where we meet the signed Lake Canyon Trail, southbound, at 4.1 miles. Bearing left, we begin winding among large, angular gray boulders, part of the landslide debris that created Lower Palisades Lake. The landslide emanated from the slopes above the mouth of Lake Canyon, about one-quarter mile to the east.

The lovely emerald-green waters of Lower Palisades Lake soon come into view as the trail approaches the western edge of the landslide dam before dipping down to the bridge at the lake's outlet.

Douglas-fir forest shades most of the lakeshore, and at the lake's inlet is a willow-clad meadow where moose can occasionally be observed. Steeply rising, thickly forested slopes bound the canyon east of the lake. To the west a discontinuous forest clings to exceedingly steep slopes of boulder fields and broken cliffs. Tall peaks and ridges jut skyward as much as 3,000 feet above the lake on all sides. Some of the peaks are rocky crags, but the slopes of others are softened by a meadowy blanket; many rise above timberline, others are feathered along their crests by stunted conifers.

Nestled deep in the forested canyon, the lake evokes feelings of great remoteness, though we are only 4.25 miles from the trailhead. The north shore near the inlet and the east shore offer the best fishing access. A few fair campsites can be found on the rocky landslide dam above the outlet and on the grassy bench near the Lake Canyon Trail junction.

From the lake, return the way you came.

Trip 18

BLOWOUT CANYON

Distance: 2.4 miles, round trip.
Low/High Elevation: 6,120'/7,160'.
Difficulty: Moderate.
Use: Low.
Suited For: Dayhike.
Best Season: Late May through early October.
Wildlife Viewing: Fair.
Grizzly Bear Danger: Low.
Map/Trailhead: 15/17.
Nearest Campgrounds: Blowout Boat Ramp/Campground, 2.7 miles, and Alpine, 10.4 miles from the trailhead.
Driving to the Trailhead: Follow U.S. 26 for 10.5 miles northwest from Alpine Junction, Wyoming, or for 17.3 miles southeast from Swan Valley, Idaho, to Blowout Canyon Road on the left, indicated by a small BLOWOUT CANYON sign. This turnoff lies 0.3 mile south of the prominently signed Blowout Boat Ramp/Campground.

Follow the narrow gravel road east into Blowout Canyon for 2.0 miles to the loop at the roadend. The road is rutted and rocky in places, but is passable to carefully driven passenger cars. Several undeveloped camping areas can be found just off the road over its length.
Introduction: Blowout Canyon is one of dozens of canyons that slice into the southwest front of the Snake River Range above Swan Valley and Palisades Reservoir. The canyon harbors scenery and vegetation typical of the range: rugged limestone peaks jutting above timberline, aspen groves,

meadow-draped slopes rich with wild-flowers, and scattered conifer forests.

The canyon's name, however, may give you a hint that it is somehow different from others in the range, and indeed it is. The canyon derives its name and its unusual landscape, from a massive rockslide that broke loose from the flanks of Peak 9426 at the canyon's head, and buried the upper two miles of the canyon in a shroud of shattered limestone blocks. In area and volume of rock, the Blowout slide rivals the more famous Greater Yellowstone rockslides, those in the Madison and Gros Ventre river canyons.

This short but steep dayhike leads into this unrenowned rockslide, and offers fine vistas of the alpine peaks above the slide, and of Palisades Reservoir and the Caribou Mountains.
Description: From the loop at the roadend at 6,120 feet, a very steep 4WD road ascends a narrow ridge to the north. Walk up that track for a few yards, then head east on the trail; a nearby TRAIL sign shows the way.

We ascend a moderate grade at first, crossing verdant slopes for 200 yards. The slopes above the slide debris are dotted with widely scattered Douglas-fir, Rocky Mountain juniper, and limber pine, and are cloaked with various shrubs and wild-flowers. Among the diverse flora on these slopes are the shrubs of Rocky Mountain maple, antelope bitterbrush, pachystima, and Oregon grape; and the blooms of arrowleaf balsamroot, penstemon, Indian paintbrush, false Solomon-seal, yarrow, and scarlet gilia.

Heaps of rocky detritus resembling a glacial moraine spread out across the canyon floor south of the trail. Tall Douglas-firs and a thick mantle of shrubs have colonized the landslide debris, suggesting the slide is old.

Soon we mount some blocky landslide debris, and ascend the rocky trail along a minor ridge. The trail maintains a moderate grade, crossing slide debris dotted with scattered conifers. The rocky landscape is mantled by shrubs that now include tobacco brush, common juniper, serviceberry, chokecherry, and birch-leaf spirea.

After emerging from the shrubby woodland, you ascend into increasingly rocky terrain. Views begin to open up, reaching down-canyon to Palisades Reservoir and to the north slopes of the Caribou Mountains. Ahead, Blowout Canyon appears to be blocked by a massive rock dam, and we soon begin to ascend the steep, rocky face of that obstacle.

At the rim of the "dam," the grade eases and we then enter a small, tree-studded basin, its floor strewn with shattered limestone blocks. A brief but moderate-to-steep ascent soon follows, leading into another minor basin. From there, we steeply ascend the face of another rock "dam" blocking the canyon.

Shortly before reaching its rim, the trail forks, 1.2 miles from the trailhead. A sign on a lone Douglas-fir just above the fork proclaims BLOWOUT CANYON, and lists mileage to Quaker Flat (1.5 miles via the left fork) and to Spaulding Basin (1.5 miles via the right fork). The right fork leads deeper into the slide-covered basin ahead, so we follow that trail another 0.2 mile to the shoulder of a minor ridge just below Point 7231 on the map.

This ridge affords fine views into the upper reaches of the Blowout Canyon slide, and to the alpine peaks rising above. The broken western flanks of Peak 9426, looming on the eastern skyline, are the source of the rockslide.

Blowout Canyon is today a peaceful place, filled with the sound of the wind through the forests, and the song of birds filling the air. Geologic processes, though usually slow and nearly imperceptible, sometimes occur suddenly and with dramatic effects. At one time this peaceful canyon thundered and shook with the sudden release of billions of tons of rock. Over time, settling and colonization by plants have softened the rough edges of the Blowout Canyon slide.

From Blowout Canyon, retrace your route to the trailhead.

Palisades Reservoir and the Caribou Mountains lie in the distance beyond Blowout Canyon

 **Chapter Three**

BEYOND JACKSON HOLE—
SOUTHEASTERN GREATER YELLOWSTONE

Introduction

The Teton Range, with its bold, serrated crags that soar 7,000 feet skyward from the floor of Jackson Hole, is an overwhelming presence, inspiring and commanding the attention of millions of visitors each year. It is not surprising then that the mountains east and southeast of Jackson Hole are often overlooked. Those mountains—the Mt. Leidy Highlands, and the Gros Ventre Range (pronounced Grow Vont)—rise gently east of Jackson Hole in a sweep of grassy foothills studded with aspen groves and scattered stands of conifers.

Farther east, beyond the foothills, densely forested slopes rise to the skyline, along with a handful of alpine summits, most notably Sheep Mountain (called the Sleeping Indian for obvious reasons) and conical Jackson Peak. Hidden from view between the two ranges is the valley of the Gros Ventre River. Gathering its waters from the distant Continental Divide and from major tributaries issuing from both the Gros Ventre Range and the Mt. Leidy Highlands, the river meanders through one of the most remote and isolated valleys in Greater Yellowstone.

This area offers colorful rock formations spanning some 500 million years of earth history, ample evidence of past glaciation and landslide activity, and opportunities to view a broad range of wildlife, from pronghorn antelope to trumpeter swans. Contrasting scenery ranging from colorful badlands to ice-chiseled alpine peaks, and the wild and remote atmosphere of the valley, all combine to offer ample incentives to abandon crowded Grand Teton National Park and to explore the enchanting Gros Ventre River valley.

Visitors traveling to this region via Teton Pass are urged to stop at the pass and drink in the tremendous panorama. Without the distraction of the Tetons, which are blocked from view at the pass by the spreading bulk of Mt. Glory to the north, your gaze stretches east and southeast, past Jackson Hole and the Snake River, to the broad expanse of the Gros Ventre Range, crowned by dozens of limestone peaks reaching above 10,000 and 11,000 feet.

On the far southeast horizon, beyond where the Snake River disappears from view into the labyrinthine depths of its Grand Canyon, two other imposing mountain ranges thrust their bold peaks skyward—the Wyoming and Salt River ranges.

The Gros Ventre Range, seen to best advantage from Teton Pass, stretches 35 miles from Jackson Hole in the northwest to Green River in the southeast. The bulk of these scenic, mostly limestone mountains lie within the boundaries of the 287,000-acre Gros Ventre Wilderness, a grand mountain landscape of vast conifer forests, rugged peaks, rich meadows, deep canyons, and broad alpine basins, many of which harbor small timberline lakes and tarns.

The Wyoming Range, on the southern fringes of the Greater Yellowstone area, is a collection of obscure mountains typically viewed only from afar. Highway 189/191 through scenic Hoback Canyon lies just north of the Wyoming Range, but from the canyon-bottom highway travelers gain only occasional views of the range's meadow-draped alpine peaks. Crowned by 10,000-foot summits, the narrow Wyoming Range extends for some 90 miles from Hoback Canyon in the north to the town of Kemmerer, Wyoming, in the south.

Ancient glaciers gouged cirques into the higher flanks of these mountains, but there are few high lakes. Most of the range is covered by a thick carpet of meadows and wildflowers, which contrast with its red and tan rocks. Only a discontinuous forest covers the slopes of the range.

The 50-mile-long Wyoming Range National Recreation Trail closely follows the crest, yet few hikers will be found on this or other trails in this beautiful but almost undiscovered mountain range. A 225,000-acre tract of roadless land within the range has been proposed for wilderness designation.

The range lies within the Overthrust Belt, and is thought to contain large reserves of gas and oil. The petroleum industry opposes wilderness designation of the Wyoming Range, and the area is threatened by increasing oil and gas exploration and development.

At the north end of Jackson Hole, near Moran Junction, the Buffalo Fork of the Snake River, a major tributary, flows westward from a broad valley that separates the Mt. Leidy Highlands to the south from the Teton Wilderness and the southern Absaroka Range (pronounced Ab-sor-ka) to the north. Within the vast reaches of the 585,468-acre wilderness are broad, forest-clad ridges, wide valleys filled with rich meadows and, near the Continental Divide and the eastern boundary of the Wilderness, vast alpine plateaus, where snowmelt feeds the beginnings of both the Snake and Yellowstone rivers.

The Teton Wilderness abuts the backcountry of southeastern Yellowstone National Park on the north and the Washakie Wilderness on the east. This two-million acre tract of wildlands is the largest contiguous roadless area in Greater Yellowstone. The area now encompassed by the Teton Wilderness was long ago recognized for its value as critical wildlife habitat. Around the turn of the century, wildlife populations were being decimated by hunters in and around Yellowstone National Park. Elk were slaughtered by the thousands, the hunters taking only their valuable "tusks"

(eye teeth). Huckleberry Ridge (see Trip 26) is reputed to have been used by poachers who lived there in earth-covered shelters. By 1907, the area that is now Teton Wilderness was set aside as the Teton Game Preserve, where hunting was outlawed for nearly 30 years. Today, the Teton Wilderness remains an exceptional habitat, and travelers here have a high probability of viewing many large mammals, including the grizzly bear.

Just north of 9,658-foot Togwotee Pass (pronounced Toe-ga-tee) on the Continental Divide, east of Jackson Hole and Moran Junction, the southernmost extension of the Absaroka Range thrusts skyward from flower-filled meadows and timberline forests in a wall of gray, stratified volcanic cliffs and spires. A few miles east of the pass, a gravel forest road leads 5 miles north into the realm of these volcanic mountains, ending at the Brooks Lake Campground and trailhead.

Brooks Lake is one of the gems of Greater Yellowstone, and its timberline surroundings offer some of the finest camping and hiking in the region. Lying just beneath the Absaroka's crest, Brooks Lake's trails offer easy access to high, sprawling meadows and timberline forests and lakes, and the area boasts a striking backdrop of lofty, splintered crags and sweeping cliffs that typify the high country of the range.

Points of Interest

NATIONAL ELK REFUGE

Jackson Hole has historically been a vital migration route and wintering area for thousands of elk that spend summers in the high meadows of southern Greater Yellowstone. With the advent of homesteading in Jackson Hole in the 1880s, fences, hayfields, and ranches began to supersede traditional elk winter range and to block migration routes. Unregulated hunting and several severe winters in the 1880s took a heavy toll on elk populations.

Steps were taken by a handful of forward-thinking local residents and the Wyoming legislature that led to the establishment of the National Elk Refuge and a feeding program for the elk in 1909. Expanded to its current size of 23,754 acres in 1933, the National Elk Refuge in the southeast corner of Jackson Hole harbors 5,000-10,000 wintering elk. During severe winters, the elk are fed hay. Wyoming is the only state in Greater Yellowstone that offers supplemental feed to wintering elk. Other feed grounds are located in the Gros Ventre valley and in the upper Green River basin near the Wind River Range.

LOWER GROS VENTRE SLIDE

The Gros Ventre Road (see Trip 19) is a favorite auto tour of visitors to the Jackson Hole area. The Gros Ventre River valley is a scenic delight, ranging from a deep and confined canyon in its lower reaches, to a wide open expanse of sagebrush-clad hills in its upper reaches. Views extend from the alpine heights of the Gros Ventre Range to the badlands of the Red Hills, and the road offers access to the foaming waters of the river and to the placid waters of Upper and Lower Slide lakes.

Within the valley are 45 sedimentary rock formations, all of them intricately folded and faulted. Steep slopes, past episodes of glaciation, and the general instability of the sedimentary rocks in the valley help to make this area the most landslide-prone in Wyoming. Dozens of landslides have helped to shape the landscape we see here today. Some actually remain in motion, though their movement is too slow to detect. Upper Slide Lake, as its name suggests, was dammed long ago by a landslide, but the most recent evidence of major landslide activity is the Lower Gros Ventre Slide and the large lake it impounded in the lower reaches of the valley.

Along the Gros Ventre Road there is a turnout with an interpretive display and a short trail into the slide area below Lower Slide Lake. Although a greater volume of rock moved in the Madison Slide in Montana (see Chapter 1), the Lower Gros Ventre Slide covers a larger area, and like the Madison Slide, was triggered by earthquake activity.

In the spring of 1925, heavy rains had saturated the sedimentary rock layers on the flanks of Sheep Mountain in the lower Gros Ventre River valley. On June 23, an earthquake set a mass of rock in motion, and within three minutes, 50 million cubic yards of rock hurtled into the canyon and surged 350 feet up the opposite slope. A rock dam, 2,000 feet wide and 250 feet high, impounded the river, forming three-mile-long Lower Slide Lake.

The dam held for nearly two years, but finally, on May 18, 1927, the dam was breached, unleashing a disastrous flood. A 15-foot wall of water rushed through the small town of Kelly, killing six people and destroying all the town's structures except the church and the school. The effects of the flood were felt as far as Idaho Falls, 135 miles away.

Access and Services

All highways that lead to the trails and campgrounds in this chapter are delightful scenic drives, passing through what is arguably the finest scenery in Greater Yellowstone. Access to this region is gained from the west via Wyoming 22 over Teton Pass, covering a distance of 24 miles from Victor, Idaho, to Jackson, Wyoming. From the southwest, U.S. 26/89 leads 23 miles from Alpine Junction, Wyoming, to Hoback Junction. And from the southeast, Highway 189/191 leads 53 miles from Daniel Junction, near Pinedale, Wyoming, to Hoback Junction, through scenic Hoback Canyon. This busy highway links Jackson with Rock Springs (180 miles) and Evanston (208 miles). This route offers tremendous views of the south front of the Gros Ventre Range as it winds through the Hoback River canyon, where the river has carved deeply into colorful sedimentary rock formations. Hoback Junction lies 13 miles south of Jackson, in the Snake River's Grand Canyon.

From the north, Jackson can be reached via U.S. 191/26/89, 31 miles south of Moran Junction, and 58 miles south of the South Entrance to Yellowstone National Park.

From the east, travelers can reach Moran Junction in Jackson Hole by following U.S. 26/287 for 128.6 miles northwest from Riverton, Wyoming, and 53.6 miles from Dubois, via Togwotee Pass.

The paved, two-lane Gros Ventre Road, beginning 7 miles north of Jackson, leads through the small town of Kelly (offering groceries and a pay telephone) and through Grand Teton National Park and into Bridger-Teton National Forest. Beyond the forest boundary, the road leads into the river's canyon, past the Lower Gros Ventre Slide, and turns into a wide gravel road beyond Atherton Creek Campground (see Trip 19 driving directions).

Jackson, Wyoming (6,209'), the cultural and economic hub of southern Greater Yellowstone, is a year-round tourist mecca. Jackson offers a wide array of services, including motels, restaurants, gas, auto and RV repair, towing, car rentals, groceries, hiking and camping supplies, several Snake River outfitters who offer guided float trips, and a hospital. Seven miles north of town is the Jackson Hole Airport—the only airport inside the boundaries of a national park—which offers connections to larger regional airports. Car rental is also available at the airport.

Bondurant, Wyoming (6,588'), is a small, isolated ranching community in the upper Hoback River valley that offers few services to travelers. Gas and a restaurant are north of the town, and a small motel and RV park are a short distance south.

Dubois, Wyoming (6,917'), lying in the upper Wind River Valley southeast of Togwotee Pass, offers a wide range of services, including nine motels, restaurants, gas, auto and RV repair, towing, groceries, and outdoor supplies. While in town, consider visiting the National Bighorn Sheep Interpretive Center, which offers fine displays on bighorn sheep in general, and information on the Whiskey Mountain herd (the largest herd of Rocky Mountain bighorn sheep), consisting of approximately 1,000 bighorns, that dwell in the Wind River Range south of town.

For further information on accommodations and services, contact the chambers of commerce listed below:

Jackson Hole Chamber of Commerce
P.O. Box E
Jackson, WY 83001
(307) 733-3316 or (800) 782-0011

Dubois Chamber of Commerce
616 West Ramshorn Street
P.O. Box 632
Dubois, WY 82513
(307) 455-2556

Campgrounds

21 • ATHERTON CREEK (6,950')

Location. Above the south shore of Lower Slide Lake, on the Gros Ventre Road, 17.8 miles northeast of Jackson (see Trip 19 driving directions for exact location); Bridger-Teton National Forest, Jackson Ranger District.

Facilities. 19 camping units, tables, fire pits and grills, water, toilets, garbage containers; boat launch; paved campground access road and campsite spurs; maximum trailer length of 25 feet; a fee is charged.

Dates Usually Open. June 5 through Oct. 30.

The Setting. This scenic, open campground is located on a hillside overlooking Lower Slide Lake in the Gros Ventre River canyon. Most campsites are located well above the lake, but a few lie next to the shore. The sites are situated among groves of small aspens.

The campground has fine views of the lake and part of the Lower Gros Ventre Slide, the bold southern peaks of the Teton Mountains, and of the densely forested slopes of the Gros Ventre Range.

22 • RED HILLS (7,000')

Location. In the Gros Ventre River valley alongside the Gros Ventre Road, 20.4 miles northeast of Jackson, Wyoming (see Trips 19 and 20 driving directions for exact location); Bridger-Teton National Forest, Jackson Ranger District.

Facilities. 5 camping units, tables, fire pits, water, toilets, garbage containers; a fee is charged.

Dates Usually Open. June 5 through Oct. 30.

The Setting. This pleasant riverside campground lies just above the south bank of the Gros Ventre River in a shady grove of Engelmann spruce. The east slopes of the Red Hills loom boldly over the campground in the northwest, providing a scenic and colorful background of red-colored ledges and corrugated slopes studded with gnarled limber pines.

Beyond the Red Hills rises the cliff face of Lavender Hills, and north of the campground lies a hilly expanse created by the Lavender Slide (see Trip 19), one of many landslides that have shaped the Gros Ventre River valley landscape.

There is ample space between campsites, and the sites are screened from one another by the spruce forest.

23 • CRYSTAL CREEK (7,010')

Location. In the Gros Ventre River valley, on the Gros Ventre Road, 0.4 mile east of Red Hills Campground (see Trips 19 and 20 driving directions for exact location); Bridger-Teton National Forest, Jackson Ranger District.

Facilities. 6 camping units, tables, fire pits, water, toilets, garbage containers; maximum trailer length of 20 feet; a fee is charged.

Dates Usually Open. June 5 through Oct. 30.

The Setting. This campground is more spacious than nearby Red Hills, though it contains only one more campsite, and lies in a more open setting. The campground is situated at the confluence of aptly-named Crystal Creek and the turbid waters of the Gros Ventre River.

Some of the campsites are in open locations, others are shaded by spruces. A few sites lie just above Crystal Creek upstream from the confluence, but most are away from the creek and river on the bench above. Crystal Creek, a clear, swift, 15-20-foot-wide stream, carries about the same volume as the Gros Ventre River above the confluence. Views of the Red and Lavender

hills are more panoramic from this campground than from Red Hills Campground.

24 • CURTIS CANYON (7,040')

Location. On the Curtis Canyon Road, 8.25 miles east of Jackson (see Trip 21 driving directions for exact location); Bridger-Teton National Forest, Jackson Ranger District.

Facilities. 12 camping units, tables, fire grills, water, toilets; maximum trailer length of 20 feet; a fee is charged.

Dates Usually Open. June 5 through Sept. 10.

The Setting. This pleasant campground is located on a grassy bench on the west slope of the Gros Ventre Range, 600 feet above the broad valley of Jackson Hole. The campsites are shaded by a grove of Douglas-fir.

There are tremendous views of Jackson Hole and the Tetons from the edge of the forested campground, and even better views from the Curtis Canyon Viewpoint, located at the end of a short spur road that begins 100 yards west of the campground entrance.

From the viewpoint, vistas also include the Snake River Range in the southwest, the cliff-bound declivity of Sheep Creek below to the north, and conical Jackson Peak on the eastern skyline.

25 • HOBACK (6,200')

Location. In Hoback Canyon, just off U.S. 189/191, 8.0 miles east of Hoback Junction and 42.5 miles northwest of Daniel Junction; Bridger-Teton National Forest, Jackson Ranger District.

Facilities. 14 camping units, tables, fire pits, fire grills, water, toilets, garbage containers; paved access road and camping spurs; maximum trailer length of 25 feet; a fee is charged.

Dates Usually Open. June 5 through Sept. 10.

The Setting. This pleasant campground lies in an open setting along the north banks of the Hoback River. Some sites are partly shaded among groves of Engelmann spruce. South of the campground, the forested slopes of the Wyoming Range rise 2,000 feet, and the slopes of the Gros Ventre Range, including the timberline summit of

9,665-foot Cream Puff Peak, rise to the north.

26 • GRANITE CREEK (6,840')

Location. In the Granite Creek valley, on the south slopes of the Gros Ventre Range, one mile north of Trailhead 21 (see Trip 22 driving directions for exact location); Bridger-Teton National Forest, Jackson Ranger District.

Facilities. 52 camping units, tables, fire grills, fire pits, water, toilets, garbage containers; maximum trailer length of 25 feet; a fee is charged.

Dates Usually Open. June 25 through Sept. 10.

The Setting. This scenic campground lies on a bench 250 yards west of large Granite Creek. Most sites are in a shady forest of lodgepole pine and subalpine fir, but a few sites at the north end of the campground lie at the forest's edge, next to a sagebrush-dotted meadow.

The campground lies in one of the most dramatic mountain settings in Greater Yellowstone. A grand array of 11,000-foot peaks rise nearly 5,000 feet above, circling the middle reaches of Granite Creek valley. The lofty pyramid of 11,095-foot Flying Buttress Mountain, rising east of the campground, is especially dramatic. The spire of The Open Door, an aptly named limestone formation, rises above the campground to the northeast.

Granite Falls, a roaring 20-foot cascade, lies one quarter mile up the road. One half mile farther is the Granite Pool parking area and the roadend. From there, a walk of 300 yards leads to the Granite Hot Springs Pool. The pool is open to the public for a fee, from 10 A.M. to 8 P.M. daily. Average summer water temperature at the hot springs is 93 degrees F.

27 • KOZY (6,350')

Location. In Hoback Canyon, just off U.S. 189/191, 12.8 miles east of Hoback Junction, 2.0 miles northwest of Bondurant, and 39.7 miles northwest of Daniel Junction; Bridger-Teton National Forest, Jackson Ranger District.

Facilities. 8 camping units, tables, fire pits, fire grills, water, toilets, garbage containers; paved access road and camping spurs; maximum trailer length of 18 feet; a fee is charged.

Dates Usually Open. June 5 through September 10.

The Setting. This scenic campground lies along the south banks of the Hoback River in an open section of the canyon. The sites are in a sagebrush-studded meadow enlivened by a variety of colorful wildflowers. Small lodgepole pines offer limited shade.

Views of the canyon are good, stretching down-river past the northern flanks of the Wyoming Range, where meadow-draped slopes and conifer groves rise to the skyline. Of interest is the prominent red butte of 7,210-foot Battle Mountain, a notable landmark rising to the northwest. The sandstones of Battle Mountain were thrust eastward over younger shales and sandstones along the Jackson-Prospect Thrust Fault. An extension of this thrust fault can be seen in lower Granite Creek. This fault marks the eastern boundary of the overthrust belt in Wyoming.

Battle Mountain is also noteworthy for the origin of its name. Under the Fort Bridger treaty of 1868, Bannock and Shoshone Indians were guaranteed "the right to hunt upon the unoccupied lands of the United States so long as game may be found thereon." In 1895, Bannocks from Idaho entered Wyoming to hunt and gather hides for the winter. The Bannocks, however, were threatened with arrest for violating state game laws established in the 1890s. A battle ensued between Bannocks and a Jackson posse in Granite Creek.

About 0.4 mile west of the campground, a parking area north of the highway, and just west of the bridge over the river, offers access to a 4WD road that ascends 600 feet in 0.75 mile to the crest of Battle Mountain. From there you have a close-up view of the thrust fault, as well as a dramatic view into Granite Creek valley and the high southern peaks of the Gros Ventre Range.

28 • Sheffield Creek (6,900')

Location. East of the John D. Rockefeller, Jr. Memorial Parkway, between Grand Teton and Yellowstone national parks, 2.9 miles south of the South Entrance to Yellowstone National Park, and 0.6 mile southeast of Flagg Ranch resort (see Trip 26 driving directions for exact location); Bridger-Teton National Forest, Buffalo Ranger District.

Facilities. 4 camping units, tables, fire pits, toilets, water (not potable), bear-resistant food storage boxes; no fee is charged.

Dates Usually Open. June 15 through Nov. 15.

The Setting. This small, seldom-used campground lies at the trailhead for Trip 26 to Huckleberry Mountain, on a bench above Snake River, and alongside small Sheffield Creek. In the summer of 1988, windblown trees fell onto a powerline across the highway and southwest of the campground, igniting the Huck Fire, a blaze that spread eastward for miles across the Teton Wilderness. As a result of the fire, the campground lies among the charred remains of a lodgepole-pine forest. There is no shade in the campground, but views are unrestricted, reaching southwest to the northern Teton Range, and west and northwest to the forested expanse of the Yellowstone Plateau.

29 • Turpin Meadow (6,920')

Location. In Turpin Meadow, just north of the Buffalo Fork of Snake River. Drive 12.9 miles east of Moran Junction via U.S. 26/287, or 12.4 miles west of Togwotee Pass, and 40.7 miles west of Dubois, and turn north where a large sign points to Turpin Meadow Recreation Area, opposite the Four Mile Meadow Picnic Area. Follow the good gravel road north for 4 miles to the campground, located just north of Turpin Meadow Lodge and the bridge over the Buffalo Fork; Bridger-Teton National Forest, Buffalo Ranger District.

Facilities. 18 camping units, tables, fire pits with grills, water, toilets, bear-resistant food storage boxes, bear-resistant garbage containers; maximum trailer length of 25 feet; a fee is charged.

Dates Usually Open. June 1 through Oct. 31.

The Setting. This pleasant campground lies in the Buffalo Fork valley in an open forest of small, scattered lodgepole pines. The open valley is bounded by rolling, sagebrush-clad hills studded with groves of pines. Views from the campground stretch west across broad Buffalo Fork valley to the imposing, snow-streaked crags of the Tetons.

Grizzly bears frequent this area, so adequate food storage is a necessity (use the food storage boxes provided in the campground). The North Buffalo Fork Trail begins at the campground, but because of a high incidence of human-grizzly bear encounters, this trail is not covered in this book.

Turpin Meadow Lodge, located across the river from the campground, offers a variety of services to guests. For reservations or for more information, contact the lodge at: Box 379, Moran, Wyoming 83013, or phone 1-800-743-2496.

30 • Hatchet (8,000')

Location. In the Buffalo Fork valley, just south of U.S. 26/287, 8.1 miles east of Moran Junction, or 0.2 mile west of Blackrock Ranger Station, 17.2 miles west of Togwotee Pass, and 45.5 miles west of Dubois; Bridger-Teton National Forest, Buffalo Ranger District.

Facilities. 9 camping units, tables, fire pits with grills, water, toilets, bear-resistant food storage containers, bear-resistant garbage containers; maximum trailer length of 25 feet; a fee is charged.

Dates Usually Open. June 25 through Sept. 10.

The Setting. This small campground, conveniently located 200 yards off the highway, lies in an open forest of small lodgepole pines. Views extend northward across the broad Buffalo Fork valley and westward to the northern reaches of the Tetons.

31 • Falls (8,250')

Location. 0.5 mile south of U.S. 26/287, 32.3 miles east of Moran Junction, 7.0 miles east of Togwotee Pass, and 21.3 miles west of Dubois, in the Absaroka Range; Shoshone National Forest, Wind River Ranger District.

Facilities. 45 camping units located along two loop roads in the campground: Pine Drive (27 units) and Spruce Drive (18 units); tables, fire pits with grills, water, toilets, bear-resistant garbage containers; maximum trailer length of 32 feet; a fee is charged.

Dates Usually Open. June 1 through Oct. 30.

The Setting. This exceptionally scenic campground is located in a forest of lodgepole pine and Engelmann spruce alongside willow-bordered Brooks Lake Creek. Views from the campground reach northeast to the jagged 11,000-foot crest of Pinnacle Buttes. The Pine Drive loop road is shaded by a canopy of spruce, pine, and subalpine fir. The Spruce Drive loop lies in an open forest of mixed conifers.

At the south end of the campground, a short trail leads 150 yards along the rim of Brooks Lake Creek canyon, offering a close-up view of Brooks Lake Creek Falls. The creek here plunges and cascades 200 feet over a series of resistant volcanic ledges.

From the trail's end there are fine views southeast into the upper reaches of Wind River Valley and beyond to the ice-clad peaks and plateaus of the Wind River Range.

32 • PINNACLE (9,100')

Location. In the Absaroka Range, above the east shore of Brooks Lake, 5.0 miles north of U.S. 26/287, 32.7 miles east of Moran Junction, 7.4 miles east of Togwotee Pass, and 20.9 miles west of Dubois, Wyoming (see Trip 27 driving directions for exact location); Shoshone National Forest, Wind River Ranger District.

Facilities. 21 camping units, tables, fire pits with grills, water, toilets, bear-resistant garbage containers; maximum trailer length of 22 feet; a fee is charged.

Dates Usually Open. June 20 through Sept. 10.

The Setting. This campground lies along a 0.3 mile road that leads from the outlet of Brooks Lake to the top of a tree-studded hill above the east shore. The campsites rest in a variety of scenic settings: some lie alongside Brooks Lake Creek, some are set in open forest beneath the towers of Pinnacle Buttes, and others lie in a peaceful, shady forest of lodgepole pine and Engelmann spruce.

This campground is more open than nearby Brooks Lake Campground, and most sites offer outstanding views, from the aptly named Pinnacle Buttes in the east, to Brooks Lake and the spreading timberline meadows that fringe its shores, and to a broad cliff band of gray volcanic rock that abuts the Continental Divide.

33 • BROOKS LAKE (9,080')

Location. In the Absaroka Range, along the south shore of Brooks Lake, 5.0 miles north of U.S. 26/287, 32.7 miles east of Moran Junction, 7.4 miles east of Togwotee Pass, and 20.9 miles west of Dubois, Wyoming (see Trip 27 driving directions for exact location); Shoshone National Forest, Wind River Ranger District.

Facilities. 14 camping units, tables, fire pits with grills, water, toilets, bear-resistant food storage boxes, bear-resistant garbage containers; maximum trailer length of 22 feet; boat launch; a fee is charged.

Dates Usually Open. June 20 through Sept. 30.

The Setting. This scenic campground lies just above the south shore of Brooks Lake (9,050') in an open forest of Engelmann spruce and lodgepole pine. Some of the campsites are situated close to the grassy lakeshore, but most sites rest on the forested slope above the lake. Splendid views are enjoyed from the campground, stretching across the three-quarter-mile-long lake to broad meadows, timberline forests, and imposing gray volcanic cliffs and spires.

Phone reservations can be made for all campgrounds in the Jackson Ranger District (Campgrounds 21-27) by dialing (800) 342-2267, or (801) 226-3564.

For Further Information

Information regarding Trips 19-25; Campgrounds 21-27:

Bridger-Teton National Forest
Jackson Ranger District
P.O. Box 1689
Jackson, WY 83001
(307) 739-5400

Information regarding Trip 26;
Campgrounds 28-30:

Bridger-Teton National Forest
Buffalo Ranger District (Blackrock
Ranger Station)
P.O. Box 278
Moran, WY 83013
(307) 543-2386

Information regarding Trips 27-29;
Campgrounds 31-33:

Shoshone National Forest
Wind River Ranger District
P.O. Box 186
Dubois, WY 82513
(307) 455-2466

Wilderness Regulations

Trails in both the Teton and Gros Ventre
wilderness areas are covered in this chapter. Backpackers planning an extended trip
into either of these wilderness areas should
study the regulations listed below, and be
prepared to follow them while in the backcountry.

TETON WILDERNESS

1. All motorized and mechanized vehicles and equipment, including bicycles and hang gliders, are prohibited.
2. Maximum group size is 20 persons.
3. Camping is not allowed within 200 feet of a designated trail.
4. The limit for occupying a backcountry campsite is 14 days.
5. Unburnable refuse must be packed out of the Wilderness.
6. The use of soaps in any water source or within 50 feet of a water source is not permitted.
7. Cutting or limbing of live trees is prohibited.
8. Using signs, tape, or flagging, or other artificial marker are not permitted.
9. Leaving a fire unattended without completely extinguishing it is prohibited.
10. Operating or using any audio devices such as portable radios or musical instruments in such a manner and at such a

time so as to disturb other persons is not permitted.
11. Discharging firearms in the vicinity of camps and over lakes or other bodies of water is prohibited.
12. Placing or maintaining a cache or leaving gear in the Wilderness is not permitted.
13. All food and beverages, including canned food, pop, beer, garbage, grease, processed livestock or pet food, and scented or flavored toiletries (toothpaste, chapstick, etc.) must be stored unavailable to bears at night and when unattended during the day.
14. Attractants must be hung at least 10 feet off the ground and four feet from any vertical support, or stored inside a bear-resistant container.

GROS VENTRE WILDERNESS

1. Group size is limited to 15 persons.
2. Maximum length of stay at backcountry campsites is 16 days.
3. Camping within 200 feet of a lake is prohibited.
4. Motorized and mechanized vehicles and equipment, including bicycles and hang gliders, are prohibited.

Trip 19

GROS VENTRE ROAD TO RED HILLS

Distance: 3.0 to 3.8 miles round trip.
Low/High Elevations: 7,100'/8,150' to 8,560'.
Difficulty: Moderate.
Use: Low.
Suited For: Dayhike.
Best Season: June through September.
Wildlife Viewing: Fair.
Grizzly Bear Danger: Low.
Map/Trailhead: 16/18.
Nearest Campgrounds: Red Hills, 1.3 miles, Crystal Creek, 1.6 miles, and Atherton Creek, 4.2 miles from the trailhead.
Driving to the Trailhead: Drive on U.S. 26/89/191 7.0 miles north from Jackson,

Wyoming, to signed Gros Ventre Junction and turn right (northeast) onto paved, two-lane Gros Ventre Road.

After 4.6 miles you pass the large Gros Ventre Campground (Grand Teton National Park), and after 6.8 miles enter the small community of Kelly. Here the road turns north, and after another 1.3 miles you reach a prominently signed junction with the eastbound Gros Ventre Road. A national forest sign here lists various destinations and mileages in the upper Gros Ventre valley.

Drivers southbound on U.S. 26/89/191 can reach that junction north of Kelly by driving 16.7 miles south of Moran Junction and 44.0 miles south of Yellowstone National Park's south entrance, to signed Antelope Flat Road, and turn left (east). That road junction is 150 yards south of the signed Blacktail Ponds Overlook in Grand Teton National Park. Follow the paved Antelope Flat Road east across the valley of Jackson Hole, then turn south at a signed four-way junction. After driving 5.8 miles from the highway, you reach the signed junction with the Gros Ventre Road north of Kelly, and turn left (east).

From that junction follow the narrow pavement of the Gros Ventre Road eastward as it winds among rolling hills and groves of aspen in Grand Teton National Park for 2.3 miles to the boundary of Bridger-Teton National Forest. After another 2.4 miles, you pass a large turnout on the south side of the road, opposite the massive Lower Gros Ventre Slide, where you will find a large interpretive display, and the start of a 0.4-mile interpretive trail leading into the canyon and to the edge of the slide.

After 6.0 miles from the junction north of Kelly, pass the turnoff to Atherton Creek Campground, beyond which the pavement ends, and the Gros Ventre Road continues eastward as a good, wide gravel road. After 11.0 miles from the junction near Kelly, and 5.0 miles from the end of the pavement, you reach the signed entrance to Red Hills Ranch, on the south side of the road. Your unmarked trail begins 50 yards east of the ranch entrance on the north side of the

road. There are wide spots off the road here in which to park.

Introduction: The red rock badlands of the Red Hills, in the Gros Ventre River valley, are one of the anomalies of Greater Yellowstone. The hills present a scene more typical of the desert Southwest than of the Middle Rocky Mountains.

This short but steep hike passes through this unusual landscape en route to a glorious vista point, where a sweeping panorama stretches from the Tetons in the west to the distant Wind River Range in the southeast.

Description: The unmarked but well-defined trail initially leads north from the Gros Ventre Road, toward the mouth of a minor canyon. Despite the relatively high elevation here (7,100'), you feel as if you were in a Southwest desert—the slopes above are nearly barren of vegetation, small ledges and cliff bands jut outward, and runoff gullies dissect the slopes into a typical badlands landscape. By contrast, the north slopes of the Gros Ventre Range to the south, with their aspen groves, dense forests, grassy parks, and alpine peaks, serve to remind you that you are indeed in the Rocky Mountains.

The red tread of the trail rises steadily from the start as we head into the mouth of the steep and narrow draw. The trailside grasslands are studded with big sagebrush and early summer wildflowers such as sulphur paintbrush, sticky geranium, and larkspur.

We curve northeast upon entering the draw, and the grade becomes moderate. The Red Hills rise abruptly from the draw to a skyline of sharply pointed summits, grassy on their lower slopes and feathered with scattered limber pines on their crests.

The Red Hills are composed of the 180-million-year-old Chugwater Formation. Within this formation are beds of red shales, siltstones, sandstones, and thin white layers of gypsum. This formation is widespread throughout Wyoming, forming dramatic badlands scenery in places such as the Bighorn Basin and east of Dubois in the upper Wind River valley.

At first, the bottom of the draw is lined with willows, but no surface water flows here. Green gentian is common near the mouth of the draw. This showy plant requires two seasons of growth to complete its life cycle. During the first year it develops a ground-hugging rosette of large, light green leaves; the following year the plant develops a tall, flowering stalk covered with small, greenish-white flowers. After the plant dies, its stalk may remain erect for many seasons.

As we continue, the grade becomes moderately steep and the trail is confined to the bottom of the increasingly narrow draw. Tall, white-boled aspens soon appear, and groves of Engelmann spruce begin to clothe the shady, north-facing slopes. Widely scattered limber pines dot the south-facing slopes of the Red Hills to the north.

The trail becomes increasingly steep as we labor up the draw but, as we approach its head, the grade begins to moderate on the conifer-dotted slopes. Indian paintbrush, sticky geranium, sagebrush, snowberry, currant, and buffaloberry appear, and finally we reach the crest of the Red Hills at an 8,150-foot saddle, 1.5 miles from the trailhead.

The view from this point easily rewards us for our efforts. To the south are the broad northern flanks of the Gros Ventre Range, crowned by ranks of 10,000-foot and 11,000-foot limestone peaks. At the western end of the range we can see the pointed "face" and round "belly" of the Sleeping Indian (Sheep Mountain).

Northward, the colorful cliff band on the south face of the Lavender Hills (composed of the purple and gray claystones of the Cloverly Formation) looms boldly above us, separated from our ridge by a shallow basin. That basin

appears to be a glacial cirque, but it was created along the trailing edge of the massive Lavender Slide, one of many landslides in the Gros Ventre valley.

This ridgetop offers a good place to observe the effect of microclimates on vegetation patterns. The open, sun-drenched south-facing slopes host only scattered limber pines, but just north of the crest, on the cool, shady north-facing slopes, a forest of Douglas-fir and subalpine fir thrives.

From the saddle, you have three options: return the way you came; turn right on a faint path that follows the ridge east then south 0.1 mile to Point 8166, where a broader view opens up; or follow the steep trail west for 0.4 mile to a higher ridge, from where the most panoramic view unfolds.

For the last option, follow the very steep trail west. The mostly open slopes are dotted with limber pine and Douglas-fir, and in early summer enjoy the large yellow blossoms of arrowleaf balsamroot. After gaining 400 feet in 0.4 mile, we mount an 8,560-foot, north-trending ridge. From this ridge there is an outstanding view of the Teton Mountains, which up to this point have been obscured by the Red Hills. From square-topped Mt. Moran (12,605') in the northwest to the ski runs of Rendezvous Mountain in the southwest, that range is displayed in all of its magnificence.

Lower Slide Lake and the Tetons from Red Hills

Below to the west, the deep canyon of the Gros Ventre River winds toward Jackson Hole past landslide-dammed Lower Slide Lake and opens up into the grassy foothills beyond. The Gros Ventre Range dominates the southward view. In the foothills of that range Grizzly Lake lies on a grassy, forested bench above the river (see Trip 20). To the southeast our view stretches up the broad Gros Ventre valley to the distant northern peaks of the Wind River Range, craggy and glacier-clad.

Eventually we must leave the grand vistas and retrace our route to the trailhead.

Trip 20
RED HILLS CAMPGROUND TO GRIZZLY LAKE

Distance: 9.0 miles round trip.
Low/High Elevations: 7,010'/7,600'.
Difficulty: Moderate.
Use: Moderate.
Suited For: Dayhike or backpack.
Best Season: Mid-June through September.
Wildlife Viewing: Good.
Grizzly Bear Danger: Low.
Map/Trailhead: 16/19.
Nearest Campgrounds: Red Hills Campground is located opposite the trailhead; Crystal Creek, 0.3 mile, and Atherton Creek, 5.6 miles from the trailhead.
Driving to the Trailhead: Follow driving directions in Trip 19 to Red Hills Ranch, then continue east on the gravel road, crossing the Gros Ventre River after 0.6 mile, and reaching the signed trailhead parking area after another 0.7 mile, opposite the entrance to Red Hills Campground, 12.3 miles from the junction north of Kelly. The Crystal Creek Campground lies 0.3 mile east of the trailhead on Gros Ventre Road.
Introduction: This pleasant hike to Grizzly Lake tours part of the northern foothills of the Gros Ventre Range. These rolling foothills are glacial moraines, dotted with erratic

boulders carried here by glacial ice from as far away as the Wind River Range, more than 35 miles distant.

The trail passes through an open landscape of grassy, sagebrush-covered slopes, aspen groves, and scattered pockets of conifer forest. Fine vistas of unusual and contrasting landforms, flower-speckled meadows, and a scenic mountain lake make this trip a rewarding choice for visitors to the Gros Ventre region.

Description: From the trailhead opposite the spruce-fringed waters of the Gros Ventre River, we pass a destination and mileage sign, briefly parallel the road below, and soon join an old jeep trail heading southeast into a narrow meadow. After 0.3 mile, we leave the jeep trail, turning right (south) onto the signed foot trail. We then ascend moderately through a lodgepole-pine and spruce grove, soon topping out on a grassy, sagebrush-clad bench. Here the trail becomes obscure for about 150 years, but 3-foot-high wooden posts guide us southward on a meandering course among scattered boulders (glacial erratics) toward the foot of a 700-foot-high red rock butte.

Fine views from the bench reach northwest to the desert-like Red and Lavender hills, west down the Gros Ventre valley to the bold peaks of the central Teton Range, and southwest up the glacier-gouged West Miner Creek canyon to the 11,000-foot summits of Sheep Mountain. Wildflowers in this sagebrush-covered expanse are colorful and diverse until midsummer. On this bench and throughout the course of the hike we will see valerian, sticky geranium, arrowleaf balsamroot, sulphur paintbrush, longleaf phlox, pussytoes, and rock daisy.

Reaching the head of a southwest-trending draw, we meet a well-worn path coming from the old, now-closed trailhead at Crystal Creek Campground, and we bear right, descending gently southwest down the draw. The smooth tread soon leads to a jackleg fence, which we follow through shady lodgepole forest. For the next 1.5 miles, much of the route follows fence lines that demarcate the boundary between private lands (lying north of the fence) and national forest lands.

Soon the forest thins and we enter another sagebrush-dotted bench, then generally follow the fence line southwest to the banks of an irrigation ditch, curve south into the East Miner Creek drainage, cross a bridge spanning the ditch, and momentarily reach the 8-foot wide stream of East Miner Creek.

During periods of high runoff, you must ford the swift, but shallow, cobble-bottomed stream. If the water is low, an easy rockhop affords a dry crossing. Beyond the crossing, the trail leads south, up-canyon, along the spruce-bordered stream for a short distance, then follows switchbacks on a moderate grade to a minor ridge, where more fine views unfold.

From the ridge we descend northwest on the faint, rocky trail, then curve west when we reach the fence line. Soon the trail becomes easier to follow as we descend to the spruce- and lodgepole-shaded banks of West Miner Creek, 1.8 miles from the trailhead. A small log offers a dry crossing of the creek, but just beyond it you must jump across a smaller branch of the creek.

Our trail then crosses faint jeep tracks that lead 200 yards south to an old cabin, but we stay on the foot trail, soon ascending a moderate grade, and gaining 175 feet to the crest of another minor ridge. Atop the ridge, the trail bends north, descending steadily down a draw shaded by lodgepole pine, Engelmann spruce, and aspen.

Shortly we leave the draw, curve west into another draw, and follow along its small stream, ascending at a moderate grade. Ignoring two right-branching trails that cross the creek, we labor up a steep pitch to a low ridge, where we reach a signed junction, 2.5 miles from the trailhead.

The left-branching, southwest-bound trail ascends 2,700 feet in another 4.5 miles to a high ridge overlooking Blue Miner Lake. But we bear right, descending slightly into a broad, grassy, willow-choked basin, and skirt the shores of a marshy pond. Alert hikers may spy a moose wad-

ing in the pond or browsing among the willows.

Now curve around the spruce-fringed bowl, jump across two small, early summer creeks, and then ascend moderately upon grassy slopes to a broad, 7,600-foot ridge dotted with aspen, lodgepole and limber pines, and subalpine fir. The ensuing gentle, 1.2-mile descent is a delightful stroll through flower-speckled meadows, aspen groves, and stands of lodgepole pine. At length we reach a bench above the east shore of Grizzly Lake, where the trail forks. The left branch skirts the south and west shores of the lake, and the right branch goes above the east shore. Both trails offer access to the lake and to good campsites shaded by spruce and lodgepole pine.

The 7,184-foot lake lies at the bottom of a broad depression, with no inlet or outlet. At first glance, Grizzly Lake may appear to be of glacial origin, lying in a depression bounded by moraines. However, the lake actually lies behind the barrier of a large landslide from the north slopes of the Gros Ventres. This is but one of six major landslides that have occurred during the last several thousand years in the landslide-prone Gros Ventre valley.

The lake's setting is not one of ice-gouged bedrock and alpine peaks typical of most high mountain lakes in Greater Yellowstone, but rather is gentle and unimposing. A discontinuous forest of pine and spruce fringes the lake's southeast shore, while the north and west shores are meadow-bordered and rise to rolling, grassy, sagebrush-dotted hills studded with scattered pines.

From the lake, retrace your route to the trailhead.

Trip 21

CURTIS CANYON ROAD TO GOODWIN LAKE

Distance: 6.0 miles round trip.
Low/High Elevations: 8,100'/9,500'.
Difficulty: Moderate.
Use: Heavy.
Suited For: Dayhike or backpack.
Best Season: July through September.
Wildlife Viewing: Fair.
Grizzly Bear Danger: Low.
Map/Trailhead: 17/20.
Nearest Campground. Curtis Canyon, 2.75 miles from the trailhead.
Driving to the Trailhead: In the prominent town square of Jackson, Wyoming, where the northbound highway leads to Grand Teton and Yellowstone national parks, proceed east through town on East Broadway Street; a sign points the way to the National Elk Refuge.

After 1.0 mile, East Broadway Street ends, and you turn left (northeast) onto a wide gravel road at the prominently signed National Elk Refuge entrance. This road leads through the rich meadows of the refuge, where thousands of elk gather each winter. After 4.6 miles, turn right (east) onto a wide, road where a national forest sign lists various destinations and mileages.

After another 1.3 miles the road smooths out where we enter Bridger-Teton National Forest, and then begins climbing the west slopes of the Gros Ventre Range via switchbacks. Soon we pass the spur road to Curtis Canyon Viewpoint (and a grand panorama of Jackson Hole and the Tetons), and 100 yards farther pass the entrance to Curtis Canyon Campground, 8.25 miles from Jackson.

From the campground, follow the road as it climbs via more switchbacks for another 1.7 miles, and bear right where Sheep Creek Road branches left. The spacious trailhead parking area lies at the roadend, beside a broad, sloping meadow, 1.0 mile

from the last junction, 2.75 miles from the campground, and 11.0 miles from Jackson.
Introduction: Conical Jackson Peak, rising to 10,741 feet, is a prominent landmark at the western end of the Gros Ventre Range, 6 miles east of the town of Jackson. The peak is unusual in the Gros Ventres, since it is composed of granite, not limestone, as are the peaks that dominate the range. Nestled in a broad cirque just below and northeast of the peak is Goodwin Lake, the most easily accessible timberline lake in the range, and a favorite dayhike of Jackson area residents.

This fine hike leads through open forests as it ascends the upper west slopes of the Gros Ventres, and ends next to the deep waters of Goodwin Lake. This trip offers numerous good campsites and brook trout fishing at the lake, and an optional scramble to the summit of Jackson Peak.

Since this trip lies within the boundaries of the Gros Ventre Wilderness, backpackers should familiarize themselves with the wilderness regulations listed earlier in this chapter.
Description: There are no signs at the trailhead to indicate a trail, and indeed, there is none. The initial 1.4 miles of our trip follow a long-closed logging road that begins at the south end of the parking area, behind the locked gate. The rocky road ascends at a gentle-to-moderate grade, passing through a forest of lodgepole pine, Douglas-fir, and subalpine fir, and across narrow clearcuts now overgrown with young pines.

Within the first half mile, ignore two right-forking spur roads. Upon reaching the first switchback in the road, pause to enjoy the fine view of ice-sculpted Jackson Peak, looming above to the south. Dramatic views of the 7,000-foot eastern escarpment of the Teton Range and of Jackson Hole help pass the time as we ascend a moderate grade to another switchback, where we turn south and continue ascending the rocky roadbed to a trail sign at 8,720 feet, 1.4 miles from the trailhead.

Here we leave the road, turn left onto the rocky trail, and ascend a moderately steep

Goodwin Lake

grade southeast. Soon, subalpine fir and whitebark pine begin to dominate the forest as we labor up a steep grade that ends in a flower-speckled meadow, rich with the blooms of lupine, arrowleaf balsamroot, and sticky geranium.

Just beyond the meadow's east edge, we mount the crest of a narrow ridge and follow it south, high above the canyon that drains audible Sheep Creek, east of our promontory. Tall, multibranched, whitebark pines and spire-topped subalpine firs shade the trail. Occasional openings between trailside trees allow views that stretch across gaping Sheep Creek canyon to a broad, 10,000-foot ridge, its slopes broken by limestone cliff bands and ledges.

A pleasant 0.4-mile jaunt along the gently rising ridge leads to the signed boundary of the Gros Ventre Wilderness, beyond which we begin to traverse rocky, east-facing slopes, from where views soon open up as the forest cover thins. Our view stretches down the heavily forested trough of Sheep Creek and broadens to the north in a panorama that includes the northern reaches of the Teton Mountains, Jackson Hole, Jackson Lake, the southern limits of the Yellowstone volcanic plateau, and the western Teton Wilderness.

Soon we pass above a shallow, boulder-choked draw and, where the trail merges with the draw ahead, we cross over the boulder field. These boulders are pushed up along the western margin of the draw; this is a small lateral moraine, left by the melting fringes of an ancient glacier.

The rocky tread leads through a timberline forest of pine and fir, on a steady but moderate grade. We soon skirt the shore of a small pond, then ascend briefly to an easy rockhop of Goodwin Lake's outlet creek. Beyond the crossing it's 150 yards to the lake's north shore. The trail continues south beyond the lake, heading deep into the Gros Ventre Wilderness.

This timberline gem is fringed on its north, east, and south shores by an open forest of Engelmann spruce and whitebark pine. Talus slopes rise steeply from the west shore to the broken north ridge of Jackson Peak; the summit of the peak is barely visible where it juts above a ridge to the southwest.

Scattered boulders and ice-polished bedrock knobs are here and there among the forest around the lake, and there are a number of good campsites. Some overused and now closed campsites lie along the east shore; restrain the urge to use those sites and remember to camp at least 200 feet from any lake in the Gros Ventre Wilderness. Brook trout averaging 10 inches are plentiful in the lake, and they promise to keep anglers busy.

Eventually we retrace our route back to the trailhead.

Trip 22

GRANITE CREEK TO BOULDER CREEK VIA THE HIGH LINE TRAIL

Distance: 7.5 miles, round trip.
Low/High Elevations: 6,760'/8,480'.
Difficulty: Moderate.
Use: Low.
Suited For: Dayhike.
Best Season: Mid-June through mid-Sept.
Wildlife Viewing: Excellent.
Grizzly Bear Danger: Low.
Map/Trailhead: 18/21.
Nearest Campgrounds: Granite Creek, 1.0 mile, Kozy, 9.3 miles, and Hoback, 11.0 miles from the trailhead.
Driving to the Trailhead: From U.S. 189/191 in Hoback Canyon, 11.4 miles east of Hoback Junction (which is 13.0 miles south of Jackson), and 9.7 miles northwest of Bondurant, turn northeast onto Granite Creek Road (Forest Road 30500), prominently signed for Granite Recreation Area.

Granite Creek Road is a good, wide gravel road, but develops a rough washboard surface through the summer. Follow this road northeast into the Granite Creek valley, ignoring the left-forking Little Granite Creek Road after 1.3 miles, and a right fork, signed for Jack Pine summer homes, after 6.6 miles.

A destination and mileage sign on the left (west) side of the road at 7.6 miles notes the beginning of the High Line Trail. Since no parking is available here, turn right just beyond the trail, where a sign points to the trailhead. Follow this road east, bridge Granite Creek, and park in the spacious trailhead parking area a few yards north of a T-intersection, 0.3 mile from the High Line Trail.

There are several undeveloped camping areas in Granite Creek valley below the trailhead, and a large campground 1.0 mile up the road. The camping limit in the Granite Recreation Area is five days.

Introduction: The southwest slopes of the Gros Ventre Range rise steadily from the depths of Hoback Canyon via a series of long ridges, mantled in profuse greenery and scattered conifer forests. These ridges undulate upward for several miles, then end abruptly at the foot of alpine summits that tower above 10,000 and 11,000 feet. The peaks form an exciting background for travelers in Hoback Canyon, but they appear to form an impenetrable barrier to backcountry travel.

Numerous long, U-shaped canyons, however, afford access through that mountain barrier. Granite Creek is the most prominent of these canyons, and is arguably the most scenic. Easy access from Hoback Canyon, numerous good trails, a large campground, Granite Falls, and the Granite Hot Springs Pool all combine to make the Granite Recreation Area the premier attraction in the Gros Ventre Range.

This scenic trip follows part of the High Line Trail along the southwest face of the Gros Ventre Range, and leads to a lovely timberline basin embraced by 10,000-foot limestone crags. The trail is well-defined and easy to follow, with occasional detours around fallen trees. Heavy traffic by mule deer, elk, and moose, and by stock parties during the autumn hunting season has created a rough, uneven tread.

Description: From the trailhead parking area, backtrack down the road 0.3 mile to the signed High Line Trail, at 6,795 feet. Ascend a moderate grade southwest over open slopes studded with sagebrush and a diverse collection of wildflowers, such as cinquefoil, sticky geranium, valerian, yellow mule's ears, lupine, larkspur, Oregon grape, arrowleaf balsamroot, woodland star, and cow parsnip.

Views are inspiring from the start, reaching across broad Granite Creek valley to the 11,000-foot peaks that surround it. Soon, however, you duck into an aspen grove and views are obscured. Continue a steady, moderate ascent, alternating between aspen groves and scattered stands of subalpine fir, and meadow-covered slopes.

The trail curves west at a minor draw, and the ascent continues beneath a canopy of subalpine fir, lodgepole pine, and Douglas-fir. As we gain elevation on the west wall of Granite Creek valley, more wildflowers begin to appear, and a variety of shrubs clothe the slopes. Mountain ash, Rocky Mountain maple, buffaloberry, and Utah honeysuckle form the shrubby understory. Common wildflowers include meadow rue, heartleaf arnica, Canada violet, Richardson geranium, waterleaf, and spring beauty.

After ascending 1,150 taxing feet in 1.2 miles, the grade abates where we curve around the shoulder of a ridge, and we begin a gently ascending, northwest-bound traverse just below the ridgecrest. Soon the forest opens up, and we head across slopes clad in aspens and carpeted with a profusion of arrowleaf balsamroot and mule's ears. Fine views from this stretch of the trail reach across Granite Creek valley to the prominent summits of 11,113-foot Antoinette Peak in the northeast, and across the southwest face of the range to the 11,131-foot crest of The Elbow in the southeast.

Soon we pass through a stand of charred snags, then cross over the ridge and continue the traverse, now on southwest-facing slopes. Here we exchange views of Granite Creek for views of Hoback Canyon and the summits of the Wyoming Range. The trail ahead dips into minor draws at times, and passes through groves of aspen and isolated stands of subalpine fir, but most often the trail stays just above timberline on open slopes. At length the small bowl harboring Boulder Creek comes into view ahead, and after 3.75 miles we reach the basin floor alongside a small, willow-bordered stream at 8,320 feet.

The bowl lies in a grand timberline setting and offers a convenient terminus for a day's outing on the High Line Trail. Isolated groves of subalpine fir dot the verdant slopes surrounding the basin, and broken walls of light gray limestone rise steeply north and northwest to an array of alpine summits: Peak 10285 to the northwest, and Peaks 10654 and 10623 to the north.

Boulder Creek basin on the High Line Trail, Gros Ventre Range

A few poor campsites lie on a low moraine just east of Boulder Creek, sheltered by fir groves. Strong hikers may wish to continue the high meadow walk as far as Little Granite Creek, in another scenic basin, 3.8 miles farther west.

Most hikers will end the trip at Boulder Creek and backtrack to the trailhead.

Trip 23

GRANITE CREEK TO SHOAL FALLS

Distance: 12.4 miles, round trip.
Low/High Elevations: 6,760'/8,520'.
Difficulty: Strenuous.
Use: Low.
Suited For: Dayhike or backpack.
Best Season: Late June through mid-September.
Wildlife Viewing: Excellent.
Grizzly Bear Danger: Low.
Maps/Trailhead: 18, 19/21.
Nearest Campgrounds: See *Nearest Campgrounds* for Trip 22.
Driving to the Trailhead: Follow driving directions for Trip 22.
Introduction: Shoal Falls, a striking 150-foot waterfall in Shoal Creek valley on the southwest slopes of the Gros Ventre Range, is the destination of this strenuous, up and down, all-day hike. The trail is easy to follow, but it involves steep grades, and two significant descents en route to the falls, which remain hidden from view until the final descent to Shoal Creek, 5.6 miles from the trailhead.

This rewarding trip offers grand vistas and passes through a scenic landscape of dense forests, aspen groves, and timberline meadows rich with wildflowers.

Description: From the trailhead parking area at 6,760 feet, where a sign points to Shoal Falls, follow the Swift Creek Trail, a rocky, long-closed road, generally east above the conifer-bordered banks of Swift Creek. Rise moderately at first upon sagebrush-

clad slopes, where yellow mule's ears put forth a memorable floral display until midsummer.

After entering a mixed conifer forest, we reach a junction less than 0.5 mile from the trailhead, near the mouth of Swift Creek's precipitous canyon. Turn right at the sign here for Shoal Falls, and proceed through the forest, for 250 yards to another signed junction. Take the left fork, signed for SHOAL LAKE TRAIL JUNCTION and head uphill to the southeast.

The trail ahead ascends very steeply at times on the east wall of Granite Creek valley, passing beneath a moderately dense canopy of Douglas-fir and lodgepole pine. We climb through the viewless forest to a small sloping meadow at 7,640 feet, 1.3 miles from the trailhead, thick with shoulder-high western coneflowers. From here an expansive vista reaches southwest to the alpine crest of the Wyoming Range.

Beyond the meadow the grade moderates, and we continue ascending forested slopes to the crest of a minor ridge at 8,160 feet, 2.1 miles from the trailhead. There we enter subalpine meadows studded with groves of lodgepole pine and subalpine fir. Massive Flying Buttress Mountain, rising to 11,095 feet, looms above the trail to the northeast.

The following 1.2 miles is a pleasant, gentle walk through scattered timberline forests and high meadows enlivened by the blooms of yarrow, arrowleaf balsamroot, blue harebell, western coneflower, subalpine daisy, Richardson geranium, and yampah. From these grasslands we enjoy fine views of the towering peaks of the Gros Ventre Range in the north, and of the distant Wyoming Range in the southwest.

After 3.3 miles we begin a gradual descent to the west rim of a small canyon, where we turn southeast and follow the rim. Soon we descend steep, cobbly switchbacks into the shallow canyon below. Reaching the canyon floor, we jump across a small stream, and begin a protracted uphill grade, ascending moderately along an east-trending draw. Meadows spread out along the floor of the draw, their borders fringed by groves of aspen, lodgepole pine, Engelmann spruce, and subalpine fir. Soon the draw becomes a rich flower garden hosting the colorful blooms of western coneflower, Richardson geranium, subalpine daisy, yampah, palish larkspur, cinquefoil, and giant-hyssop.

The draw eventually merges into the slopes of a minor ridge, and after 4.5 miles, at 8,480 feet, we crest that ridge, then head east across the open expanse of a broad, grassy bowl. One final, short ascent leads out of the bowl and onto a tree-fringed saddle high above Shoal Creek valley at 8,520 feet, 4.8 miles from the trailhead.

A memorable panorama of rugged Gros Ventre peaks unfolds from this vantage. Soaring more than 2,500 feet above to the north are the broad alpine slopes of Flying Buttress Mountain. Northeast into Shoal Creek valley we see a limestone cliff band cutting across the canyon. Shoal Falls, presently invisible, plunges through a recess in this cliff. Rising above Shoal Creek are the summits of 11,404-foot Palmer Peak, 11,682-foot Doubletop Mountain, 11,180-foot Hodges Peak, 10,979-foot Eagle Peak, and the long gray crest of The Elbow.

The trail descends steeply east from the saddle, carving through dense, shoulder-high greenery. Midway down the slope, you enter the Gros Ventre Wilderness, and enjoy your first good views of Shoal Falls. After descending 720 feet in 0.8 mile, you reach the banks of Shoal Creek, just below a wide meadow flooded with beaver ponds. From this point you have the best view of the 150-foot waterfall.

Now you can either enjoy the view of the falls from a distance and return the way we came or, for a closer look at the falls, follow a rough, obscure path up the canyon.

For the latter, first cross Shoal Creek (an easy 15-foot-wide ford, or possibly a log crossing), then walk uphill for 150 yards to a junction. Here an unmarked trail, well worn by cattle that graze here in summer, leads northeast, following above the east banks of Shoal Creek. Turn left onto that trail, but the way becomes obscure in the forest after

crossing a small stream and a passing a good, large packer campsite.

Up the canyon beyond the campsite you soon relocate the trail. Shortly you cross another small stream, then a branch of Shoal Creek. The route beyond is a bushwhack and a rockhop, but around a bend in the creek you soon reach the shadowed amphitheater where the falls plunge over the gray limestone cliff.

Eventually, we must retrace our rigorous up and down route back to the trailhead.

Trip 24

CLIFF CREEK FALLS

Distance: 11.8 miles, round trip.
Low/high Elevations: 6,940'/8,000'.
Difficulty: Moderate.
Use: Low.
Suited For: Dayhike or mountain bike trip.
Best Season: Late June through mid-Sept.
Wildlife Viewing: Good.
Grizzly Bear Danger: Low.
Map/Trailhead: 20/22.
Nearest Campgrounds: Kozy, 9.2 miles, and Hoback, 13.8 miles from the trailhead.
Driving to the Trailhead: Follow U.S. 189/191 for 7.2 miles northwest from the small town of Bondurant, Wyoming, or 14.8 miles east from Hoback Junction (13.0 miles south of Jackson), to Cliff Creek Road, signed Forest Road 30530. Follow this good gravel road as it ascends south up Cliff Creek canyon and into the Wyoming Range.

After 6.9 miles, bear right at a junction; a sign here points the way to the trailhead. The spacious trailhead parking area lies another 0.1 mile up the right fork, next to a large information sign, above the banks of Cliff Creek. Numerous undeveloped camping areas can be found all along Cliff Creek Road and at the trailhead.

Introduction: This fine dayhike leads deep into the Wyoming Range above Hoback Canyon, passing through cool forests, bucolic meadows, and following Cliff Creek to a memorable waterfall in a shadowed amphitheater. This trail, well-worn and easy to follow, is much less strenuous than Trip 23 to Shoal Falls. Expect to see cattle grazing on the slopes and in the meadows along much of the trail.

Description: From the trailhead at 6,940 feet, the trail leads several yards down to Cliff Creek, a 20-foot-wide stream that we must ford. Its waters are shin-deep with a gentle current.

Beyond the ford, follow a 4WD road south up the canyon, quite soon reaching a fork in the road. Follow the left fork of the road along the willow-bordered banks of the creek for 0.4 mile, to where the signed Cliff Creek Trail branches right, and leads uphill away from the road.

The ensuing 1.9 miles of the trail ascends the canyon through stands of lodgepole pine and subalpine fir. Grassy openings in the forest are painted with the vivid colors of a myriad of wildflowers, including arrowleaf balsamroot, western coneflower, subalpine daisy, yarrow, cinquefoil, monkshood, Richardson geranium, yellow mule's ears, and yampah. Shrubs in the narrow but open canyon stud the slopes above the trail, and include buffaloberry, common juniper, sagebrush, serviceberry, and wildrose.

Views are infrequent from the confines of the canyon, but there are occasional glimpses of tundra-capped alpine summits to the south. After following the banks of Cliff Creek for 2.3 miles, we rockhop small Cabin Creek, a Cliff Creek tributary, and soon ascend a grassy draw to a signed junction at 7,273 feet, 2.5 miles from the trailhead.

The signed Bondurant Creek Trail forks left at the junction, but we bear right, then head southwest through a profusion of mule's ears. Soon we return to the banks of Cliff Creek in a willow-studded meadow and follow the canyon toward the west. We gain views of the forested ridges that bound the canyon, rising more than 1,000 feet to the skyline, and cliffs of red rock begin to appear on the slopes. We also enjoy glimpses into the distant head of the canyon, flanked by high ridges and verdant slopes.

The trail ahead alternates between stands of mixed conifers and open, rich meadows. At 4.1 miles, we cross the creek a second time. If no logs are in place, ford the 10-foot-wide, shin-deep waters. Beyond that crossing, above the creek's shady south banks, Engelmann spruce joins the pine and fir forest.

Soon we return to the creek, at 4.5 miles, and cross back to the north bank. There may be stout logs in place at the crossing and just downstream. The trail continues rising gently for 0.5 mile beyond the third crossing, till we reach the rocky slopes of an alluvial fan, cut by numerous runoff channels, and pass beneath the overhanging branches of narrowleaf cottonwoods.

At the western edge of the fan, a short, steep ascent leads to the shore of an algae-green pond. After skirting that pond, our undulating trail leads over rocky, sparsely forested terrain, passing below two cold springs that nurture a pair of ponds.

Beyond the ponds, there are fine views of the lofty ridges and red cliffs that embrace the upper reaches of the canyon. After 5.8 miles, a 20-foot waterfall comes into view up the canyon to the west, plunging down an overhanging limestone ledge. This fall, however, is not the one we seek, and we soon reach a sign pointing the way south to the falls. A final ascent leads 200 yards to the foot of Cliff Creek Falls, hidden in a cliff-bound amphitheater.

Cliff Creek Falls

The falls are dramatic, plunging 150 feet over the limestone cliffs. Tall pines and firs on the rim of the amphitheater lend a sense of scale to the falls.

After enjoying the cool spray of Cliff Creek Falls, backtrack to the trailhead.

Trip 25

UPPER HOBACK CANYON TO ROOSEVELT MEADOWS

Distance: 9.0 miles, round trip.
Low/high Elevations: 7,755'/8,320'.
Difficulty: Moderate.
Use: Low.
Suited For: Dayhike or backpack.
Best Season: Late June through mid-September.
Wildlife Viewing: Good.
Grizzly Bear Danger: Low.
Map/Trailhead: 21/23.
Nearest Campgrounds: Kozy, 25.5 miles, and Hoback, 30.3 miles from the trailhead.
Driving to the Trailhead: From U.S. 189/191, 3.8 miles southeast of Bondurant, Wyoming, or 28.5 miles northwest of Daniel Junction (10.0 miles from Pinedale, and 110.0 miles from Rock Springs), turn south onto Upper Hoback Road, signed for FOREST ROAD 30700, and SUBLETTE COUNTY ROAD 23-174.

Follow this good gravel road generally southwest into Upper Hoback Canyon, passing numerous large ranches during the first several miles. After 9.0 miles the road becomes rocky and rutted. Ignore a left-branching road 11.1 miles from the highway, and after driving 13.9 miles, you reach the loop at the roadend, where the trail begins. Several undeveloped campsites are at the trailhead, and along the banks of Hoback River about 200 yards east of the trailhead.

Introduction: This scenic, seldom-used trail follows the course of the upper Hoback River, crosses the crest of the Wyoming Range at a low pass, and leads to the broad timberline spread of Roosevelt Meadows, bounded by alpine peaks and ridges.

The trail is easy to follow, with minimal elevation gain. However, numerous stream crossings make the trip more rigorous than its moderate rating suggests.

Description: The signed Upper Hoback Trail, open to horse and foot traffic only, begins at the west edge of the parking area at 7,755 feet. Follow the trail west, skirting an old beaver pond, and then enter a forest of lodgepole pine and subalpine fir.

The trail gently ascends Upper Hoback Canyon, alternating between stands of conifers and willow-clad meadows. Wildflowers in the canyon are colorful and diverse, including subalpine daisy, monkshood, cinquefoil, sticky geranium, white clover, and yarrow.

At 0.5 mile avoid the signed High Line Trail and stay left, continuing up the canyon. Soon we begin jumping across some of the innumerable small streams that cascade across the trail. Many inactive beaver dams pond the river in the meadows, where we may spot moose browsing among the willow thickets. Good views from the trail extend up the canyon to the timberline ridges.

At 1.5 miles (7,857 feet) we reach the first of eight fords of the Hoback River, a 10-foot-wide, knee-deep stream here in its headwaters, with a moderate current. We then traverse benches above the river's south bank, staying mostly in pine and fir forest. Western coneflower and hairy arnica join the ranks of wildflowers in the meadow openings along the trail.

At length the benches merge with the canyon's slopes, then the trail ascends steeply but briefly. Soon we drop back to the river and wade across it to the north bank. Within a few yards the trail leads to another crossing, this one only ankle-deep where the river spreads out across a 25-foot-wide bed. Mountain bluebells and pink monkeyflower deck the stream banks at both crossings.

About 100 yards beyond the previous crossing, in a confined part of the canyon, we drop back to the river's channel, ford the

Roosevelt Meadows, near the crest of the Wyoming Range

stream to the north bank, and then almost immediately cross back to the south banks. The canyon becomes even more confined up ahead, and the rocky slopes force our trail next to the boulder-strewn riverbed. We soon cross the river again, and again quickly cross back to the south banks at the seventh ford.

We then briefly ascend a steep, westbound grade, and the canyon begins to open up. Notice the contrasting forest cover on the opposite slopes of the canyon. Above the trail, on the cool, shady, north-facing slopes, is a dense forest of Engelmann spruce and subalpine fir. On the rocky, sun-drenched south-facing slopes to our north, only a scattering of drought-tolerant limber pine dots the slopes.

Soon we emerge from the canyon and enter an expansive, soggy meadow, flooded in places by several inactive beaver ponds. We skirt the southern rim, and midway around it reach a signed junction. The unsigned, seldom-used left fork continues southwest to the head of Hoback River, to

the southwest. Follow the right fork, signed for various destinations.

Our northwest-bound trail leads across the willow-studded meadow, and becomes ill-defined where it dips into muddy depressions but is easy to follow where it carves through willow thickets. About 200 yards from the junction, we reach the eighth and final ford of the Hoback River. Here the water is shallow and it may be possible to rockhop the river in late summer. There may also be logs offering a dry crossing.

A short ascent from the crossing leads to a grassy bench and past a well-used packer campsite, beyond which we ascend a northwest-trending draw. The grade abates at a flower-rich meadow, incorrectly signed ROOSEVELT MEADOWS. Continuing up the draw, we soon reach the crest of the Wyoming Range at a broad, grassy saddle at 4.4 miles from the trailhead and 8,320 feet.

After 200 yards you enter Roosevelt Meadows, a peaceful, verdant expanse at the headwaters of Little Greys River. A luxuriant display of wildflowers paints the landscape in shades of yellow, lavender, white, and blue. In addition to hosting many of the blooms cited above, the meadows here also support western coneflower, yellow mule's ears, and bracted lousewort.

From Roosevelt Meadows, we retrace our steps to the trailhead.

Trip 26

SHEFFIELD CREEK CAMP-GROUND TO HUCKLE-BERRY MOUNTAIN

Distance: 11.0 miles, round trip.
Low/High Elevations: 6,900'/9,615'.
Difficulty: Strenuous.
Use: Low.
Suited For: Dayhike.
Best Season: Late June through Sept.
Wildlife Viewing: Good.
Grizzly Bear Danger: High.
Map/Trailhead: 22/24.
Nearest Campground. Sheffield Creek, located at the trailhead.
Driving to the Trailhead: From U.S. 191/89/287 (the John D. Rockefeller, Jr. Memorial Parkway), 2.9 miles south of Yellowstone National Park's south entrance, 0.6 mile south of Flagg Ranch resort, and 0.1 mile south of a bridge over the Snake River, turn east onto a dirt road where a small national forest sign points to Sheffield Creek and Teton National Forest. Drivers coming from the south will find this turnoff 24.6 miles north of Moran Junction.

The dirt road leads through a forest of charred lodgepole-pine snags, crosses shallow Sheffield Creek, and enters Teton National Forest after 0.3 mile, ending after 0.7 mile at a small trailhead parking area and information sign at the south end of the campground. Pit toilets and water are available at the campground, but the Bridger-Teton National Forest Service warns that the water is not potable.
Introduction: This rigorous but rewarding all-day hike ascends from the valley of the

Snake River to a high timberline ridge in the northwest corner of the Teton Wilderness, just 3 miles south of Yellowstone Park. On the summit of Huckleberry Mountain is a well-preserved log lookout tower (circa 1938), one of few remaining lookouts in Greater Yellowstone.

The entire trip passes through the path of the 227,525-acre Huck Fire of 1988, one of 249 wildfires that consumed nearly one million acres of forest in Greater Yellowstone during that dry, windy summer. Although the fire destroyed much of the rich huckleberry thickets the mountain was named for, this trip offers hikers a first-hand lesson in forest and meadow regeneration following a fire, as well as far-ranging vistas from the summit.

Grizzly bears are sometimes seen on this trail; hikers should follow the guidelines for traveling in bear country (see *Hiking in Grizzly Country*, pg. 8).
Description: From the trailhead, Huckleberry Mountain is obscured from view by the intervening ridges rising to the east. From the trail sign we wind east across a low bench among blackened snags. Soon we enter the signed Teton Wilderness, and then begin a steady, prolonged, moderate-to-steep ascent on dusty trail.

After gaining 500 feet in one mile, the trail curves northeast, steeply ascending a narrow ridge. From this ridge we gain fine views down to the forest- and meadow-fringed Snake River, the Flagg Ranch resort complex, and the southwestern reaches of the Yellowstone volcanic plateau. Surrounding us are the charred remains of a lodgepole-pine forest, with slopes below thickly mantled in a carpet of green vegetation. Forest fire is a natural process (though the Huck Fire started when wind-blown trees fell across a powerline near the trailhead) that has occurred in Greater Yellowstone at intervals of 200-400 years. Fires help thin overgrown forests and recycle nutrients locked up in logs, snags, and dead forest litter. Fires also create sunny openings in the forest, and vegetation quickly rebounds on the enriched soil.

Lodgepole pine is well adapted to fire. Most mature lodgepoles bear some serotinous cones, cones that remain closed and do not release their seeds until they are subjected to high temperatures, as in a fire. Lodgepoles are the first conifers to become reestablished after a burn, as they thrive in sunny openings. Even-aged stands of lodgepoles throughout Greater Yellowstone testify to that species' ability to regenerate after a burn.

Throughout much of this trip we will see a profusion of young pines naturally reforesting the charred slopes. We will also pass groves of green trees that somehow managed to escape the heat and flames of the Huck Fire. In some places the fire burned with such intensity there are no saplings, only bare soil.

Grasses and wildflowers grow in colorful abundance on trailside slopes, and will continue to do so until the new forest casts too much shade. From early to midsummer you will see the blooms of fireweed, sticky geranium, red clover, lupine, birchleaf spirea, arrowleaf balsamroot, wild hollyhock, dogbane, and Oregon grape, and shrubs such as tobacco brush, serviceberry, and snowberry.

The ascent abates briefly where we hop across a small Sheffield Creek tributary at 1.8 miles (7,950 feet). The steep ascent continues beyond the crossing, leading through a burned Engelmann-spruce forest. The ground on these slopes is barren of saplings, since spruce requires the shade cast by other trees to become established. Once a lodgepole forest develops on these slopes, it may take another 200-300 years, barring another fire, for spruces to reforest the mountainside.

The steep, rocky, and dusty ascent ends on an 8,800-foot ridge after another 1.4 miles. A broad grassy bowl, studded with timberline forest trees, spreads out to the east, and the rocky, volcanic ridge of Huckleberry Mountain rises to the skyline beyond.

From the ridge, a steep but brief descent leads to a crossing of an early summer creek, and beyond it we ascend steeply once again, at first on grassy slopes, then among scattered groves of whitebark pine

The historic Huckleberry Mountain lookout tower

and subalpine fir, where green trees now outnumber burned snags. Expansive views stretch southwest to the tall peaks of the northern Teton Mountains.

Soon the trail curves southeast around the bowl, and we briefly dip into two minor gullies that may have flowing water. At Huckleberry Ridge (9,200 feet and 4.4 miles), the grade finally abates. A well-earned rest on this open, grassy ridge allows us to enjoy good views deep into the backcountry of southern Yellowstone National Park and the Teton Wilderness, to the northeast and east.

The stretch of trail ahead is a pleasant, nearly level walk across sloping meadows and timberline groves of whitebark pine, subalpine fir, and Engelmann spruce. Most of the evidence of the fire is behind as we proceed through unscathed forest.

After 0.4 mile from the crest of Huckleberry Ridge we reach a southwest-trending draw and a sign that proclaims FIRE TOWER. The lookout is visible on the crest of Huckleberry Mountain above to the southwest. But the old trail that once led there, branching right from the trail farther ahead, has been reclaimed by meadows and blocked by fallen trees, and is now very difficult to locate.

The best way to reach the lookout is to leave the trail at the FIRE TOWER sign and proceed cross-country west-southwest, ascending the sloping meadow into the open forest above. Head for the saddle on the crest of Huckleberry Mountain, north of the lookout tower.

After about 300 yards, you should intersect the old trail to the top, on the steep slopes northeast of the saddle. This part of the old trail is well-worn and easy to follow. Steep, rocky switchbacks lead to the saddle, and then south along the ridge to the end of the trail and the lookout tower at 9,615 feet, 5.5 miles from the trailhead. En route we pass a few charred trees just north of the lookout, but fortunately the historic structure was spared.

The unoccupied lookout commands an unobstructed panorama that easily compensates us for our efforts. From this lofty vantage point, the vast forest-clad Yellowstone volcanic plateau stretches to the horizon. Here and there the plateau is punctuated by tall volcanic prominences. Eastward lies the wild interior of the Teton Wilderness, a landscape of rolling, forested, meadow-covered ridges and deep canyons stretching away in waves of progressively higher ridges for 35 miles to the Continental Divide.

Far to the southeast rise the peaks of the Gros Ventre Range. To the south, sprawling Jackson Lake can be seen at the north end of Jackson Hole, above which the majestic Tetons soar skyward. This unusual perspective of the Tetons from the northeast exposes the range in profile, accentuating the abrupt eastern face of the range rising 7,000 feet from the valley floor. From its north end, the range rises out of forested plateaus to broad alpine summits, which in turn rise to an aggregate of towering crags and pinnacles hosting small icefields on their flanks.

The two-story log lookout tower, listed in the National Register of Historic Places,

was built by Civilian Conservation Corps crews in 1938. The Forest Service used this lookout tower from 1938 until 1957, after which aerial observations became the principal means of fire detection. An exterior stairway offers access to the second-story observation deck, from which the finest views unfold.

From Huckleberry Mountain allow ample time to return to the trailhead before dark.

Trip 27

BROOKS LAKE CAMP-GROUND TO UPPER BROOKS LAKE

Distance: 7.0 miles round trip.
Low/High Elevations: 9,060'/9,105'.
Difficulty: Easy.
Use: Moderate.
Suited For: Dayhike or backpack.
Best Season: July through September.
Wildlife Viewing: Fair.
Grizzly Bear Danger: Moderate.
Map/Trailhead: 23/25.
Nearest Campgrounds: Brooks Lake Campground is at the trailhead; Pinnacle, 0.8 mile, and Falls, 5.4 miles from the trailhead.
Driving to the Trailhead: Follow U.S. 26/287 east for 32.7 miles from Moran Junction in Jackson Hole, or west for 20.9 miles from Dubois, to the signed Brooks Lake Recreation Area and the Brooks Lake Road, Forest Road 515. (This turnoff is 7.8 miles east of Togwotee Pass, and 0.4 mile east of the turnoff to Falls Campground.)

Follow the good, gravel-surfaced Brooks Lake Road north 4.0 miles to a junction with Forest Road 516, signed for Bonneville Pass Trailhead (Trip 29 takers will turn right onto that road). Bear left at that junction toward Brooks Lake (signed), passing the turnoff to Pinnacle Campground after 0.3 mile. After driving another 0.8 mile, turn right next to the entrance to Brooks Lake Lodge, and proceed north, downhill, 0.2 mile to the entrance to Brooks Lake

Brooks Lake and the Pinnacle Buttes

Campground. Instead of turning right into the campground, bear left onto the boat-ramp loop road. Parking is in the west half of the loop.

Introduction: The pleasant, scenic hike to Upper Brooks Lake is one of the finest high meadow walks in Greater Yellowstone. Tall volcanic peaks approaching 11,000 feet embrace the meadows that stretch from the trailhead to the lake, where good cutthroat trout fishing (to 10 inches) and a variety of good, scenic campsites in the timberline forest await.

The only drawback to this hike is the presence of cattle in the meadows during the summer. But the scenery passed en route is so absorbing, you'll probably find the early summer mosquitoes to be more annoying than the cows.

Description: From the lakeside trailhead at 9,060 feet, proceed west through a gate, where a sign designates our route as the Yellowstone Trail. Here our delightful stroll through the vast meadows begins, and we enjoy inspiring views from the start. Pyramidal Sublette Peak anchors the southern end of the great wall of volcanic cliffs to the west, and to the east loom the bold spires of Pinnacle Buttes.

The trail leads through the broad meadows west of Brooks Lake, bridging a few minor, willow-bordered streams en route to a signed junction at 0.6 mile. Here you part company with hikers on Trip 28, and bear right, continuing our lakeside stroll. After you leave the lake behind, a minor ascent leads into the spreading reaches of a 2-mile-long meadow. From the top of the ascent, follow a low, grassy moraine that reaches down into the meadow. From the moraine the view stretches north up the shallow trough of Brooks Lake Creek, beyond the low gap of Bear Cub Pass, and to the broad summit of Peak 10,794, deep within the Teton Wilderness.

At 1.9 miles, a sign points right to Upper Brooks Lake, and another trail (unsigned) forks left, heading northwest. That trail can be used by Trip 28 hikers on their return from Jade Lakes.

Following the right fork, we continue north, soon dropping to a small stream that we easily rockhop. About 200 yards beyond that stream is Brooks Lake Creek, about 20 feet wide and shallow. If the water level is low, we can also rockhop across. From that creek follow a short, steep grade into a light forest of Engelmann spruce and whitebark pine. Topping out on a grassy slope, we meet a right-branching trail leading southeast. This trail, used primarily by equestrians, ultimately leads to the Bonneville Pass Trail (Trip 29).

We bear left at that junction and proceed north through the forest, soon dropping back to the meadow where the trail forks once again. The right fork stays just inside the forested margin of the meadow, but the way has many minor ups and downs, and the tread is flooded by springs. The lower (left) trail is the better route since it gains minimal elevation as it skirts the meadow's edge. Fireweed, lupine, bracted lousewort, groundsel, and Richardson geranium splash their vivid colors across the seemingly endless spread of meadows.

Eventually, however, the meadow narrows and becomes choked with willows, and suddenly Upper Brooks Lake (9,105 feet) spreads out before us. The trail leads across a small creek, beyond which we merge with the upper (right) trail.

The lake sits nearly astride the Continental Divide, which rises just above to the north. Lovely meadows and groves of pine and spruce surround the lake in the shallow bowl at the head of Brooks Lake Creek. Good campsites can be found above the north and west shores, sheltered by conifer groves.

The trail continues around the east shore of the lake and quickly ascends 50 feet to Bear Cub Pass, a popular Teton Wilderness entry point. Unfortunately, tall spruces obscure wilderness views from the pass.

From the lake, retrace your route to the trailhead.

Trip 28
BROOKS LAKE TO JADE LAKES

Distance: 4.6 miles, round trip; or 5.3 miles, loop trip.
Low/High Elevations: 9,060'/9,600'.

Difficulty: Moderately easy.
Use: Heavy.
Suited For: Dayhike or backpack.
Best Season: July through September.
Wildlife Viewing: Good.
Grizzly Bear Danger: Moderate.
Map/Trailhead: 23/25.
Nearest Campgrounds: See *Nearest Campgrounds* for Trip 27.
Driving to the Trailhead: Follow driving directions for Trip 27.
Introduction: This exceptionally scenic short hike leads from the open meadows fringing Brooks Lake to a pair of timberline gems resting beneath the stratified volcanic cliffs of the Continental Divide, in the southern reaches of the Absaroka Range.

At the Jade Lakes you will find good fishing for pan-sized cutthroat trout and a few fair campsites. Once you reach Lower Jade Lake, you have the option of extending the trip by following a trail that loops back to the trailhead via the meadows of Brooks Lake Creek.

Description: From the trailhead at 9,060 feet, follow the first 0.6 mile of Trip 27 to the signed junction, and turn left toward Jade Lakes. Our well-worn trail ascends northwest up a finger of the meadow that reaches into the timberline forest above. The trail has been worn into multiple, parallel paths, and we ascend moderately at first, then steeply.

Catching our breath on this short grind, we see Richardson geranium, yarrow, buckwheat, lupine, subalpine daisy, and cinquefoil on the slopes alongside the trail, as well as more distant features such as the meadow-fringed waters of Brooks Lake, and the jagged profile of the Pinnacle Buttes rising beyond the lake. On the distant southeast horizon are the ice-clad plateaus of the northern Wind River Range.

The steep grade abates soon after we enter timberline forest, and we then traverse west across steep slopes, enjoying memorable views of peaks, meadows, and forests. We soon reach the margin of a long, narrow meadow next to a small stream and curve northwest, ignoring a left-branching path that crosses the stream.

As our trail skirts the meadow's edge, on the western skyline ahead is an imposing, 2-mile-long wall of stratified volcanic cliffs abutting the crest of the Continental Divide. After you leave the meadow, a moderate ascent through the forest leads to a meadow-bordered tarn. A brief stroll around its west shore is followed by a gentle ascent up a narrow draw. Trailside meadows here sport the blooms of groundsel, hairy arnica, lupine, and mountain bluebells.

The grade ends atop a minor 9,600-foot saddle, 1.75 miles from the trailhead. From there our trail quickly descends to the east shore of deep, emerald-green Upper Jade Lake, at 9,532 feet. Backpackers will find a few fair campsites in the willow-clad meadow above the southwest shore, next to a small stream.

Upper Jade Lake

The fluted gray cliffs of the Continental Divide loom boldly above the west shore of the lake. The dark gray layers of volcanic breccia and the light gray ash layers that together compose the cliffs offer silent testimony to the extensive volcanic activity that built the Absaroka Range about 50 million years ago.

Although footpaths encircle Upper Jade Lake, the main trail follows the east shore. Most hikers go no farther than this lake, but those who wish to extend the hike will continue following the lakeshore trail. After an easy rock-hop of the lake's outlet, descend a moderate grade beneath a canopy of whitebark pine, Engelmann spruce, and subalpine fir to more isolated Lower Jade Lake, at 9,420 feet, 2.3 miles from the trailhead. Campsites at this lake are poor, as there is little level ground. Steep slopes clothed in timberline forest rise from

the lake's green waters, blocking out most views.

From Lower Jade Lake, we can either retrace our steps to the trailhead, or follow a distinct but unmaintained trail that loops back to the trailhead via a different route. For the latter, follow the trail north along the west shore. Soon you reach a junction above the lake's northwest corner. Turn right here, descend steeply at first, and then follow the rough, undulating

Trail to Jade Lakes

trail above the north shore of Lower Jade Lake. Beyond the lake we follow a minor draw to the east, then soon curve north around the shoulder of a ridge.

Beyond the ridge the trail bends eastward and then descends through pine and spruce forest. The grade ends 0.8 mile from the lower lake at the margin of a long meadow along Brooks Lake Creek. Follow the trail out into the meadow, and soon reach a fork in the trail beside the small creek draining Jade Lakes. Turn right here and immediately rockhop the creek. Thereafter follow the grassy trail southeast across the meadow, jump across another small stream, and meet the Yellowstone Trail between Brooks Lake and Bear Cub Pass, after another 0.3 mile.

Here you turn right (south), and follow the first 1.9 miles of Trip 27 in reverse to the trailhead.

Trip 29

BONNEVILLE PASS

Distance: 4.6 miles, round trip.
Low/High Elevations: 9,280'/9,960'.
Difficulty: Easy.
Use: Moderate.
Suited For: Dayhike.
Best Season: July through September.
Wildlife Viewing: Good.
Grizzly Bear Danger: Moderate.
Map/Trailhead: 23/26.
Nearest Campgrounds: Pinnacle, 2.0 miles, Brooks Lake, 3.0 miles, and Falls, 5.1 miles from the trailhead.
Driving to the Trailhead: Follow the driving directions for Trip 27 to Forest Road 516, and turn right. This narrow and rough, dirt road leads 1.7 miles to the roadend and trailhead parking area, next to two large information and destination/mileage signs.
Introduction: The Bonneville Pass Trail is a major thoroughfare leading into the western reaches of the Du Noir Special Management Area. This area of glacial cirques, volcanic cliffs and buttes, timberline lakes, and wildflower-rich meadows is a 26,000-acre proposed addition to the 704,000-acre Washakie Wilderness, which protects the east slopes of the Absaroka Range to the north.

But you don't have to commit yourself to an extended backpack trip to enjoy the area. This easy hike leads to the broad, 10,000-foot meadows of Bonneville Pass, where inspiring views reach deep into the Du Noir country and across the scenic Brooks Lake basin.

Description: From the trailhead at 9,280 feet, broken volcanic cliffs, spires, and grass-crested ridges soar skyward to the north, east, and south, and we follow a long-closed logging road east beneath those lofty prominences. The route narrows to true trail after 300 yards, just before we reach shallow, 8-foot wide Bonneville Creek.

After rockhopping to the north bank, proceed up-canyon on a gentle grade, passing beneath a canopy of Engelmann spruce and whitebark pine. Small meadow openings in the forest are adorned with the blooms of bracted lousewort, Richardson geranium, yampah, fireweed, subalpine daisy, lupine, buckwheat, and yarrow.

A narrow band of the timberline forest stretches along the south slopes of the canyon, opposite the trail. This is a good example of where forest trees should not be harvested. In a cold timberline environment, 200 years or more are necessary for a spruce forest to reach maturity.

At 1.0 mile we reach the end of the logged forest, opposite the gaping cirque of Jules Bowl. That scenic cirque, embraced on three sides by the 11,000-foot spires of Pinnacle Buttes, is a worthwhile cross-country side trip if time and energy allow.

Beyond Jules Bowl the grade steepens as we ascend a willow-clad meadow, and then enter groves of timberline forest, where the spire shapes of spruces and subalpine firs contrast with the spreading, multi-branched forms of whitebark pines. As the ascent continues, we step across three small, spring-fed streams and finally reach the western edge of the Bonneville Pass meadows, where the grade abates.

In the meadows we soon rockhop a small stream, then ascend gently along the dense forest fringe of the meadows. At 2.2 miles we reach the watershed divide in the long pass, where a sign proclaims our entry into the Du Noir Special Management Area.

At the 9,960-foot pass, take time to soak in the beauty of the surroundings. The three-quarter-mile-long meadows are painted with the vivid colors of a variety of wildflowers, including the lavenders of subalpine daisy and lupine, the whites of valerian and bracted lousewort, and the yellow blooms of hairy arnica.

The meadows are bounded on the southwest by the somber gray Pinnacle Buttes, forming a dramatic background of broken cliffs and stony towers. North of the pass rise the more gentle slopes and rounded ridges of the Continental Divide, dotted with gnarled and stunted conifers. To the east, massive Du Noir Butte dominates the view above the remote headwaters of West Du Noir Creek. To the west is a memorable view of pyramidal Sublette Peak and of the banded cliffs of the Continental Divide.

From the high point of the pass the meadow stretches northeast for another 0.4 mile, and we follow the trail as it gently descends past a marshy tarn to the rim above Dundee Creek. From there the trail descends 800 steep feet in 1.0 mile to the verdant opening of Dundee Meadows.

After enjoying the meadows of Bonneville Pass, retrace your steps to the trailhead.

Pinnacle Buttes and Bonneville Pass

Chapter Four

NORTH OF YELLOWSTONE

Introduction

North and northeast of Yellowstone National Park, the rolling ridges and vast meadows of the Yellowstone volcanic plateau shed their mantle of dense forest and rise abruptly to the alpine crests of three major mountain ranges—the Gallatin, Absaroka, and Beartooth mountains.

The Gallatins, composed of volcanic rocks similar to those found in the Park, extend north in a series of gently rolling alpine hills, ending after 50 miles in a wall of jagged peaks near the town of Bozeman, Montana. The north part of the Absaroka Range also stretches about 50 miles north from the Park, but the Absarokas are capped by rugged crags and form the most jagged, breathtaking crest in Greater Yellowstone, save for the Tetons.

The broad, semi-arid grasslands of Paradise Valley separate the two ranges, and the mighty Yellowstone River flows through this valley for some 50 miles between Gardiner and Livingston, Montana. U.S. Highway 89 follows Paradise Valley to the North Entrance to the Park. Besides being the windiest valley in Greater Yellowstone, it is also one of the most spectacular. Bounded on the west by the forested, 4,000-foot face of the Gallatins, and on the east by the 6,000-foot front of the Absarokas, this dry, grassy valley offers one of the most dramatic low-elevation approaches to Yellowstone.

Near the northeast corner of the Park, the Absaroka Range takes on its more familiar face of somber gray volcanic rocks, and the bold peaks of the range form the eastern boundary of the Park. Beyond the Park's Northeast Entrance, near Cooke City, Montana, another range of mountains extends north and east from the Absarokas. These mountains, the Beartooths, are the focus of this chapter.

The Beartooth Mountains, part of the 943,377-acre Absaroka-Beartooth Wilderness, support the most extensive area of alpine tundra in the Rocky Mountains outside of Colorado. The range contains more than 900 lakes, many of them stocked with a variety of trout, and more than 20 summits in the range reach above 12,000 feet in elevation. Among them is Montana's highest—12,799-foot Granite Peak.

The southern flanks of the Beartooth range are a gently sloping, plateau-like surface dominated by granite domes and shallow lake basins. This rocky slope of the range, called the Beartooth Plateau, was long ago scoured by a vast sheet of ice that gouged out the lake basins and flowed around, but not over, the 12,000-foot peaks on the crest, hence the peaks' flat, unglaciated summit surfaces.

The northern flanks of the plateau, in contrast, were deeply carved by glaciers, and deep, U-shaped canyons bounded by rugged, soaring peaks and cliff-edged plateaus dominate the landscape there.

To enjoy alpine scenery in the Greater Yellowstone area usually requires a long day-hike or, more often, an extended backpack trip. But in the Beartooths, the ascent into the high country is accomplished in your car, thanks to the Beartooth Scenic Byway. This byway (U.S. 212), called "the most beautiful drive in America," extends for 62 miles through a landscape of alpine grandeur unrivaled in the Rocky Mountains. Between the gateway community of Cooke City at the Park's Northeast Entrance, and Red Lodge, Montana, this highway, opened in 1936, follows the southern and eastern edges of the lofty Beartooth Mountains. The highway's apex at 10,947-foot Beartooth Pass is the highest point reached by a road in the Rockies outside of Colorado.

These are among the most majestic mountains in Greater Yellowstone, and from the comfort of your car you will pass through a breathtaking landscape dotted by high lakes, groves of gnarled timberline trees, and vast meadows and tundra painted in shades of yellow, white, lavender, and red by the myriad wildflowers that thrive here.

Views are ever-changing as you travel the Beartooth Scenic Byway. North of the highway rise the ice-scoured south slopes of the Beartooths. South of the highway rise the dark brown and gray battlements of the Absaroka Range, dominated by Matterhorn-like Pilot Peak, a landmark that has guided Native Americans, trappers, and miners through the region for centuries.

Between the two mountain ranges lies the broad, forested valley of the Clarks Fork of the Yellowstone River, Wyoming's only Wild and Scenic River. The Beartooth Scenic Byway follows the upper reaches of Clarks Fork downstream before ascending to Beartooth Pass. Farther downstream, Chief Joseph Scenic Highway (Wyoming Highway 296) follows above Clarks Fork Canyon, a spectacular gorge carved in the river's lower reaches, northwest of Cody, Wyoming.

Although the highway offers grand panoramas, travelers are urged to detour to Clay Butte Lookout (see Trip 36), and to the West Summit Rest Area at Beartooth Pass, where some of the finest far-ranging vistas in Greater Yellowstone unfold.

The Beartooth Scenic Byway also affords easy access to numerous trailheads, where hikers enjoy a high elevation start to their backcountry trips. And there are more than one dozen national forest campgrounds situated next to the highway between Cooke City and Red Lodge.

This highway is one of the busiest highways in the northern reaches of Greater Yellowstone. Many visitors choose the Beartooths for their summer vacation, and many more travel through en route to the Northeast Entrance to the Park. Hence campgrounds fill early in the day during peak season (late July through mid-August). Exceptions include the campgrounds in Rock Creek near Red Lodge (campgrounds 44-49), and those located along the Chief Joseph Scenic Highway (campgrounds 40 and 41).

There are several undeveloped camping areas along the Beartooth Scenic Byway, but these sites also fill early. Visitors who use undeveloped sites here must take steps to minimize their impact on the delicate alpine terrain—build no campfires, use established sites only, and stay on developed roadways.

Grizzly bears use the area covered in this chapter, and hikers should remain alert at all times. Special food storage regulations are in effect, and are posted at campgrounds.

The Beartooths are snow country, and the highway remains closed between Cooke City and Rock Creek (southwest of Red Lodge) throughout winter, and may not re-open until late May or early June. Travelers on this highway should expect sudden snowstorms at any time during summer, when the highway may be temporarily closed.

Access and Services

Access to the area covered in this chapter is provided by U.S. 89, which leads 52 miles south from Interstate 90 at Livingston, Montana, to the North Entrance of Yellowstone Park at Gardiner, Montana.

The Beartooth Scenic Byway (U.S. 212), leads 62.5 miles from Cooke City, Montana (4.0 miles from Yellowstone's Northeast Entrance), to Red Lodge, Montana. Red Lodge can be reached by following U.S. 212 southwest for 60 miles from Interstate 90 at Billings, Montana; or by following Montana Highway 78 south 48 miles from Interstate 90 at Columbus, Montana.

The Beartooth Scenic Byway can also be reached in the canyon of Clarks Fork Yellowstone River by following Chief Joseph Scenic Highway (Wyoming 296) northwest for 46 miles from that highway's junction with Wyoming 120, 16.5 miles northwest of Cody, Wyoming.

Livingston, Montana (4,487'), in the upper Yellowstone Valley alongside Interstate 90, is the last major resupply point en route to Yellowstone's North Entrance. This full-service town offers numerous motels, groceries, camping and recreation supplies, gas, auto and RV repair and towing, restaurants, and a hospital.

Billings, Montana (3,117'), is also in the Yellowstone Valley on Interstate 90. With a population of 70,000, Billings is Montana's largest city, and it offers the most complete array of services in the Greater Yellowstone area.

Cody, Wyoming (5,016'), also offers a full complement of services to travelers (see Chapter 5), and the town is the last one en route to the Beartooth Scenic Byway from the east.

Gardiner, Montana (5,267'), lies above the banks of Yellowstone River at the North Entrance to Yellowstone National Park. Much like West Yellowstone, Montana, this town depends on tourist dollars to support its economy, and Gardiner offers a wide range of services. Twelve motels, two large RV parks, restaurants, groceries, gas, auto and RV repair and towing, and camping and recreation supplies are all available in this small gateway community.

Silver Gate, Montana (7,389'), is 1.0 mile east of Yellowstone's Northeast Entrance, on the Beartooth Scenic Byway. This hamlet offers three lodges, a cafe, and gas.

Cooke City, Montana (7,651'), 4.0 miles east of Yellowstone Park, offers seven motels, an RV park, restaurants, auto and RV repair and towing, gas, and limited camping and recreation supplies.

The Top of the World Store (9,350'), is on the north side of the Beartooth Scenic Byway, 24.5 miles east of Cooke City and 37.6 miles southwest of Red Lodge, between Beartooth and Island lakes. The store offers groceries, gas, and motel cabins.

Red Lodge, Montana (5,555'), is a full-service town located along the banks of Rock Creek in the northeast foothills of the Beartooths. The town offers seven motels, an historic downtown hotel, a medical clinic, restaurants (Red Lodge claims to have more restaurants per capita than any other town in Montana), groceries, gas, and auto and RV repair and towing.

For further information on accommodations and services, contact the chambers of commerce listed below:

Gardiner Chamber of Commerce
P.O. Box 81
Gardiner, MT 59030
(406) 848-7971

Red Lodge Chamber of Commerce
P.O. Box 988
Red Lodge, MT 59068
(406) 446-1718

Cooke City Chamber of Commerce
P.O. Box 1146
Cooke City, MT 59020

(For information by phone, contact Yellowstone Trading Post at (406) 838-2265.)

Campgrounds

34 • TOM MINER (7,100')

Location. In the Gallatin Range, at the end of Tom Miner Creek Road (see driving directions for Trip 30 for exact location); Gallatin National Forest, Gardiner Ranger District.

Facilities. 16 camping units, tables, fire pits with grills, water, toilets; maximum trailer length of 20 feet; a fee is charged.

Dates Usually Open. June 1 through October 30.

The Setting. This lightly used, end-of-the-road campground lies in a shady forest of spruce, alongside small Trail Creek, near the head of the broad grassy bowl of Tom Miner Basin. Views reach to the bold volcanic summits of 10,095-foot Sheep Mountain and to aptly named Sawtooth Mountain to the southeast. Stratified volcanic cliffs and ledges hosting rich greenery and scattered conifers rise northwest of the campground.

Whitetail deer, uncommon in Greater Yellowstone, are frequently seen in the campground.

35 • SODA BUTTE (7,800')

Location. On U.S. 212, 0.6 mile east of Cooke City, Montana and 13.0 miles west of the junction with the Wyoming 296; Gallatin National Forest, Gardiner Ranger District.
Facilities. 21 camping units, tables, water, fire pits with grills, toilets, bear-resistant garbage containers; maximum trailer length of 20 feet; a fee is charged.
Dates Usually Open. June 15 through Sept. 15.
The Setting. This pleasant campground lies alongside Soda Butte Creek in an open forest of lodgepole pine and subalpine fir. Small meadows among the trees support a rich assortment of wildflowers.

36 • COLTER (8,040')

Location. On U.S. 212, 1.9 miles east of Cooke City, Montana, and 9.8 miles west of the junction with the Wyoming Highway 296; Gallatin National Forest, Gardiner Ranger District.
Facilities. 23 camping units, tables, water, fire pits with grills, toilets, bear-resistant garbage containers; some sites have bear-resistant food storage boxes; maximum trailer length of 20 feet; a fee is charged.
Dates Usually Open. June 15 through September 15.
The Setting. This partly forested campground lies near the head of Soda Butte Creek, just north of Highway 212. Most sites lie in an open forest of subalpine fir and lodgepole pine, but sites near the west end of the campground are in an area burned by the Storm Creek Fire in 1988. Visitors will notice a rich variety of greenery and many conifer saplings in the burned area. Views from the campground contrast the volcanic summits of the Absaroka Range to the south with the granite peaks of the Beartooth Mountains to the northwest.

37 • CHIEF JOSEPH (8,040')

Location. On U.S. 212, 3.2 miles east of Cooke City, Montana, and 10.4 miles west

of the junction with the Wyoming 296; Gallatin National Forest, Gardiner Ranger District.
Facilities. 7 camping units, tables, water, fire pits with grills, toilets, bear-resistant garbage containers; maximum trailer length of 15 feet; a fee is charged.
Dates Usually Open. June 15 through September 15.
The Setting. This small campground, shaded by a dense canopy of subalpine fir, lies just off the highway, 50 yards west of the turnoff to Trailhead 29, where Trip 33 begins.

38 • FOX CREEK (7,100')

Location. On U.S. 212, 7.2 miles east of Cooke City, Montana, and 6.4 miles west of the junction with the Wyoming Highway 296; Shoshone National Forest, Clarks Fork Ranger District.
Facilities. 27 camping units, tables, water, fire pits with grills, toilets, bear-resistant garbage containers; maximum trailer length of 32 feet; a fee is charged.
Dates Usually Open. June 1 through Sept. 30.
The Setting. This peaceful campground lies on a bench, just above and southwest of Clarks Fork Yellowstone River, in a shady forest of conifers. Dramatic views stretch upward to the dark spire of 11,708-foot Pilot Peak and to the blocky tower of 11,313-foot Index Peak 2 miles to the west.

39 • CRAZY CREEK (6,900')

Location. On U.S. 212, 11.0 miles east of Cooke City, Montana, and 2.5 miles west of the junction with the Wyoming 296; Shoshone National Forest, Clarks Fork Ranger District.
Facilities. 15 camping units, tables, water, fire pits with grills, toilets, bear-resistant garbage containers; maximum trailer length of 32 feet; a fee is charged.
Dates Usually Open. June 1 through October 20.
The Setting. This small campground lies just south of U.S. 212 on a bench above Clarks Fork of Yellowstone River. The foaming whitewater of Crazy Creek cascades behind the campground. Sites are shaded by lodge-

pole pine and Engelmann spruce. Grand views reach northwest to Pilot and Index peaks.

40 • LAKE CREEK (6,902')

Location. In the canyon of Clarks Fork Yellowstone River, just north of Wyoming 296, from a point 1.2 miles southeast of the junction with U.S. 212, and 61 miles northwest of Cody, Wyoming; Shoshone National Forest, Clarks Fork Ranger District.
Facilities. 6 camping units, tables, fire pits with grills, water, toilets, bear-resistant garbage containers; maximum trailer length of 22 feet; a fee is charged.
Dates Usually Open. July 1 through Sept. 7.
The Setting. This pleasant campground is conveniently located just off the highway, in a shady lodgepole-pine forest alongside tumbling Lake Creek. Views extend south from the campground to the high ridge of the Hunter Peak massif, 2,000 feet above, and this ridge is crowned by snags charred in the Clover-Mist Fire of 1988. Views from the footbridge spanning Lake Creek west of the campground reach up to the Matterhorn-like summit of 11,708-foot Pilot Peak and its companion summit, 11,313-foot Index Mountain.

41 • HUNTER PEAK (6,560')

Location. In the canyon of the Clarks Fork of the Yellowstone River, just west of Wyoming 296, 4.75 miles southeast of the junction with U.S.212, and 57.25 miles northwest of Cody, Wyoming; Shoshone National Forest, Clarks Fork Ranger District.
Facilities. 9 camping units, tables, fire pits with grills, water, toilets, bear-resistant food storage boxes, bear-resistant garbage containers; maximum trailer length of 32 feet; a fee is charged.
Dates Usually Open. June 1 through November 30.
The Setting. This small campground is conveniently located just off the highway in a peaceful forest of lodgepole pine and Engelmann spruce, along the banks of the wide, slow waters of Clarks Fork Yellowstone River. Hunter Peak, at 9,034 feet, looms

over the campground to the south, its limestone cliff bands covered by a forest of charred snags.

42 • BEARTOOTH LAKE (8,960')

Location. In the Beartooth Mountains, 0.6 mile northeast of U.S 212, 22.7 miles east of Cooke City, Montana, 9.1 miles east of the junction with Wyoming 296, and 39.7 miles southwest of Red Lodge, Montana; Shoshone National Forest, Clarks Fork Ranger District.
Facilities. 21 camping units, tables, water, fire grills, toilets, bear-resistant garbage containers; boat launch and picnic area 0.4 mile from highway; maximum trailer length of 32 feet; a fee is charged.
Dates Usually Open. July 1 through Sept. 7.
The Setting. This very scenic campground rests on a low moraine above 110-acre Beartooth Lake (8,901'), in a shady forest of lodgepole pine and Engelmann spruce. The colorful sedimentary rock slopes of 10,514-foot Beartooth Butte rise northwest of the lake. Beartooth Lake offers good fishing for brook, lake, rainbow, and cutthroat trout, and grayling.

43 • ISLAND LAKE (9,550')

Location. In the Beartooth Mountains, 0.3 mile north of U.S. 212, 25.7 miles east of Cooke City, 12.1 miles east of the junction with Wyoming 296, and 36.4 miles southwest of Red Lodge; Shoshone National Forest, Clarks Fork Ranger District.
Facilities. 20 camping units, tables, water, fire grills, bear-resistant garbage containers, boat launch; maximum trailer length of 32 feet; a fee is charged.
Dates Usually Open. July 1 through Sept. 7.
The Setting. This scenic campground lies in a timberline setting on a low, grassy and tree-dotted ridge south of 9,518-foot Island Lake. Several rocky, tree-studded islands dot the 140-acre lake, which offers good fishing for brook trout. Grand views stretch north across the lake, past nearby Night Lake, to bold alpine peaks, including 11,409-foot Lonesome Mountain, 12,612-foot Castle Mountain, and 12,377-foot Beartooth Mountain.

44 • PARKSIDE (7,120')

Location. In Rock Creek canyon, Beartooth Mountains, west of U.S. 212 (see driving directions for Trip 40 for exact location); Custer National Forest, Beartooth Ranger District.
Facilities. 25 camping units, tables, fire pits with grills, water, toilets, bear-resistant garbage containers; paved access road and campsite spurs; maximum trailer length of 30 feet; a fee is charged.
Dates Usually Open. May 22 through September 6.
The Setting. This pleasant campground is divided into two loops, with sites 1 through 15 lying above the south bank of large Rock Creek, and sites 16 through 25 lying above the north bank, reached via a bridge. The campground lies in a shady pine forest, deep in the U-shaped, glacier-carved trench of Rock Creek canyon.

45 • GREENOUGH LAKE (7,200')

Location. In Rock Creek canyon, Beartooth Mountains, west of U.S. 212 (see driving directions for Trip 40 for exact location); Custer National Forest, Beartooth Ranger District.
Facilities. 18 camping units, tables, fire pits with grills, water, toilets, bear-resistant garbage containers; paved access road and campsite spurs; maximum trailer length of 30 feet; one camping unit for handicap use and handicap-accessible toilet; a fee is charged.
Dates Usually Open. May 22 through September 6.
The Setting. This pleasant campground lies in a shady pine forest, deep in the canyon of Rock Creek. The Parkside Trail leads 0.25 mile from the campground to small Greenough Lake, and thence another 1.75 miles to M-K Campground, following Rock Creek much of the way.

46 • LIMBER PINE (7,200')

Location. In Rock Creek Canyon, Beartooth Mountains, west of U.S. 212 (see driving directions for Trip 40 for exact location); Custer National Forest, Beartooth Ranger District.
Facilities. 15 camping units (three of which are walk-in, tent camping sites), tables, fire pits with grills, water, toilets, bear-resis-

tant garbage containers; paved access road and campsite spurs; maximum trailer length of 30 feet; a fee is charged.
Dates Usually Open. May 22 through September 6.
The Setting. The sites are partly shaded by scattered lodgepole pines on the north banks of Rock Creek. Good views northwest from the campground reach to the alpine rim of Hellroaring Plateau.

47 • M-K (7,400')

Location. In Rock Creek canyon, Beartooth Mountains, west of U.S. 212 (see driving directions for Trip 40 for exact location); Custer National Forest, Beartooth Ranger District.
Facilities. 11 camping units, tables, fire pits with grills, toilets, no water or garbage collection; maximum trailer length of 20 feet; no fee.
Dates Usually Open. May 22 through September 6.
The Setting. This pleasant campground lies in a peaceful forest of lodgepole pine, above the south banks of Rock Creek. Alpine plateaus rise to the southern skyline above the campground, and on the plateau slopes you can see part of the switchbacks of the Beartooth Scenic Byway below Beartooth Pass.

48 • BASIN (6,902')

Location. In the West Fork Rock Creek canyon, west of Red Lodge in the Beartooth Mountains (see driving directions for Trips 41 and 42 for exact location); Custer National Forest, Beartooth Ranger District.
Facilities. 30 camping units, tables, fire pits with grills, water, toilets, bear-resistant garbage containers; paved access road and campsite spurs; maximum trailer length of 25 feet; a fee is charged.
Dates Usually Open. May 22 through September 6.
The Setting. Shaded by tall, slender lodgepole pines, this pleasant campground is located deep in the shady confines of West Fork Rock Creek. Forested slopes and ridges embrace the canyon, rising 2,000 feet above to the north and south. The Basin Lakes

Trail begins 0.1 mile east of the campground entrance (see Trip 41).

49 • CASCADE (7,580')

Location. In the West Fork Rock Creek canyon, west of Red Lodge, Montana, in the Beartooth Mountains (see driving directions for Trips 41 and 42 for exact location); Custer National Forest, Beartooth Ranger District.

Facilities. 30 camping units, tables, fire pits with grills, water, toilets, bear-resistant garbage containers; maximum trailer length of 25 feet; a fee is charged.

Dates Usually Open. May 22 through September 6.

The Setting. This is a very pleasant and expansive campground, located on a bench just north of West Fork Rock Creek. Sites are shaded by a forest dominated by slender lodgepole pines. Set deep in the forested canyon, views extend upward to the west and southwest, where rugged canyon walls rise to alpine plateaus.

Reservations for some sites in Basin Creek (#48) and Cascade (#49) campgrounds can be made in advance by phoning (800) 280-2267.

For Further Information

For information regarding Trips 30-33; Campgrounds 34-37, contact:

Gallatin National Forest
Gardiner Ranger District
P.O. Box 5
Gardiner, MT 59030
(406) 848-7375 or 7376

For further information regarding Trips 34-39; Campgrounds 38-43, contact:

Shoshone National Forest
Clarks Fork Ranger District
1002 Road 11
Powell, WY 82435
(307) 754-7207

For further information regarding Trips 40-42; Campgrounds 44-49, contact:

Custer National Forest
Beartooth Ranger District
Route 2, Box 3420
Red Lodge, MT 59068
(406) 446-2103

Wilderness Regulations

Since many trips in this chapter lead to areas in the Absaroka-Beartooth Wilderness, backpackers should become familiar with the regulations below before entering the Wilderness.

1. Except at designated campsites with bear-resistant food storage boxes, campsites and campfires must be located at least 200 feet from lakes and 100 feet from streams.
2. Group size is limited to 15 people.
3. Do not camp in sites posted closed to camping.
4. Maximum length of stay in a site is 16 days.
5. Garbage must be packed out, and camp structures, including fire rings, must be dismantled.
6. Motorized and mechanized equipment, including bicycles and hang gliders, is prohibited.

Trip 30

TOM MINER CAMPGROUND TO PETRIFIED FOREST TRAIL

Distance: 2.0 miles, round trip.
Low/High Elevations: 7,080'/7,720'.
Difficulty: Moderately easy.
Use: Moderate.
Suited For: Dayhike.
Best Season: Late June through mid-September.
Wildlife Viewing: Excellent.
Grizzly Bear Danger: Moderate.
Map/Trailhead: 24/27.

Nearest Campground. Tom Miner, located at the trailhead.

Driving to the Trailhead: Follow U.S. 89 north 16.0 miles from Gardiner, Montana, at the North Entrance to Yellowstone National Park, or south 36.0 miles from Interstate 90 at Livingston, Montana, to the westbound Tom Miner Creek Road, signed for TOM MINER BASIN.

This good, wide gravel road leads west to a bridge spanning the Yellowstone River, and then after 0.4 mile to a T-intersection where you turn left (south); a sign here points the way to Tom Miner Basin. After another 0.75 mile, bear right where the Old Yellowstone Trail road branches left, and follow the steadily ascending road into the broad grassy bowl of Tom Miner Basin.

Ignore the signed, northbound Divide Creek Road, 6.4 miles from the highway, and after 8.2 miles, bear left where a road branches right to the B-Bar Ranch. Beyond that junction the road narrows and becomes rough, with occasional potholes and rocky stretches. At 11.0 miles from the highway, the Sunlight Road forks left, but you bear right and enter Tom Miner Campground after another 0.3 mile. The trailhead parking area is at the west, upper end of the campground, 11.7 miles from the highway.

The national forest boundary is 0.5 mile east of the campground entrance, and there are no undeveloped camping areas. Overnight visitors are restricted to Tom Miner Campground.

Introduction: About 50 million years ago, eruptions of two chains of volcanoes in the Greater Yellowstone area caused widespread mudflows that buried vast forests. Over time, these forests were fossilized, and today more than 40 square miles of fossil forests have been exposed by erosion in the northeast corner of Yellowstone Park, and in the Gallatin Petrified Forest northwest of the Park.

These fossil forests are the most extensive in the world, and many petrified trees can be found standing upright in the same positions in which they grew. Some trees are so well-preserved that their growth rings and cellular structure have enabled botanists to identify the species. Leaves, needles, cones, and pollen grains are found in these volcanic sediments.

The preserved temperate species such as pines, willows, firs, spruces, elms, and redwoods are believed to have grown in cool climates near the tops of the high volcanoes. But trees similar to those found today in such places as the southeastern U.S. and in Central America are preserved here as well, including bays, figs, laurels, dogwoods, and magnolias. Probably these trees grew in humid tropical lowlands at the bases of the volcanoes.

This short dayhike follows a well-defined trail into the Gallatin Petrified Forest above Tom Miner Campground. The trail leads past petrified logs and wood fragments exposed in the bluffs northwest of the campground. Interpretive signs along the way offer insights into the events that created the petrified forest.

Visitors may collect up to 20 cubic inches of petrified wood in this area, but first you must obtain a collection permit, available free of charge from the Gardiner Ranger District office in Gardiner, Montana (see *For Further Information* above). Be sure to read the regulations attached to the permit carefully.

Description: From the roadend at 7,080 feet follow the trail west for a few yards to a gate (please keep closed) that bars cattle from entering upper Trail Creek. The trail ahead ascends a moderate grade through meadows decorated with the pink blooms of sticky geranium and the bluish flowers of lupine. Groves of white-boled aspen are scattered above the trail, and a dense ribbon of Engelmann spruce hugs the banks of Trail Creek below to the south.

Verdant slopes dotted with conifer groves and broken by bluffs of brown volcanic rocks rise above the canyon to the north, and the trail soon leads into those bluffs. After crossing a dry, cobbly stream bed, we reach a signed junction at 0.25 mile. Hikers en route to Buffalo Horn Pass (see Trip 31) will continue straight ahead, but we bear right (northwest) onto the Petrified Forest Trail (open to foot traffic only).

This trail leads into the mouth of a northwest-trending draw via a flower-filled meadow. Where we enter the draw, volcanic boulders litter the nearby slopes. After ascending the draw for 0.3 mile, we reach a series of switchbacks. The switchbacks lead up a moderate grade on southwest-facing slopes, beneath a shady canopy of Douglas-fir and limber pine. Good views from these slopes reach across the valley of Trail Creek to high, tree-crested ridges on the southern skyline. The switchbacks end at the foot of the rocky bluffs, and the trail turns north and follows the base of a low cliff.

Interpretive signs point out pieces of petrified logs, and if you look carefully, you will find many more fossilized wood fragments. The trail ends in a small alcove about 1.0 mile from the trailhead, where a petrified tree stump hangs from overhead. The growth rings in the stump are clearly visible.

Hikers have worn paths beyond the trail's end, leading over and around the bluffs. You'll likely find much petrified wood if you explore further, but exercise caution—the slopes are steep and the rocks are unstable.

Eventually, you backtrack to the trailhead.

Trip 31

TOM MINER CAMPGROUND TO BUFFALO HORN PASS

Distance: 4.6 miles, round trip.
Low/High Elevations: 7,080'/8,523'.
Difficulty: Moderate.
Use: Low.
Suited For: Dayhike or mountain bike trip.
Best Season: July through mid-September.
Wildlife Viewing: Excellent.
Grizzly Bear Danger: Moderate.
Map/Trailhead: 24/27.

Nearest Campground. Tom Miner, located at the trailhead.
Driving to the Trailhead: Follow driving directions for Trip 30.
Introduction: This short but rewarding dayhike ascends from Tom Miner Campground to the crest of the Gallatin Range at Buffalo Horn Pass, the divide between the Yellowstone and Gallatin river drainages. The trail, which is only occasionally rocky with a moderate grade, passes through rich natural flower gardens throughout much of its length. The tread, however, is very slippery during and shortly after rainfall.

Your chances of observing wildlife along this trail are better than on any other trail in this book. Mule and whitetail deer, elk, moose, coyote, and black and grizzly bear frequent this area. An easy 0.3-mile side trip leads from the pass to a low grassy knob on the Gallatin crest, where inspiring vistas unfold.
Description: From the trailhead at Tom Miner Campground, follow the trail west into upper Trail Creek canyon (see Trip 30) for 0.25 mile, and continue straight ahead at the junction with the Petrified Forest Trail. We ascend generally west on a gentle grade at first, crossing meadow-draped slopes rich with the colorful blooms of lupine, cinquefoil, sticky geranium, mountain dandelion, and arrowleaf balsamroot.

After 0.6 mile from the junction, we dip slightly down to a rockhop crossing of small Dry Creek. Beyond the crossing we rise steeply, but the grade soon moderates on verdant slopes above conifer-lined Trail Creek. More blooms join the ranks of the wildflowers here, now including yellow mule's ears, larkspur, birch-leaf spirea, and woods forget-me-not. Looking closely, we will see pieces of petrified wood strewn across the smooth trail bed.

Lodgepole pines soon appear in groves above the trail, but the trailside slopes remain open and allow fine views to the east, where the slopes of Trail Creek canyon frame the distant high peaks of the Absaroka Range.

At length we curve around the headwaters bowl of Trail Creek, where mountain bluebells and willows hug the banks of the infant stream below the trail. Beyond the bowl, the grade briefly abates in a meadow hosting a profusion of the purple blooms of larkspur. Then one final, moderate ascent through a conifer forest leads to the pretty, round meadow atop the crest of the Gallatins at 8,523-foot Buffalo Horn Pass, 2.3 miles from the trailhead.

A four-way junction lies at the pass, with trails leading west to Buffalo Horn Creek, south to Yellowstone Park, and north to Ramshorn Peak, the bold summit rising nearly 2,000 feet above the pass. The pass offers no views, but the meadow supports a fine display of wildflowers, including American bistort, yarrow, cinquefoil, white mule's ears, larkspur, lupine, sticky geranium, and dandelion.

Although Ramshorn Peak offers dramatic vistas, the route to its summit is strenuous and beyond the reach of some dayhikers. There is a fine viewpoint, however, only a few minute's walk from the pass (0.6 mile round trip) that is accessible to any hiker.

To get there, follow the southbound trail, signed for Yellowstone National Park, 0.3 mile to the south shoulder of a minor knob (Peak 8,598 on the map). Leave the trail here (mountain bikers should proceed on foot from this point), and easily ascend for several yards to the summit of the knob.

Only scattered whitebark pines dot the crest, affording a nearly unobstructed panorama of northwest Greater Yellowstone. Spreading out below the knob to the west is the broad forested valley of Buffalo Horn Creek, dotted with emerald-green meadows and several small tarns. On the western horizon lies the jagged Madison Range, among the most majestic mountains in Greater Yellowstone. From the Spanish Peaks in the northwest to the Hilgard Peaks in the southwest, the view encompasses more than 30 miles of 10,000-foot and 11,000-foot peaks of the Madison crest. To the north rises the tall cone of 10,296-foot Ramshorn Peak, and beyond it is the rugged west face of 9,771-foot Fortress Mountain. Far to the east we can see the jagged alpine summits of the Absaroka Range.

After enjoying the memorable vistas, retrace the flower-decked trail back to Tom Miner Campground.

Trip 32
FISHER CREEK TO LADY OF THE LAKE

Distance: 4.8 miles, round trip.
Low/High Elevations: 8,749'/8,960'.
Difficulty: Easy.
Use: Moderate.
Suited For: Dayhike or backpack.
Best Season: July through mid-Sept.
Wildlife Viewing: Good.
Grizzly Bear Danger: Moderate.
Map/Trailhead: 25/28.
Nearest Campgrounds: Colter, 2.1 miles, Soda Butte, 3.3 miles, Chief Joseph, 3.4 miles, Fox Creek, 7.8 miles, and Crazy Creek, 11.6 miles from the trailhead.
Driving to the Trailhead: Eastbound drivers on U.S. 212 will find the trailhead access road—the Lulu Pass Road—by following the highway 1.8 miles east from Cooke City, Montana, just beyond a series of low-speed "S" curves. If you reach the entrance to Colter Campground, you've gone 0.1 mile too far.

Westbound drivers will find the access road by following the Beartooth Scenic Byway west for 11.8 miles from the junction with Wyoming 296, and 8.8 miles from the Montana/Wyoming border.

A sign at the access road shows mileage to the Goose Lake Jeep Road via Lulu Pass Road, and indicates that the access road is not maintained. The road is steep, rough, and rocky, but passable to carefully driven cars. The road leads steadily uphill northwest from the highway. Avoid two westbound roads (to the left) along the way, at 0.1 mile and at 0.8 mile.

After 1.0 rough mile from the highway, at a Y-junction, turn right where a small sign points to Lady of the Lake Trail. After 200 yards, the road forks. You will find parking just beyond this junction. Do not follow the left fork; it ends at a washout above Fisher Creek after 100 yards, and there is no turnaround there.

Several undeveloped camping areas can be found near the roadend above Fisher Creek.

Introduction: This scenic, easy hike is a fine choice for hikers with limited time or energy, and is an especially good choice for families with children. The trail, with minimal elevation gain, leads through subalpine forests to 42-acre Lady of the Lake in the western reaches of the Beartooth Mountains. Anglers will find productive fishing for pan-sized brook trout. Absaroka-Beartooth Wilderness regulations apply to backpackers staying overnight.

Description: The only obstacle on this trip is Fisher Creek, and you must ford this cold, shallow stream at the road washout just beyond the trailhead, at 8,749 feet. A sign opposite the ford points to the trail, actually an old road, which you follow gently uphill, first east, then north, through a conifer forest.

After 0.25 mile we pass above the charred remains of an old stamp mill, remnants of the heyday of gold mining in the Cooke City Mining District. Only two miles west, on the flanks of Henderson Mountain, work has begun on a modern open-pit gold mine. This highly controversial operation, above timberline near the headwaters of three tributaries to Yellowstone River, is only two miles from the boundary of the Absaroka-Beartooth Wilderness, and less than three miles from Yellowstone National Park.

Shortly thereafter we pass two well-preserved cabins and a sign pointing to Lady of the Lake. Continue following the old road northeast and, after 0.6 mile from the trailhead, leave the road and bear right onto the trail. The trail ahead is rocky as we proceed northeast on an undulating traverse, where huckleberry and grouse whortleberry carpet the shady forest floor. Soon the

trail begins a gentle ascent and after 1.3 miles, we enter the Absaroka-Beartooth Wilderness.

Next we descend easily to a long, narrow meadow, its upper reaches splashed with the blooms of marsh marigolds until midsummer. Its lower reaches, bisected by a small stream, are enlivened by mountain bluebells, Indian paintbrush, and cow parsnip. At the lower, eastern end of the meadow, we jump across a small stream and quickly reach the shores of Lady of the Lake.

This beautiful, long lake is bordered by a scattered forest of Engelmann spruce, subalpine fir, and whitebark pine. Glacier-smoothed ridges of granite rise east and west of the lake, and to the north 11,550-foot Mount Zimmer rises beyond tree-fringed ridges. Some campsites at the lake bear the scars of past overuse, and these are posted NO CAMPING.

The trail follows the west shore of the lake generally north, and midway around it are several good camping areas. At that point, the lake lies in the foreground of a fine view that reaches south to the prominent, somber gray Absaroka Range summits of Pilot Peak and Index Mountain. The shoreline is alternately rocky, grassy, and tree-fringed. As we approach the shallow, swampy north end of the lake, at 2.4 miles, we enjoy another fine view to the dark cone of Mount Zimmer. Beyond the lake, the trail begins ascending, leading deeper into the Wilderness.

After enjoying this easily accessible lake, return to the trailhead.

Trip 33

CLARKS FORK TRAILHEAD TO ROCK ISLAND LAKE

Distance: 6.2 miles, round trip.
Low/High Elevations: 8,000'/8,166'.
Difficulty: Moderately easy.
Use: Moderate.
Suited For: Dayhike or backpack.

Best Season: Late June through mid-Sept.
Wildlife Viewing: Good.
Grizzly Bear Danger: Moderate.
Map/Trailhead: 26/29.
Nearest Campgrounds: Chief Joseph, 0.3 mile, Colter, 1.25 miles, Soda Butte, 2.5 miles, Fox Creek, 4.0 miles, and Crazy Creek, 7.9 miles from the trailhead.
Driving to the Trailhead: Follow U.S. Highway 212 for 10.4 miles northwest from the junction with Wyoming 296, and 1.5 miles northwest from the Montana/Wyoming border; or 3.2 miles east from Cooke City to a turnoff signed for CLARKS FORK PICNIC AREA AND TRAILHEAD. The turnoff lies 50 yards southeast of the entrance to Chief Joseph Campground.

Follow this dirt road for 0.3 mile to its end at the spacious trailhead parking area above the banks of Clarks Fork Yellowstone River. Picnic tables and toilets are located at the trailhead.

Introduction: Most lakes in the Beartooth Mountains lie at or above timberline, but Rock Island Lake lies in a forested setting in the "temperate zone" of the range. The trail to the lake, which can be muddy after recent rainfall, gains little elevation en route to the lake.

A peaceful walk through the forest, fishing for cutthroat and brook trout, and good, pine-shaded campsites at the lake are ample reasons for choosing this trip for a day's outing, or for an overnight stay. Absaroka-Beartooth Wilderness regulations apply to backpackers who stay overnight.

Description: Our trail leaves the northeast corner of the loop at the roadend at 8,000 feet, and we follow it northeast through open forest to a sturdy footbridge spanning Clarks Fork Yellowstone River, where it cascades through a narrow, rocky gorge.

A pleasant stretch of trail follows, leading through a shady forest of Engelmann spruce, lodgepole pine, and subalpine fir. After 0.3 mile, the trail bends east just above a narrow pond on the Clarks Fork. At this point, a wide, roadlike horse trail nearly joins our foot trail from the west, and then parallels our trail for another 0.7 mile.

Our trail through the forest ahead is mostly smooth, with only occasional roots and rocks. The shady forest floor is carpeted with a mat of low-growing grouse whortleberry shrubs and taller huckleberry bushes. Heartleaf arnica, a common wildflower in moist, shady forests in Greater Yellowstone, is the dominant bloom here.

Continuing through the forest on a gentle uphill grade, we pass the signed Broadwater Trail (a jeep road), branching north at 0.8 mile. The signed Vernon Lake Trail branches right at 1.3 miles, beyond which our trail and the horse trail converge and our route becomes much rougher and rockier. After another 0.2 mile, we pass just above the outlet of 8,070-foot Kersey Lake. An anglers trail branches left here, following the south shore of the lake, which offers good fishing for brook trout.

Our trail, however, leads away from the lake as we traverse above the south shoreline. Midway around the lake and 100 feet above it, we pass through a strip of forest charred in the lightning-caused Storm Creek Fire of 1988. Fireweed is common on this steep, rocky, north-facing slope, but very few new trees have begun to reforest the area.

The open, burned forest allows fine views of lofty Beartooth summits rising beyond Kersey Lake. From northwest to north we see

Rock Island Lake

10,603-foot Sheep Mountain, 11,550-foot Mount Zimmer, Iceberg Peak, Mount Wilse, 12,351-foot Glacier Peak, and the cockscomb crest of 12,337-foot Mount Villard.

Kersey Lake fades from view as we head deeper into the forest, but soon we reach the fringes of a long, soggy meadow that stretches away to the north. We cross a corrugated bridge over a swampy section of the spread, then stroll through lodgepole pine forest to the Absaroka-Beartooth Wilderness boundary and a junction.

Our trail, signed for Rock Island Lake, branches right and leads southeast. The Russell Creek Trail, to the left, leads 50 yards to a junction with the Big Moose Trail, which passes just north of Rock Island Lake en route to the Crazy Lakes chain.

Bearing right toward Rock Island Lake, we take a nearly level stroll through lodgepole forest for 0.7 mile to the northwest shore of the lake, where the trail ends. Good campsites lie in the forest north of the trail several yards west of the lake.

The irregular shoreline of this large, 137-acre lake is fringed with conifers, and numerous rocky, pine-studded islands rise from its deep water. The alpine crest of 10,100-foot Bald Knob looms on the northern skyline, and low, tree-covered knobs encircle the lake.

From Rock Island Lake, retrace your route to the trailhead.

Trip 34

CRAZY CREEK CAMP-GROUND TO IVY LAKE

Distance: 8.2 miles, round trip.
Low/High Elevations: 6,920'/8,080'.
Difficulty: Moderate.
Use: Moderate.
Suited For: Dayhike or backpack.
Best Season: Late June through mid-September.
Wildlife Viewing: Good.
Grizzly Bear Danger: Moderate.

Cascades on Crazy Creek, north of Crazy Creek Campground, on the trail to Ivy Lake

Map/Trailhead: 27/30.
Nearest Campgrounds: Crazy Creek, 100 yards east of the trailhead; and Lake Creek, 3.7 miles, Fox Creek, 3.9 miles, Hunter Peak, 7.3 miles, Chief Joseph, 7.9 miles, Colter, 9.2 miles, Soda Butte, 10.4 miles, Beartooth Lake, 11.7 miles, and Island Lake, 14.8 miles from the trailhead.
Driving to the Trailhead: The trailhead is located on the north side of the U.S 212, 100 yards west of the entrance to Crazy Creek Campground and 2.6 miles west of the junction with Wyoming 296, 51.1 miles southwest of Red Lodge, Montana, and 11.0 miles southeast of Cooke City.
Introduction: This trip, beginning at the lowest trailhead on the Beartooth Scenic Byway, ascends through aspen groves and sagebrush-covered slopes en route to pretty Ivy Lake, one of the Crazy Lakes chain. Although the forest around part of the lake was charred in 1988 by the Storm Creek Fire, the lake is still a scenic destination for a day's outing, and good campsites in green forest at the lake offer backpackers the opportunity for a pleasant overnight stay.

Fishing can be productive for rainbow and brook trout. Absaroka-Beartooth Wilderness regulations apply to overnight camping.
Description: From the 6,920-foot trailhead the trail leads northwest through lodgepole pine forest to the banks of vigorous

Crazy Creek, where we meet a trail on the left coming from the campground. Our trail follows the creek upstream, and after 200 yards, Crazy Creek thunders in a series of cascades plunging over granite ledges.

The trail soon forks, the left fork following the creek to the cascades. Stay to the right, and ascend gentle-to-moderate grades through an open forest of lodgepole pine, Douglas-fir, and aspen, staying above and east of Crazy Creek. Wildflowers along this stretch include the lavender blossoms of sticky geranium, the white blooms of Richardson geranium, and blue harebell, lupine, yarrow, and groundsel.

At 0.3 mile we enter Absaroka-Beartooth Wilderness, and 0.2 mile farther we pass through a gate in a fence line, behind which cattle graze in summer. Beyond the gate we stroll down to an easy rockhop crossing of a shallow stream, then ascend open, sagebrush-studded slopes. From these warm, sunny slopes we have fine views of Jim Smith Peak, Pilot Peak, and Index Mountain in the Absaroka Range.

The trail ahead, rocky in places, ascends moderately on brushy slopes to crest a broad ridge at 2.0 miles. There we enter lodgepole-pine forest, then begin a gentle downhill grade. Soon we enter an area of charred snags, and shortly reach a soggy meadow. We can't avoid wet feet here, so we slog ahead through the swamp for 100 yards to the forest fringe on the meadow's north side.

Beyond the meadow, we rise moderately through increasingly rocky terrain. There are few green trees here—mostly blackened poles—but young lodgepole pines are reforesting the slopes, grow-

ing among profuse greenery. The grade moderates when we enter a sagebrush-clad clearing, and shortly we exit the Wilderness just above the tarn of Little Moose Lake. From this opening we have the first good views of the lofty Beartooth crest, streaked with snow and crowned by an array of prominent summits in the northwest, including Sheep Mountain, Mount Zimmer, Mount Wilse, Glacier Peak, Mount Villard, and Granite Peak, which at 12,799 feet is the highest point in Montana.

Shortly after leaving the Wilderness, we reach the Crazy Lakes Jeep Trail at 3.3 miles, and turn left (north). The signed Crazy Lakes Trail, a single path, branches right after another 0.25 mile, but we stay left and follow the winding 4WD road for another 0.3 mile to a vehicle barricade at the Wilderness boundary.

From there we follow the trail as it winds down through charred forest to the southern end of Ivy Lake, near its outlet, at 7,972 feet, 4.1 miles from the trailhead. Blackened snags hug the banks of the outlet, where Crazy Creek cascades over granite slabs. Low granite ridges dotted with pines circle the lake, and we enjoy good views across the lake's broad waters to 10,312-foot Jim Smith Peak to the south, and west to the dome of Rock Island Butte.

Ivy Lake

The forest above the west and north shores managed to escape the 1988 fire, and backpackers will find good campsites there in lodgepole pine forest, accessible by shoreline trails.

From Ivy Lake, retrace your steps to the trailhead.

Trip 35

MUDDY CREEK TO GRANITE LAKE

Distance: 9.6 miles, round trip.
Low/High Elevations: 8,080'/8,720'.
Difficulty: Moderate.
Use: Moderate.
Suited For: Dayhike or backpack.
Best Season: Mid-July through mid-September.
Wildlife Viewing: Good.
Grizzly Bear Danger: Moderate.
Map/Trailhead: 28/31.
Nearest Campgrounds: Beartooth Lake, 4.8 miles, Lake Creek, 5.5 miles, Island Lake, 6.2 miles, Crazy Creek, 6.9 miles, and Hunter Peak, 9.1 miles from the trailhead.
Driving to the Trailhead: From U.S. 212, turn north onto signed Muddy Creek Road. Find this turnoff by driving 4.4 miles northeast from the junction with Wyoming 296; or 17.9 miles east from Cooke City, Montana; or 44.2 miles from Red Lodge, Montana.

Follow this dirt road north for about 200 yards, where you will find ample parking just off the road. Several undeveloped camping areas lie west of the road in this area.

The road ahead, passable only to

high-clearance vehicles, is extremely rocky and narrow for the remaining 0.4 mile to the trailhead. You can probably walk to the trailhead in the same time it would take to drive.

Introduction: This rewarding trip follows the forested valley of Muddy Creek to a low divide, then quickly descends to sprawling Granite Lake. Encompassing 228 acres, this lake is one of the largest in the Absaroka-Beartooth Wilderness. The lake offers several excellent campsites, and good fishing for pan-sized brook trout.

This trip ends near the outlet of the lake, in Wyoming, but the upper (north) half of the lake lies within Montana. Absaroka-Beartooth Wilderness regulations apply in this area.

Description: Most people will park about 200 yards north of the Beartooth Scenic Byway, at 8,080 feet, and walk the remaining 0.4 mile of the rocky road to the trailhead. From there, proceed north past a vehicle barricade, and follow the closed road—the Muddy Creek Trail—through a shady forest of Engelmann spruce and lodgepole pine.

After 0.25 mile, dip down to the banks of a muddy stream, jump over its trickling waters, and continue ahead on the trail proper. Soon thereafter pass a wilderness information sign, then briefly skirt the western fringe of a small meadow. After re-

Granite Lake

entering forest, follow the crest of a low moraine up-canyon. About 0.8 mile from the roadend, an expansive, wet meadow, rimmed by tree-fringed granite knobs, spreads out before us, covering the entire valley floor.

The trail follows the eastern margin of the meadow, staying mostly just inside the forest. At times, however, the trail is forced into the meadow, where the tread is likely to be wet and muddy prior to August.

After skirting the meadow for 1.1 miles, we reach a signed junction with the Upper Granite Loop Trail, its invisible tread lost in the tall grass. We stay left on the obvious trail, soon entering forest and rockhopping a small stream. The route quickly returns to the meadow in an especially wet area, and the trail ahead often becomes obscure. Following the edge of the spread, we curve west, soon entering the mouth of a northwest-trending draw. There the now-rocky trail becomes well-defined, and we ascend via gentle to moderate grades in a forest of spruce, lodgepole pine, and subalpine fir. Huckleberry and grouse whortleberry clothe the nearby slopes in a mantle of green foliage, and rocky knobs rise above the confines of the draw to the skyline.

At length we mount a narrow, forest-clad saddle at 8,720 feet, 4.3 miles from the trailhead. From the saddle a steep grade quickly leads to the shore of large Granite Lake, at 8,620 feet. The trail briefly touches the shoreline, then ascends above it, crossing rock-studded, forested slopes. Soon we drop back to the lakeshore, pass a narrow meadow next to a spacious, pine-shaded campsite, then curve south to a crossing of Lake Creek, the 40-foot-wide stream draining the lake, 4.8 miles from our cars. The ford can be knee-deep, but the current is gentle. Good campsites lie opposite the ford, and farther west along the trail above the lake's south shores.

This beautiful lake is circled by forest-fringed granite knobs and domes, with a backdrop of lofty Beartooth peaks, including square-edged Castle Rock Mountain, at 12,408 feet. A timberline forest of spruce, lodgepole, and subalpine fir hugs the shoreline, and numerous rocky points jut into the lake's waters, offering anglers good access to deep water.

From Granite Lake, retrace your steps to your car.

Trip 36
CLAY BUTTE TO NATIVE LAKE

Distance: 7.6 miles, round trip.
Low/High Elevations: 9,280'/10,000'.
Difficulty: Moderate.
Use: Moderate.
Suited For: Dayhike or backpack.
Best Season: Early July through early Sept.
Wildlife Viewing: Good.
Grizzly Bear Danger: Moderate.
Map/Trailhead: 28/32.
Nearest Campgrounds: Beartooth Lake, 3.8 miles, Island Lake, 5.0 miles, Lake Creek, 10.5 miles, and Crazy Creek, 16.5 miles from the trailhead.
Driving to the Trailhead: Follow U.S. 212 to the prominently signed road to Clay Butte Lookout Tower. Find this turnoff on the north side of the highway, 21.2 miles east of Cooke City, Montana, and 7.6 miles northeast of the junction with Wyoming 296; or 40.9 miles southwest of Red Lodge, Montana.

Follow this good gravel road (which becomes quite slippery when wet) northwest for 1.8 miles to the signed trailhead for the Upper Granite Loop Trail. The trailhead parking area is just below and west of the main road, accessed via a short but steep and rough spur road.

Don't miss the unforgettable panorama of the Beartooths and the Absaroka Range from the Clay Butte Lookout Tower, at the roadend 0.8 mile above the trailhead.
Introduction: Panoramic views of some of Greater Yellowstone's highest mountains, miles of wildflower-rich meadows, and a scenic timberline lake offering good campsites and fishing for large brook trout are

major attractions of this memorable timberline trip in the Beartooth Mountains.

The trail is mostly smooth and easy to follow, but the limestone tread can become very slippery during and shortly after a rainfall. Absaroka-Beartooth wilderness regulations apply to backpackers staying overnight.

Description: From the trailhead at 9,550 feet, follow the Upper Granite Loop Trail on a descending, north-bound traverse. After several yards pass a wilderness information sign, then emerge from the timberline forest of subalpine fir, Engelmann spruce, and whitebark pine into a sloping meadow, and enter the Absaroka-Beartooth Wilderness.

Grand vistas, rivaling those from the Clay Butte Lookout, unfold from this meadow, and accompany us throughout the rest of the trip. The most prominent landmark, Pilot Peak, has guided Native Americans through this region for thousands of years, as well as guiding mountain men in search of beaver streams more than 150 years ago. Rising to 11,708 feet, Pilot Peak is one of the most striking peaks in the Rocky Mountains. Its isolated, Matterhorn-like spire juts skyward more than 4,500 feet from the depths of Clarks Fork canyon. Pilot and its companion summit, 11,313-foot Index Mountain,are the foreground of a more distant view of the somber gray peaks and ice-gouged cirques of the Absaroka Range.

The gently sloping southern flanks of the Beartooth Mountains, once engulfed in a sheet of ice, spread before us to the north and northwest. The lush meadows the trail traverses contrast with the ice-polished granite bedrock that dominates the Bear-

tooth landscape. Along the trail we see the blossoms of yarrow, one-flower daisy, American bistort, mountain dandelion, palish larkspur, mountain goldenrod, mountain bluebells, cinquefoil,and Richardson geranium.

The soils that enrich these mountainside flower gardens are derived from the limestone flanks of Clay Butte, above the trail to the east. Clay Butte and Beartooth Butte are remnants of the veneer of sedimentary rocks that long ago covered this part of the Beartooths.

The first mile of the smooth trail descends 300 feet at a moderate grade, alternating between open meadows and groves of timberline conifers. En route we cross the muddy banks of five small springs that trickle across the trail. At 1.0 mile bear right onto the signed Clay Butte Trail. The Upper Granite Loop Trail, continuing the descent northwest, leads four more miles to sprawling Granite Lake.

The following 1.5 miles are a continuation of the first mile of the trail, except that the trail gradually ascends through spectacular meadows and groves of pine, spruce, and fir, beneath the gray battlements of Clay Butte's north ridge. At 2.5 miles you jump across a small creek at the west edge of a wet, sloping meadow. The trail curves north into a minor draw, then returns to the

Native Lake

creek. Hop across it to the south bank, beyond which the trail disappears in the grassland.

Occasional cairns help guide us on a moderate ascent east up an increasingly narrow draw, toward a prominent saddle at the north end of Clay Butte. As you approach the saddle, notice the sharp contrast along our route between the deep, nutrient-rich soils derived from Clay Butte to the south and the shallow granitic soils that dominate to the north. The Clay Butte soils support a rich carpet of grasses and wildflowers, while the granitic soils have only a sparse covering of grasses.

At 3.2 miles, we crest the 10,000-foot saddle, fringed by a few hardy, ground-hugging spruces and whitebark pines. Here we meet the Beartooth High Lakes Trail, leading southeast to the Beartooth Lake Campground and northwest to more than two dozen alpine lakes.

Turning left (northwest) onto that trail, descend steadily among a scattering of stunted conifers and ice-scoured granite bedrock, enjoying more grand views along the way. After 0.6 mile, reach the shallow bowl harboring 9,800-foot Native Lake, 3.8 miles from the trailhead.

This lovely, seven-acre lake, surrounded by gentle slopes mantled in meadows and stunted trees, with a backdrop of massive alpine peaks, is typical of the hundreds of lakes that dot the range. Good campsites can be found above the west and northeast shores of the lake. From a base camp here one can spend several days fishing or exploring more than one dozen lakes that lie within a two-mile radius of Native Lake.

From Native Lake, retrace your route to the trailhead.

Trip 37

BEARTOOTH LAKE CAMPGROUND TO BEAUTY LAKE

Distance: 7.6 miles, loop trip.
Low/High Elevations: 8,904'/9,920'.
Difficulty: Moderate.
Use: Moderate.
Suited For: Dayhike or backpack.
Best Season: Mid-July through early September.
Wildlife Viewing: Good.
Grizzly Bear Danger: Moderate.
Map/Trailhead: 29/33.
Nearest Campgrounds: Beartooth Lake, located at the trailhead; and Island Lake, 4.0 miles, Lake Creek, 8.5 miles, Crazy Creek, 9.0 miles, and Hunter Peak, 12.1 miles from the trailhead.
Driving to the Trailhead: Follow U.S. 212 to the prominently signed turnoff to the Beartooth Lake Campground, on the north side of the highway just east of the outlet of Beartooth Lake. Find the turnoff 9.1 miles northeast of the junction with Wyoming 296, and 22.7 miles east of Cooke City, or 39.4 miles southwest of Red Lodge.

Drive northeast from the highway on the gravel road 0.6 mile to Beartooth Lake Campground. Just before you enter Campground Loop C, a spur road forks left and a sign points to the trailhead. This very rough and rocky spur road leads 0.1 mile down to the small parking area at the trailhead.

Introduction: This memorable loop trip is perhaps the most rewarding Beartooth trail in this book. This trail, like Trip 38, leads to Beauty Lake, and from there leads past a chain of lakes to timberline, then returns to the trailhead across the verdant slopes of Beartooth Butte.

Hikers can follow all or part of this rewarding trail, and the loop can be followed in either direction. By following the loop as it is described, you encounter more gradual uphill grades. This trip requires seven trouble-free fords of cold, shin-deep streams.

Fishing can be productive in many of the lakes along this trail. The trail lies outside of the Absaroka-Beartooth Wilderness, but backpackers should nevertheless employ no-trace techniques to minimize impact on the fragile timberline landscape.

Description: From the trailhead at 8,904 feet the trail leads north for 150 yards above the east shore of Beartooth Lake to a signed junction, where we bear right. The return leg of the loop is on the left branch.

The trail is faint as it leads east to the banks of Little Bear Creek, which we must ford. The creek is shin-deep, about 25 feet wide, with a moderate current. Beyond the ford he tread becomes more obvious through the willows bordering the creek. The next 1.2 miles are uneventful, ascending gently at first, then moderately, through a viewless forest of Engelmann spruce, and lodgepole pine.

At 1.2 miles the grade abates above rockbound Crane Lake, where we pass a trail of use leading down to its shores. Amid increasingly rocky terrain, we traverse above Crane Lake, follow above the southeast banks of the large stream that flows into it, and soon large Beauty Lake spreads out before us.

True to its name, this is a lovely 90-acre lake, lying in a broad timberline bowl bounded by granite domes. Slopes and benches of rock and meadow studded with groves of conifers are above the shoreline, and in the distance rise the tundra-covered flanks of alpine plateaus. The lake harbors brook trout, and good campsites can be found above its south and west shores.

The trail leads above the lake's east shore, crossing steep slopes and undulating at times to avoid rocky outcrops. The way is ill-defined where we cross stretches of soggy meadows. At length we leave the lakeshore and mount rocky benches, meeting the Beartooth High Lakes Trail at 2.5 miles. Go left (west) onto that trail, quickly drop to the lake's 50-foot-wide inlet creek, and wade the shin-deep waters over a slippery, cobbly bed.

Leave your wading shoes on after fording this stream, for after topping a grassy rise the trail dips down to ford another stream within 300 yards of the last. This stream is much smaller and ankle-deep.

From that crossing we ascend generally northwest in stairstep fashion, climbing steeply into a series of minor basins. The timberline terrain in this area is a scenic delight: knobs of glacier-scoured granite, meadows strewn with slabs, erratic boulders, and wildflowers, and a scattering of stunted spruce and whitebark pines on trailside slopes.

From a minor ridge at 9,680 feet, 3.0 miles from the trailhead, you descend into a meadow, follow a small creek upstream past a series of tarns, and then skirt the north shore of a larger tarn, shown as Claw Lake on some maps. There are several excellent campsites sheltered by groves of spruce and whitebark pine at this timberline

Beartooth Lake and Beartooth Butte lie adjacent to the Beartooth Lake Campground

gem, and more at nearby Grayling Lake to the south, reached via a trail that follows the east shore of Claw Lake for 0.4 mile. Both lakes support an abundance of pan-sized brook trout.

Just west of the lake we reach its inlet creek at a swift, 15-foot-wide ford. Upstream boulders in the streambed afford a dry crossing. Then follow its south banks westward, soon entering an open basin at timberline and passing above an island-studded lake. Alpine meadows, abundant granite bedrock, and stunted patches of conifers dominate the scene in the basin, with the rocky pyramid of 11,409-foot Lonesome Mountain looming above to the north.

Soon we ascend slopes above the island-studded lake, then traverse alpine tundra, passing above a trio of tarns. Then the trail turns south and shortly crests a ridge at 9,920 feet and 4.5 miles. Enjoy the memorable vista here before descending the far side of the ridge. An array of lofty summits forms the crest of the Beartooths to the north and northeast, including aptly named Castle Rock Mountain (12,408'), Castle Mountain (12,612'), and Beartooth Mountain (12,377').

As we descend the south slopes of the ridge, the verdant slopes and colorful cliffs of Beartooth Butte dominate the view. After reaching a small basin, we rockhop the infant Beartooth Creek, then follow cairns over an obscure stretch of trail that leads first west, then southwest. The trail reappears as we cross a low moraine, and soon we reach a junction and bear left, leaving the Beartooth High Lakes Trail and continuing the descent.

Numerous small streams flow across the trail as we cross the slopes of Beartooth Butte, and soon the tread changes from sand and granite bedrock to limestone, which becomes very slippery when wet. Notice the sudden increase in the richness and the diversity of trailside flora after reaching the limestone slopes. A wealth of colorful blooms decks the trail, including shooting star, buttercup, marsh marigold, alpine laurel, alpine cinquefoil, pussytoes, mountain bluebells, larkspur, and valer-

ian, with yellow columbine growing in the shelter of nearby boulders.

As we descend gentle to moderate grades, Beartooth Lake eventually comes into view. At length we reach the meadow bordering the lake and curve east, quickly rockhopping small Beartooth Creek. Now on level terrain, we stroll east to a shallow, 15-foot-wide ford of a channel of the large creek draining Crane and Beauty lakes. Soon we ford a larger but shallow channel of the creek, and then reach the third, and largest channel. This ford is about 75 feet wide, and the stream bed is filled with small, slippery rocks. The current is gentle, and the waters are about shin-deep.

Beyond the crossings, the trail soon disappears in a soggy, willow-studded meadow, and we slog ahead through mud and water, curving through the spread northeast of the lake. After about 300 yards we reach drier ground, where the trail reappears in the forest fringing the meadow. A brief stint along the meadow's edge leads to the final ford, that of Little Bear Creek, several yards downstream from our first crossing. The creek here is wider than it is above, and the shin-deep waters are filled with slippery rocks.

After fording Little Bear Creek, we cut through willow thickets, then gently ascend the meadow back to the trailhead.

Trip 38
ISLAND LAKE CAMP-GROUND TO BEAUTY LAKE

Distance: 6.0 miles, round trip.
Low/High Elevations: 9,430'/9,680'.
Difficulty: Easy.
Use: Heavy.
Suited For: Dayhike or backpack.
Best Season: Mid-July through early Sept.
Wildlife Viewing: Fair.
Grizzly Bear Danger: Moderate.
Map/Trailhead: 29/34.

Nearest Campgrounds: Island Lake, located at the trailhead; and Beartooth Lake, 4.0 miles, Lake Creek, 11.9 miles, and Crazy Creek, 12.4 miles from the trailhead.

Driving to the Trailhead: Follow U.S. 212 to the signed turnoff to Island Lake Campground. Find this turnoff by driving 25.7 miles east from Cooke City, Montana, and 12.1 miles east from the junction with Wyoming 296; or 36.4 miles southwest from Red Lodge, Montana.

Follow the wide gravel road north from the highway, past Loops A, B, and C in the campground, and turn right where a sign points to TRAILHEAD and LAKE ACCESS. The trailhead parking area lies just above (south of) the boat launch, 0.4 mile from the highway.

Introduction: This fine dayhike is a delightful, easy stroll at timberline, passing six high-elevation lakes, notable for their beauty and their good fishing. And an array of 11,000-foot and 12,000-foot peaks are constantly in view from the start. Whether you are out for a few hours or overnight, this trail offers the greatest rewards for the smallest investment of time and energy of any other trail in the Beartooths.

Virtually every sizable lake and stream en route contain an abundance of brook trout. Absaroka-Beartooth Wilderness regulations apply to backpackers.

Description: From the trailhead at 9,520 feet take the signed Beartooth High Lakes Trail west along the south shore of Island Lake. Good views extend northwest beyond the lake to the broad granite pyramid of 11,409-foot Lonesome Mountain, its flanks rounded and scoured by the vast ice sheet that long ago capped the range. Beyond that peak on the distant skyline are 12,377-foot Beartooth Mountain and 12,612-foot

Beauty Lake

The Beartooth High Lakes Trail leads into the alpine landscape of the Beartooth Mountains

Castle Mountain, both featuring the distinctive unglaciated plateau typical of the highest peaks in the range.

The nearly level lakeside stroll follows the grassy shoreline beneath a scattering of whitebark pines and Engelmann spruces. After 250 yards, rockhop the lake's outlet, Little Bear Creek, then continue along the southwest and west shores. An imperceptible rise beyond Island Lake leads to the meadow-fringed and boulder-studded shores of 9,535-foot Night Lake which like Island Lake harbors abundant brook trout.

The rocky but nearly level trail leads across meadows and among scattered conifers as we follow Night Lake's southwest shoreline. The meadows throughout the trip support a variety of wildflowers, such as alpine groundsel, mountain dandelion, lupine, cinquefoil, pussytoes, one-flower daisy, American bistort, and elephanthead.

Soon we rise gently alongside Night Lake's inlet stream, then skirt the marshy shores of an unnamed tarn. Beyond that tarn is the only noticeable ascent en route, where the rocky trail climbs 50 feet through the timberline forest to a minor watershed divide. From here we descend slightly through meadows, passing between a pair of tarns, then traversing above Lake 9624.

The trail then curves west, enters forest, and descends a moderately steep grade, losing 160 feet of elevation to a junction with the Beauty Lake Trail (see Trip 37) above the northeast shore of Beauty Lake, 3.0 miles out. We can reach its shores by following either trail, west or south, or by walking cross-country over grassy slopes and granite ledges for about 300 yards to the lakeshore. (For more information on Beauty Lake, see Trip 37).

From Beauty Lake, retrace your steps to the trailhead.

Trip 39

BEARTOOTH LOOP NATIONAL RECREATION TRAIL TO LOSEKAMP AND STOCKADE LAKES

Distance: 5.6 miles, round trip.
Low/High Elevations: 9,409'/9,820'.
Difficulty: Moderately easy.
Use: Moderate.
Suited For: Dayhike or backpack.
Best Season: Early July through early Sept.
Wildlife Viewing: Good.
Grizzly Bear Danger: Moderate.
Map/Trailhead: 30/35.
Nearest Campgrounds: Island Lake, 2.6 miles, Beartooth Lake, 6.3 miles, Lake Creek, 15.6 miles, Crazy Creek, 17.0 miles, and Hunter Peak, 19.2 miles from the trailhead.
Driving to the Trailhead: The small trailhead parking area, signed BEARTOOTH LOOP NATIONAL RECREATION TRAIL, HAUSER LAKE TRAILHEAD, lies on the northwest shoulder of U.S. 212. Find the trailhead by driving 14.5 miles northeast from the junction with Wyoming 296, or 4.9 miles southwest from the West Summit of Beartooth Pass.

The trailhead lies along the steady uphill grade above (northeast of) signed Long Lake, 0.7 mile beyond the lake's outlet, and 0.5 mile beyond the signed turnoff for the Morrison 4WD Road.

Introduction: This rewarding trip begins at the highest elevation trailhead covered in this book. The trail leads through flower-filled meadows and groves of timberline forest, passing three scenic, brook-trout-filled lakes resting in high cirques south of Beartooth Pass. Elevation gain is minimal, and most of the trail is easy to follow. The trail lies outside of the Absaroka-Beartooth Wilderness, but mountain bikes are barred anyway.

Description: From the trailhead at 9,790 feet the trail begins as an ill-defined route marked by cairns. We proceed southeast through the tundra, beneath low knolls fringed by gnarled timberline conifers. We rise gently to a minor gap between two knolls, then descend a grassy draw, now on well-defined trail, where Engelmann spruce and whitebark pine begin to appear.

Soon meadow-fringed Hauser Lake comes into view, and the serrated crest of 10,262-foot Sawtooth Mountain rises in the southeastern background. After 1/4-mile the trail bends east and then skirts the north shore of Hauser Lake. Cinquefoil and American bistort grow in abundance in the lakeside meadows here. An easy rockhop crossing of the lake's inlet stream soon follows, and we then ascend gently southeast, passing a small, shallow tarn, and proceed through rock-studded meadows encircled by forested knolls.

After a rockhop of another small stream, we follow a rocky, moderate grade into sub-

alpine forest. The grade abates where we crest a ridge fringed by stunted conifers, and views from here stretch southeast across the far reaches of the Beartooths, where grassy alpine ridges rise above deep canyons and dense forests. Sawtooth Peak and 10,423-foot Tolman Mountain dominate the view. Descend the rocky trail from the ridge and wind among boulders and granite knobs down to an expansive dry meadow, then boulderhop the stream that drains the spread. Alpine ridges near Beartooth Pass loom above the meadow to the north, and the rubbly dome of Tibbs Butte rises on the eastern skyline. An array of wildflowers blankets this broad grassland, including cinquefoil, American bistort, lupine, whorled penstemon, pussytoes, one-flower daisy, and Parry's townsendia.

A moderate grade leads through the meadows to their northeast margin, reenters forest and winds over a minor rise. Proceed gently downhill through small meadows and forest groves to a signed junction, above the west shore of long, narrow Losekamp Lake, at 2.3 miles and 9,539 feet. From here the Beartooth Loop National Recreation Trail (10 miles long) leads north and south, but the south fork is signed as the STOCKADE LAKE TRAIL.

Losekamp Lake

Losekamp Lake lies in a very attractive setting, and some may elect to end the trip here. The lake rests in a broad bowl, its shoreline bordered by flower-filled meadows and ice-polished granite bedrock. A narrow band of timberline forest clings to the lower slopes of 10,673-foot Tibbs Butte, which raises its alpine crown above the eastern shores. Looming over the basin to the north is the splintered summit of 11,029-foot Stockaid Peak, blocking Beartooth Pass and Highway 212 from our view.

Those who choose to continue to Stockade Lake will bear right (south) at the junction, briefly following Losekamp Lake's west shore. Soon you begin descending a grassy draw, following the lake's outlet stream down-canyon. After strolling downhill for 0.4 mile from the junction, you reach a ford of the stream. Avoid the ford by following a well-worn trail beside the stream for another 250 yards down to the shores of Stockade Lake, at 2.8 miles and 9,409 feet.

This beautiful lake lies in an open bowl, with grassy slopes rising above the east shore and low granite bluffs rising to the west. Good campsites can be found among slabs and boulders west of the lake, and they are sheltered by a scattering of Engelmann spruce and whitebark pine.

From Stockade Lake, retrace the scenic route back to the trailhead.

Trip 40

ROCK CREEK TO GLACIER LAKE

Distance: 3.2 miles, round trip.
Low/High Elevations: 8,700'/9,920'.
Difficulty: Strenuous.
Use: Moderate.
Suited For: Dayhike or backpack.
Best Season: Mid-July through early September.
Wildlife Viewing: Fair.
Grizzly Bear Danger: Low.
Map/Trailhead: 31/36.

Nearest Campgrounds: M-K, 5.9 miles, Limber Pine, 7.7 miles, Greenough Lake, 7.8 miles, and Parkside, 8.3 miles from the trailhead.

Driving to the Trailhead: Follow U.S. 212, northeast down the switchbacks for 18.6 miles from the West Summit of Beartooth Pass, or 10.6 miles southwest from Red Lodge to the signed turnoff for Rock Creek Road, Forest Road 421.

Follow paved Rock Creek Road west, passing the signed turnoffs to Parkside Campground at 0.4 mile, Greenough Lake Campground at 0.9 mile, and Limber Pine Campground at 1.0 mile. Immediately beyond Limber Pine Campground, the pavement ends and the road forks; the sign points up the left fork to M-K Campground and Glacier Lake Trail.

Turn left here and follow the rough gravel road up the deep canyon of Rock Creek. After 1.8 miles from the end of the pavement, you pass the entrance to M-K Campground. The road ahead deteriorates, becoming very rough, rocky, and potholed. A high-clearance vehicle is advised, though many make the drive in passenger cars.

After another rough, slow, 5.9 miles (8.7 miles from the highway), you reach the trailhead parking area at the roadend. Toilets are located here, and numerous undeveloped camping areas can be found throughout Rock Creek canyon.

Introduction: Large Glacier Lake, visible from the highway switchbacks east of the West Summit of Beartooth Pass, lies in a cliff-rimmed cirque at the head of Rock Creek, on the north slopes of the Beartooth Mountains. The trail to this often-windy lake is short, but the rocky tread and steep grades make the trip arduous.

Large brook trout inhabit the lake's deep, cold waters, but as in most high country lakes, fishing success is unpredictable. Emerald Lake, south of Glacier Lake, supports a population of cutthroat trout. That lake and the south shores of Glacier Lake lie in Wyoming, but much of Glacier lies within Montana.

Description: The trail, open to foot traffic only, begins as an old road at 8,700 feet. After 100 yards the route narrows to a foot trail. A moderate ascent via the rocky trail follows, climbing the slopes of a broad, rockbound draw.

Numerous small streams cascade down the slopes, but all are bridged by culverts. A forest fire started by a troop of Boy Scouts in the 1940s consumed much of the scant timberline forest here in upper Rock Creek canyon, and we ascend among gray and sunburnished snags. Small whitebark and lodgepole pines and subalpine firs are slowly reclaiming the rocky terrain. This stretch of the trail is hot and shadeless, but the lack of forest cover affords inspiring views of towering canyon walls and alpine plateaus.

A variety of colorful wildflowers helps divert our attention from the relentless grind, including mountain bluebells, whorled penstemon, shrub cinquefoil, fireweed, Indian paintbrush, and yarrow.

At 0.5 mile we reach a log footbridge spanning the small stream that cascades down the draw. Despite its decrepit appearance, the bridge is sturdy and safe. Beyond the bridge, more switchbacks lead into a west-trending draw where green trees form a scattered timberline forest.

The ascent finally ends at 9,920 feet, 1.2 miles from the trailhead, on the shoulder of a broad granite dome. Here trees are reduced to krummholz, growing in shrub-like mats that reach five feet above the ground at most. The rocky trail descends west from the dome toward presently visible Glacier Lake. Approaching the lake, we dip into a minor draw that holds snow until late summer in some years. A brief ascent out of the draw leads to the shores of massive Glacier Lake at 1.6 miles. The concrete dam at its outlet was constructed in 1937 by Rock Creek irrigators to ensure a steady flow of irrigation water throughout the dry summer months.

Glacier is a large (175 acres), spectacular lake, embraced by boulder fields and knobs of ice-polished granite. Canyon walls soar skyward as much as 2,000 feet above the lake to the rims of the alpine plateaus above. Only scattered groves of gnarled, wind-flagged spruces and whitebark pines dot the bedrock around the lake.

Glacier Lake

There are few camping areas above Glacier's shores, but a trail beyond the shallow ford of the lake's outlet curves around the east shore, then leads southeast past a smaller lake, and ends at Emerald Lake after 0.75 mile. Better campsites can be found in the tree-fringed tundra along the course of that trail.

From Glacier Lake, return the way you came.

Trip 41

BASIN LAKES NATIONAL RECREATION TRAIL

Distance: 7.6 miles, round trip.
Low/High Elevations: 6,902'/8,960'.
Difficulty: Moderately strenuous.
Use: Moderate.
Suited For: Dayhike or backpack.
Best Season: Early July through early September.
Wildlife Viewing: Fair.
Grizzly Bear Danger: Low.
Map/Trailhead: 32/37.
Nearest Campgrounds: Basin, 0.1 mile, and Cascade, 3.5 miles from the trailhead.
Driving to the Trailhead: From U.S. 212, near the south end of Red Lodge, `0.2 mile north of the Beartooth District Ranger Station, turn west where a prominent sign points to WEST FORK ROAD 71, and RED LODGE MOUNTAIN SKI AREA.

Follow this good paved road west through the outskirts of Red Lodge and into West Fork Rock Creek canyon. After 2.8 miles, bear left onto West Fork Road 71, signed for Basin and Cascade campgrounds. After another 4.3 miles, you reach the signed turnoff to BASIN LAKES TRAILHEAD. Turn left here and proceed 200 yards to the spacious trailhead parking area. Toilets are located at the trailhead.

Basin Campground lies 0.1 mile west of the trailhead turnoff.
Introduction: The trail to Basin Creek Lakes, open to foot traffic only, ascends through

heavy forest from West Fork Rock Creek canyon to a broad cirque on the flanks of Silver Run Plateau. En route you pass remnants of logging roads and dilapidated cabins, evidence of horse logging activity dating back to the turn of the 20th century. Logging operations in Basin Creek supplied timbers to underground coal mines in the Red Lodge area.

Lower Basin Creek Lake, at 8,380 feet, lies 2.7 miles from the trailhead, and is a popular hike with visitors staying in nearby Basin Campground. Although the trail is moderately steep, it is frequently used by families with small children. The lower lake offers fair fishing for brook trout, but the upper lake is more productive, and anglers often land brookies to 12 inches.

Description: From the trailhead at 6,902 feet, follow the wide, rocky and gravelly trail on a southeast course through open lodgepole-pine forest, shortly approaching the banks of cascading Basin Creek. Here the trail curves southwest, briefly following the brawling creek upstream to the mouth of a rugged gorge.

Upper Basin Creek Lake

Now ascend west, away from the creek, via a switchback on moderately open slopes where blown-down trees outnumber standing ones and the trail is decked with shrubby mountain alders and red raspberry bushes. Soon the trail bends south, leading back into the confines of Basin Creek canyon on a gentle grade.

Now you cross a channel of the creek via a log footbridge, then continue the ascent through a more open part of the canyon. At 1.2 miles, begin a moderately steep ascent away from the canyon, heading southwest through the forest. The grade soon abates and climbs a minor draw. Small lodgepole pines clothe the draw, and an old horse logging road, deeply cut by years of use, parallels the trail. Shortly the trail and the logging road coalesce, and you then follow the wide path toward the head of the draw. At length the trail curves north, ascends away from the draw, and becomes smooth and carpeted with pine needles.

At 1.8 miles, curve south around the nose of a minor ridge, and then enter a broad, densely forested basin. Occasional openings between the trees reveal glimpses of the alpine rim of Silver Run Plateau on the southwest skyline. The steady ascent resumes shortly after you enter the basin, and soon curves around a roofless cabin, then bridges a stream in a small meadow studded with rotting stumps. Pass the remains of two other cabins, then continue ascending through a heavy forest of small lodgepole pines. Pass several swaths cutting through the forest to the left and right, marking the paths of skid trails about one hundred years old.

At length you crest a rock-strewn moraine and curve south, leaving the logging road and proceeding on trail. The trail skirts the east shore of lower Basin Creek Lake, at 8,380 feet and 2.7 miles, a shallow tarn covered with pond lilies in late summer. Beyond the lake continue ascending through a viewless pine forest. Minor switchbacks lead southwest up the basin and, near the head of the ascent, we skirt a small tarn, where we obtain a brief view of the distant Pryor Mountains to the east, framed by the forested walls of West Fork Rock Creek canyon.

Beyond the tarn the trees become increasingly stunted toward the upper lake. Eventually a slight downhill grade on the slopes of a low moraine brings us to the north shore of beautiful upper Basin Creek Lake, at 8,960 feet, 3.8 miles from the trailhead.

A dense forest of timberline trees surrounds the slopes above the lake, contrasting with the barren cliffbound cirque headwall and the rocky alpine arms of Silver Run Plateau that embrace the basin. Good, sheltered campsites can be found above the west, north, and northeast shores.

During winter when the lake is a frozen and snowbound, the prevailing southwesterly winds drift snow against the low moraine north of the lake. There the trees have been reduced to a ground-hugging mat of krummholz that contrasts with the tall, straight trees growing in more sheltered parts of the basin.

From Basin Creek Lakes, retrace your steps back to the trailhead.

Trip 42

WEST FORK ROCK CREEK TO TIMBERLINE LAKE

Distance: 8.8 miles, round trip.
Low/High Elevations: 7,600'/9,619'.
Difficulty: Moderately strenuous.
Use: Moderate.
Suited For: Dayhike or backpack.
Best Season: Mid-July through early Sept.
Wildlife Viewing: Fair.
Grizzly Bear Danger: Low.
Map/Trailhead: 33/38.
Nearest Campgrounds: Cascade, 0.75 mile, and Basin, 4.1 miles from the trailhead.
Driving to the Trailhead: Follow the driving directions for Trip 41 to the turnoff to Basin Lakes Trailhead, and continue west up West Fork Road 71. You pass the turnoff to Basin Campground after 0.1 mile (7.2 miles

from Red Lodge), and reach the end of the pavement 0.1 mile farther.

The road ahead is a good gravel road, occasionally narrow and winding with rough and rocky stretches. You pass Cascade Campground 3.2 miles from the end of the pavement (10.5 miles from Red Lodge), and after another 0.75 mile, 300 yards west of a bridge spanning the West Fork, you reach the signed turnoff to Timberline Lake Trailhead. Turn left and go 25 yards to the parking area, where there are toilets and an information sign.

There are very few undeveloped camping areas along West Fork Rock Creek. Overnight visitors are largely restricted to staying in one of the two campgrounds here.

Introduction: Many veteran Beartooth hikers consider Timberline Lake to be the most beautiful lake in the range. True to its name, this gem lies at timberline, resting in a deep cirque beneath the flanks of 12,500-foot Silver Run Peak. Although the trail to the lake gains considerable elevation—over 2,000 feet— the grade is rarely steep and the ascent is steady but gradual. The trail is well-defined and easy to follow, but the tread is rocky at times.

This trip visits both Timberline Lake and Lake Gertrude. The lakes offer many good, scenic campsites, and they support an abundance of fat brook trout. Absaroka-Beartooth Wilderness regulations apply along this trail.

Description: From the trailhead at 7,600 feet follow the trail southwest on a gentle, traversing ascent. At first these north-facing slopes are clothed in spindly lodgepole pines, but soon we enter a shady forest.

The tread is often rocky as we wind into and out of numerous minor draws until, at 0.5 mile, we curve southeast around a switchback, then rise on forested slopes at a steady, moderate grade. At 1.1 miles the trail bends southwest, the grade abates, and we begin a protracted traverse high above the canyon of Timberline Creek. The trees on these slopes are scattered enough to allow occasional glimpses to the alpine heights of Silver Run Plateau on the southern skyline.

At 8,918 feet, 2.6 miles from the trailhead, we reach a signed junction with the south-

Timberline Lake

bound Beartrack Trail, alongside the tumbling waters of Timberline Creek. That trail leads 3.0 miles to the 10,700-foot crest of Silver Run Plateau.

Bear right at the junction, and begin another steady, moderate ascent through an open forest of increasingly stunted trees. At 3.7 miles, we reach a crossing of rock-strewn Timberline Creek, spanned by footlogs. Beyond the crossing proceed on a more gradual uphill grade, passing through groves of timberline forest, and crossing meadows enlivened by the blooms of groundsel, mountain dandelion, bracted lousewort, pussytoes, Indian paintbrush, subalpine daisy, hairy arnica, and mountain bluebells.

At 3.9 miles from the trailhead pass above Lake Gertrude, a meadow-bordered tarn at 9,520-feet. Soon the trail leads down to the south shore of the pretty lake, where we cross two channels of its inlet stream via footlogs. A few good campsites lie in groves of spruce and whitebark pine several yards south of the crossings.

The trail goes up the inlet, then shortly curves west away from the stream and ascends a short but steep grade to a grassy saddle. From there we quickly descend to the outlet of beautiful Timberline Lake at 9,619 feet, 4.4 miles from the trailhead.

This timberline gem rests on the floor of a broad cirque, embraced by the alpine arms of Silver Run Plateau. To the southwest, the plateau reaches its apex at 12,500-foot Silver Run Peak, featuring a bold granite tower on its northeast face. Below the peak lies a mile-long, 300-acre glacier, but part of that icefield is blocked from view by the 500-foot walls of the prominent dome of Peak 10359, jutting above the southwest shore of the lake.

A scattering of gnarled spruces and whitebark pines dots the rocky slopes around the lake where backpackers will find many good sheltered campsites. A trail of use follows the south shore, offering access to campsites and fishing.

After enjoying this memorable lake, return the way you came.

Chapter Five

EAST OF YELLOWSTONE—FROM CODY TO THE EAST ENTRANCE

Introduction

The wild and rugged Absaroka Range is a land of high plateaus, broad peaks, splintered crags, long and deep canyons, vast forests, and rich meadows. The distant high country of the range can be viewed from highways in Greater Yellowstone, but to reach the range's remote basins or the high passes, you must, with few exceptions, walk for days on rugged, seldom-used trails. The Absarokas remain the wildest and most inaccessible wilderness in Greater Yellowstone.

The range is made up of volcanic debris. Its flanks show the distinct layering of lava flows and ash falls in varying shades of brown and gray. Spectacular pinnacles project from slopes and crown ridges where softer rock layers have been stripped away by erosion, leaving these more resistant rocks standing in isolation. The range's high country is the deeply dissected remains of a once vast volcanic plateau.

Between the edge of Wyoming's high desert at Cody and the East Entrance to Yellowstone National Park, U.S. Highway 14/16/20 follows the canyon of North Fork Shoshone River deep into the Absaroka Range. Steeped in history and endowed with an array of erosional forms unmatched in Greater Yellowstone, the East Entrance Highway is a unique and breathtaking approach to Yellowstone. President Theodore Roosevelt called this road "the most beautiful 50 miles in America."

Although volcanic rocks are common around Yellowstone National Park, only in the North Fork canyon have these rocks been carved into such a striking array of reddish-brown erosional forms. The rock formations here are reminiscent of those in Bryce Canyon National Park in Utah, though the North Fork's rocks lack Bryce's varied colors. The descriptive names applied to some of the North Fork's rocks—Camel Rock, Anvil Rock, Holy City, Goose Rock, Elephant Head Rock, Chimney Rock, The Palisades—suggest some of the fantastic rock formations that make the canyon so unusual.

The North Fork is dry country lying in the rain shadow of the Yellowstone plateau and the Absaroka Range. Vegetation here is sparse and widely scattered. The lower half of the canyon is desert-like in appearance, where the rocky slopes, cliffs, and pinnacles are dotted with drought-tolerant limber pines and Rocky Mountain junipers. The upper reaches of the canyon, west of Eagle Creek Campground, are more typical of a mountain canyon, where dense forests of pine, spruce, and fir clothe the slopes that rise to tall ridges, and few rock outcrops are visible.

The East Entrance Highway offers a wealth of recreational opportunities. The highway closely follows the large North Fork, and numerous dirt spur roads branch off to undeveloped picnic sites and fishing access sites along the river, most of them in pleasant stands of conifers or in groves of tall cottonwoods.

Ten national forest campgrounds, offering a total of 187 campsites, are located at intervals along the highway, between the Shoshone National Forest and Yellowstone National Park boundaries. The campgrounds range from open, low-elevation sites in cottonwood groves to high elevation sites in conifer forests. Most campgrounds are close to the broad waters of the North Fork.

Camping within 0.5 mile of the highway in Shoshone National Forest is prohibited, so there are no undeveloped camping areas in the canyon. Visitors must stay overnight in one of the ten campgrounds. Plan on arriving as early as possible, since most campgrounds fill by late afternoon or early evening during peak season (late July through mid-August).

Three developed picnic areas are located in the North Fork canyon, all of them along the banks of the river in settings as varied as those of the campgrounds. Nine trailheads are located just off the highway, and diverse trails offer access into the wild and remote interior of the Absaroka Range. North of the highway lies the 350,538-acre North Absaroka Wilderness, and to the south is the 704,000-acre Washakie Wilderness (pronounced Wash-uh-kee).

With so much wild country surrounding the North Fork, and with Yellowstone National Park to the west, it is not surprising that the North Fork is home to a variety of large mammals. Large elk herds gather in the grasslands of the lower canyon during winter, and in summer they range throughout the high meadows and alpine tundra in the mountains above. Wapiti Valley, near the Wapiti Ranger Station in the lower reaches of the canyon, was named for the large elk herds ("wapiti" is a Native name meaning elk) that thrive here.

Mule deer dwell throughout the canyon, and moose are commonly observed in shallow ponds and among willow thickets. Grizzly bears also range throughout the Absarokas, which are considered to be the best grizzly habitat in Greater Yellowstone. Special food storage regulations are in effect throughout the canyon and are posted at campgrounds.

Visitors who prefer to sleep indoors in the North Fork have 15 lodges to choose from. Contact the Cody Chamber of Commerce for more information. Most lodges offer meals, lodging, guided trail rides, and horses for hire.

Points of Interest

WAPITI RANGER STATION

In March 1891 President Benjamin Harrison designated the 1.25-million-acre Yellowstone National Park Timberland Reserve along the eastern and southern boundaries of the Park. These mountainous lands were destined to become the first areas within the national forest system— Teton National Forest to the south, and Shoshone National Forest to the east.

To administer the newly designated forest reserve, rangers were hired and a log ranger station was built in Wapiti Valley between 1903 and 1905. The Wapiti Ranger Station, the first national forest ranger station, is still in use today, and it stands just north of the highway between Big Game and Wapiti campgrounds. A trailer at the site houses interpretive displays, offering an informative stop on your travels through the North Fork.

MUMMY CAVE

About 0.2 mile east of Rex Hale Campground, just above the highway at a prominent horseshoe bend in the canyon, lies a small, fenced-off alcove in the face of a low cliff.

The cave entrance has been filled with earth, but in 1962, archeologists excavated the site, which then extended about 40 feet into the wall of the cliff. Not only did they uncover the well-preserved remains of a man who died 1,300 years ago, but they also unearthed layers representing 38 different human occupations of the cave, dating back to 7280 B.C. Artifacts discovered in the cave included bone pipes, chipped stone knives and scrapers, and basketry. Fragments of the remains of birds, marmots, bighorn sheep, and horses were also found.

PAHASKA TEPEE

William F. "Buffalo Bill" Cody left an indelible mark on Western history both in fact and in myth. From his exploits as a Pony Express rider and a buffalo hunter, and his legendary Wild West Show, to his role as co-founder of the town that bears his name, Buffalo Bill epitomizes the "taming" of the West.

Cody, who was given the name Pahaska ("long hair") by the Sioux, loved the

River country. In 1901 he built a log hunting lodge—Pahaska Tepee—near the East Entrance to Yellowstone National Park. Cody entertained many notable dignitaries at his lodge, including the King of Monaco, whom Cody guided on a hunting trip along the Pahaska-Sunlight Trail in 1913.

The original lodge, listed on the National Register of Historic Places, still stands among newer buildings 2.2 miles east of the Park, and can be seen from the Pahaska-Sunlight Trailhead (see Trip 46).

Access and Services

Access to the trails and campgrounds covered in this chapter is provided by U.S. 14/16/20, which extends 50.8 miles from Cody, Wyoming, to the East Entrance to Yellowstone National Park.

Cody, Wyoming (5,016'), offers a full complement of services and attractions that make the town as much a destination as it is a resupply point. Restaurants, groceries, camping and recreation supplies, gas, auto and RV repair and towing, and numerous motels are available.

While you are in Cody, consider stopping at the four-museum complex of the Buffalo Bill Historical Center. The center includes the Whitney Gallery of Western Art; the Buffalo Bill Museum (featuring one of the finest collections of Western artifacts and displays); the Winchester Museum (featuring the most complete collection of firearms in the world); and the Plains Indian Museum.

Cody also features Old Trail Town, a collection of cabins and historic buildings; the Cody Wildlife Exhibit; the Irma Hotel, which Bill Cody built in 1902 and named for his daughter (listed on the National Register of Historic Places); and nightly rodeo exhibitions from June through August.

West of Cody, above the shores of Buffalo Bill Reservoir, are two spacious campgrounds within Buffalo Bill State Park. Between the state park and the national forest boundary are numerous lodges (reservations required, contact Cody Chamber of Commerce for more information). Pahaska Tepee Lodge, located 2.2 miles from Yellowstone's East Entrance, is the last place to refuel your car before entering the Park.

For further information on accommodations and services, contact the chamber of commerce:

Cody Chamber of Commerce
836 Sheridan Avenue
Cody, WY 82414
(307) 587-2297

Campgrounds

50 • BIG GAME (5,900')

Location. In North Fork Shoshone River canyon, Absaroka Range, just north of U.S. 14/16/20, 26.7 miles west of Cody and 24.1 miles east of the East Entrance to Yellowstone Park; Shoshone National Forest, Wapiti Ranger District.

Facilities. 17 camping units (two are pull-through sites), tables, fire pits with grills, water, toilets, bear-resistant food storage boxes, bear-resistant garbage containers; paved access road and gravel campsite spurs; maximum trailer length of 32 feet; a fee is charged.

Dates Usually Open. June 1 through September 30.

The Setting. This scenic low elevation campground lies in an open stand of narrowleaf cottonwood above the south banks of North Fork Shoshone River. Striking views extend north from the campground to brown volcanic cliffs and pinnacles.

(Note: this campground is signed BIG GAME TRAILER PARK, though it is open to visitors for tent camping as well.)

51 • WAPITI (5,950')

Location. In North Fork Shoshone River canyon, Absaroka Range, just north of U.S. 14/16/20, 27.6 miles west of Cody, Wyoming, and 23.2 miles east of the East Entrance to Yellowstone National Park; Shoshone National Forest, Wapiti Ranger District.

Facilities. 41 camping units, tables, fire pits with grills, water, toilets, bear-resistant food storage boxes, bear-resistant garbage containers; paved access road and gravel campsite spurs; maximum trailer length of 22 feet; a fee is charged.

Dates Usually Open. June 1 through September 30.

The Setting. This pleasant wooded campground lies just above the south banks of North Fork Shoshone River. Sites are partly shaded by an open forest of Rocky Mountain juniper, limber pine, and narrowleaf and black cottonwood. Good views reach north from the campground to a low ridge of reddish-brown volcanic rock, the slopes broken by cliffs and pinnacles.

52 • ELK FORK (5,960')

Location. In North Fork Shoshone River canyon, Absaroka Range, just south of U.S. 14/16/20, 27.8 miles west of Cody and 23.0 miles east of the East Entrance to Yellowstone National Park; Shoshone National Forest, Wapiti Ranger District.

Facilities. 13 camping units, tables, fire pits with grills, water, toilets, bear-resistant food storage boxes, bear-resistant garbage containers; paved access road and gravel campsite spurs; maximum trailer length of 22 feet; a fee is charged.

Dates Usually Open. June 1 through September 30.

The Setting. This pleasant, open campground lies along a 0.3-mile spur road, just south of North Fork Shoshone River canyon, above the east banks of wide and shallow Elk Fork, a North Fork tributary. The sites are shaded by a canopy of black cottonwood and a scattering of Rocky Mountain juniper. Views from the campground reach south up the Elk Fork to alpine peaks rising above the canyon's head, and to the rugged slopes and pinnacles that jut above the campground. Three natural arches can be seen on the volcanic ridges above the campground.

A trailhead parking area is at the end of the road at the south end of the campground (see Trip 43).

53 • CLEARWATER (6,000')

Location. In North Fork Shoshone River canyon, Absaroka Range, just south of U.S.

14/16/20, 30.0 miles west of Cody and 20.8 miles east of the East Entrance to Yellowstone National Park; Shoshone National Forest, Wapiti Ranger District.

Facilities. 7 camping units with a common parking area, (plus a large group camping area, reservable through the Wapiti Ranger District, and a group picnic site), tables, fire pits with grills, water, toilets, bear-resistant food storage boxes, bear-resistant garbage containers; paved access road; restricted access for trailers in common parking area; a fee is charged.

Dates Usually Open. June 1 through September 30.

The Setting. This open campground, shaded by a scattering of Douglas-firs and Rocky Mountain junipers, lies just north of the North Fork. Fine views reach north from the campground to sparsely forested volcanic slopes and ridges, punctuated by a myriad of pinnacles.

54 • REX HALE (6,150')

Location. In North Fork Shoshone River canyon, Absaroka Range, just south of U.S. 14/16/20, 34.6 miles west of Cody and 16.2 miles east of the East Entrance to Yellowstone National Park; Shoshone National Forest, Wapiti Ranger District.

Facilities. 8 camping units, tables, fire pits with grills, water, toilets, bear-resistant food storage boxes, bear-resistant garbage containers; paved access road and gravel campsite spurs; maximum trailer length of 16 feet; a fee is charged.

Dates Usually Open. June 1 through September 30.

The Setting. This small, scenic campground lies just above North Fork Shoshone River, in an open stand of Rocky Mountain juniper and Douglas-fir. Good views from the campground reach north and east to rugged volcanic cliffs and pinnacles.

55 • NEWTON CREEK (6,239')

Location. In North Fork Shoshone River canyon, Absaroka Range, just south of U.S. Highway 14/16/20, 36.0 miles west of Cody, Wyoming, and 14.8 miles east of the

East Entrance to Yellowstone National Park; Shoshone National Forest, Wapiti Ranger District.

Facilities. 31 camping units, tables, fire pits with grills, water, toilets, bear-resistant food storage boxes, bear-resistant garbage containers; maximum trailer length of 22 feet; a fee is charged.

Dates Usually Open. June 1 through September 30.

The Setting. This shady campground lies on a bench just above North Fork Shoshone River. A canopy of Douglas-fir shades the sites but obscures views of the rugged canyon walls. Small Newton Creek trickles through the center of the campground.

56 • EAGLE CREEK (6,480')

Location. In North Fork Shoshone River canyon, Absaroka Range, just south of U.S. 14/16/20, 43.5 miles west of Cody and 7.3 miles east of the East Entrance to Yellowstone National Park; Shoshone National Forest, Wapiti Ranger District.

Facilities. 20 camping units, tables, fire pits with grills, water, toilets, bear-resistant food storage boxes, bear-resistant garbage containers; maximum trailer length of 22 feet; a fee is charged.

Dates Usually Open. June 1 through September 30.

The Setting. This campground lies in a shady forest of Douglas-fir and lodgepole pine, on a bench just above North Fork Shoshone River. Forest-covered slopes rise north and south of the campground; few pinnacles are seen here in the upper reaches of the canyon. Views reach to the southwest up the canyon of Eagle Creek, where charred snags are massed on skyline ridges—evidence of the Mink Creek Fire of 1988, which began in the southeast corner of Yellowstone National Park and spread northeast into the Shoshone National Forest.

From the center of the campground, a footbridge spans the North Fork, offering access to a group of summer cabins. A trail leads south for 150 yards from the footbridge, passing between the two westernmost cabins, to join the Eagle Creek Trail,

which follows the deep canyon of Eagle Creek into the Washakie Wilderness.

57 • SLEEPING GIANT (6,600')

Location. In North Fork Shoshone River canyon, Absaroka Range, just south of U.S. 14/16/20, 46.5 miles west of Cody and 4.3 miles east of the East Entrance to Yellowstone National Park; Shoshone National Forest, Wapiti Ranger District.

Facilities. 6 camping units, tables, fire pits with grills, water, toilets, bear-resistant food storage boxes, bear-resistant garbage containers; maximum trailer length of 22 feet; a fee is charged.

Dates Usually Open. June 15 through September 30.

The Setting. This is the smallest campground in the North Fork. Its sites are shaded by a forest of scattered lodgepole pines, set on a bench just above the river. Good views reach north and south to forested ridges, and northwest to the bold crag of 10,267-foot Cody Peak.

58 • THREE MILE (6,640')

Location. In North Fork Shoshone River canyon, Absaroka Range, just south of U.S. Highway 14/16/20, 47.6 miles west of Cody, Wyoming, and 3.2 miles east of the East Entrance to Yellowstone National Park; Shoshone National Forest, Wapiti Ranger District.

Facilities. 20 camping units, tables, fire pits with grills, water, toilets, bear-resistant food storage boxes, bear-resistant garbage containers; maximum trailer length of 22 feet; a fee is charged.

Dates Usually Open. June 15 through September 30.

The Setting. This pleasant campground lies on a bench just above the North Fork. An open forest of lodgepole pine shades the campsites.

59 • PAHASKA (6,680')

Location. In Middle Creek canyon, Absaroka Range, just south of U.S. 14/16/20, 48.7 miles west of Cody and 2.1 miles east of the East Entrance to Yellowstone National Park;

Shoshone National Forest, Wapiti Ranger District.

Facilities. 24 camping units, tables, fire pits with grills, water, toilets, bear-resistant food storage boxes, bear-resistant garbage containers; maximum trailer length of 22 feet; a fee is charged.

Dates Usually Open. June 15 through September 30.

The Setting. This campground lies on a bench just north of wide, shallow Middle Creek, a tributary of North Fork Shoshone River. A forest of lodgepole pine and Engelmann spruce casts ample shade over most sites in the campground. The historic Pahaska Tepee lodge (Buffalo Bill Cody's original hunting lodge) lies within a few minutes walking distance, northeast of the campground.

For Further Information

For further information regarding Trips 43-46 and Campgrounds 50-59, contact:

Shoshone National Forest
Wapiti Ranger District
203 A Yellowstone Ave.
P.O. Box 1840
Cody, WY 82414
(307) 527-6921

Wilderness Regulations

Although none of the trail trips covered in this chapter are recommended for backpacking, Trips 43 and 46 offer backcountry campsites. Only Trip 46 lies in a wilderness area (North Absaroka), but hikers may also choose to enter the Washakie Wilderness. If you intend to backpack in either of these areas, be sure to follow the regulations listed below.

NORTH ABSAROKA AND WASHAKIE WILDERNESS AREAS

1. Camping is not allowed within 50 feet of Forest Service system trails (trails shown on the Shoshone National Forest map.
2. Shortcutting switchbacks is prohibited.

3. Maximum group size is 20.
4. Use of motorized and mechanized equipment, including bicycles, is prohibited.
5. Maximum length of stay at a single location is 14 consecutive days.
6. Damaging or removing any natural feature is prohibited.
7. Digging in, excavating, disturbing, injuring, destroying, removing, or in any way damaging any paleontological, prehistoric, historic, or archeological structure, resource, site, or artifact is prohibited.

Trip 43
ELK FORK CAMPGROUND TO ELK FORK

Distance: 6.2 miles, round trip.
Low/High Elevations: 6,000'/6,320'.
Difficulty: Easy.
Use: Low.
Suited For: Dayhike or mountain bike trip.
Best Season: Late May through September.
Wildlife Viewing: Good.
Grizzly Bear Danger: Moderate.
Map/Trailhead: 34/39.
Nearest Campgrounds: Elk Fork, located at the trailhead; and Wapiti, 0.2 mile, Big Game, 1.1 miles, Clearwater, 2.2 miles, Rex Hale, 6.8 miles, Newton Creek, 8.2 miles, Eagle Creek, 15.7 miles, Sleeping Giant, 18.7 miles, Three Mile, 19.8 miles, and Pahaska, 20.9 miles.
Driving to the Trailhead: Follow U.S. 14/16/20 for 27.8 miles west from Cody, Wyoming, or 23.0 miles east from the East Entrance to Yellowstone National Park, then turn south into Elk Fork Campground. The trailhead parking area is located at the south end of the campground, 0.3 mile off the highway. Toilets and water are available at the campground.
Introduction: Large Elk Fork creek is a major tributary of North Fork Shoshone River. Its broad valley stretches south from the confluence with the North Fork for 20 miles to

the birthplace of its waters, on the flanks of the 11,000-foot peaks of the Absaroka Range crest. This aptly named valley provides excellent habitat for large elk herds, which summer in high meadows and alpine tundra in the headwaters, and winter in the broad grasslands of the lower valley.

This fine dayhike explores the lower reaches of Elk Fork valley, passing among grassy hills flanked by rugged slopes and ridges of intricately eroded volcanic rock. The openness of the terrain in the valley affords sweeping panoramas of 11,000-foot and 12,000-foot volcanic peaks and buttes. The trail is smooth throughout the trip, and involves minimal elevation gain.

Mountain bikers can follow the trail 6.0 miles to the boundary of the Washakie Wilderness. Only the first 3.1 miles are recommended for a leisurely dayhike; the remaining distance to the Wilderness boundary involves four fords of the deep, swift waters of Elk Fork.

Description: From the 6,000-foot trailhead at the south end of Elk Fork Campground, walk south up the road several yards to a Washakie Wilderness information sign adjacent to the horse corrals. Avoid the road that branches right here; instead follow the trail south past the sign.

The first 0.3 mile of the trail traverses the east slopes of the valley above Elk Fork, crossing grassy slopes dotted with Rocky Mountain juniper, limber pine, and Douglas-fir. The open woodland allows fine views of the rugged canyon walls, and observant hikers may notice two small natural arches on the ridge to the west.

After 0.3 mile, jump across small Grace Creek in a Douglas-fir grove, then quickly ascend to the shoulder of a minor ridge, where the lower Elk Fork valley spreads out before you. Tall black cottonwoods border large, meandering Elk Fork in the valley below. Slopes carpeted in grass and studded with sagebrush rise from the valley floor. Higher up the valley slopes are forests of pine, spruce, and fir.

The trail ahead follows a mildly undulating course over rolling hills cut by shallow draws. The grassy slopes are open, dotted here and there with sagebrush and rabbitbrush. The west walls of the valley display a variety of erosional forms in the reddish-brown and gray volcanic rocks. Good views reach up the valley to the square-edged northeast ridge of Clayton Mountain, its flat crest fringed with tall conifers and bounded by tall cliffs. Over-the-shoulder views, which we will enjoy to the best advantage on the return trip, stretch across the canyon of North Fork Shoshone River to extensive alpine plateaus crowned by blocky, 12,000-foot towers.

The valley becomes more confined at 2.7 miles, and views of conical alpine sum-

High plateaus of the Absaroka Range are framed by lower Elk Fork valley

mits far up the valley begin to unfold. Here the trail bends southeast into a juniper-clad draw, then briefly ascends beyond the draw to an unsigned junction, at 6,320 feet and 2.8 miles, with a left-branching trail leading up Cougar Creek Canyon to the southeast.

Bear right, staying on the well-defined trail, and shortly reach cottonwood-bordered Cougar Creek. The creek is shallow, but you must wade across the ankle-deep, 15-foot-wide waters. Beyond Cougar Creek, the valley becomes increasingly confined, and the Elk Fork and our trail are soon funneled between broken slopes of volcanic rocks. You now descend gently to a grassy bench just above the alder-lined waters of Elk Fork.

At 3.1 miles, the trail crosses Elk Fork at a wide, swift, rock-strewn ford. The wooded bench just before the ford offers a convenient, peaceful place to end the trip. Here, just above the banks of Elk Fork, the leaves of black cottonwoods flutter in the slightest breeze, and a scattering of junipers and Douglas-firs cast scant but welcome shade.

From the crossing, retrace your steps to the trailhead.

Trip 44
CLEARWATER CREEK

Distance: 2.2 miles, round trip.
Low/High Elevations: 6,040'/6,200'.
Difficulty: Easy.
Use: Low.
Suited For: Dayhike or mountain bike trip.
Best Season: Late May through September.
Wildlife Viewing: Good.
Grizzly Bear Danger: Moderate.
Map/Trailhead: 34/40.
Nearest Campgrounds: Clearwater, 0.1 mile, Elk Fork, 2.3 miles, Wapiti, 2.5 miles, Big Game, 3.4 miles, Rex Hale, 4.5 miles, Newton Creek, 5.9 miles, Eagle Creek, 13.4 miles,

Sleeping Giant, 16.4 miles, Three Mile, 17.5 miles, and Pahaska, 18.6 miles from the trailhead.
Driving to the Trailhead: Follow U.S. 14/16/20 for 30.1 miles west from Cody or 20.7 miles east from the East Entrance to Yellowstone National Park, to a CLEARWATER TRAIL sign, located on the north side of the highway. Turn here and follow the narrow dirt road for 100 yards to the small trailhead parking area.
Introduction: This short trip is a good leg-stretcher for travelers heading to or from Yellowstone's East Entrance. The trip offers a sampling of the varied and spectacular volcanic landscape that dominates the scenery in the middle reaches of North Fork Shoshone River canyon.

The Clearwater Trail leads above cottonwood- and aspen-lined Clearwater Creek, upon slopes supporting sparse, desert-like vegetation. Good views from the trail reach up to the rugged slopes, cliffs, and pinnacles that typify the scenery in the North Fork.

The trail is smooth and well-defined for 1.1 miles to the first ford of Clearwater Creek. Beyond, the trail enters North Absaroka Wilderness, and becomes obscure and hard to follow. Since that part of the trail lies in the Wilderness, mountain bikers must be sure to go no farther than the first ford.
Description: From the trailhead at 6,040 feet, you make a brief ascent north to a sagebrush-dotted bench. Head north across the bench above Clearwater Creek, soon crossing grassy slopes studded with widely scattered Rocky Mountain junipers.

Ridges of reddish-brown volcanic rock, with cliffs and pinnacles projecting from their slopes, rise above the canyon on three sides. Very little vegetation grows in this rugged landscape, and the rawbacked ridges are fully exposed. The cliffs and pinnacles present an ever-changing scene as you proceed, and you may spy some of the natural arches that are common in the North Fork country.

The creek bottom, in contrast to the somber volcanic rocks that embrace it, supports a shady woodland of aspen, black cottonwood, and Douglas-fir. Up-canyon,

The pleasant, wide Clearwater Creek Trail

the trail eventually edges closer to the creek bottom, where limber pines, Douglas-firs, and conical junipers begin to cloak the trailside slopes.

After 1.0 mile, we dip to the canyon bottom and follow the east bank of Clearwater Creek upstream, winding among the boles of tall aspens and cottonwoods for about 200 yards to a ford of the creek. The creek here is easily crossed via a shin-deep wade, but the trail beyond is unmaintained and hard to follow.

The crossing is a pleasant locale in which to enjoy the shady confines of the canyon, especially on a hot summer day, before retracing the easy, scenic trail back to the trailhead.

Trip 45
BLACKWATER FIRE MEMORIAL TRAIL

Distance: 7.2 miles, round trip.
Low/High Elevations: 6,600'/8,360'.
Difficulty: Moderate.
Use: Moderate.
Suited For: Dayhike.
Best Season: Late June through Sept.
Wildlife Viewing: Good.
Grizzly Bear Danger: Moderate.
Map/Trailhead: 35/41.
Nearest Campgrounds: Rex Hale, 2.4 miles, Newton Creek, 2.6 miles, Clearwater, 7.0 miles, Elk Fork, 9.2 miles, Wapiti, 9.4 miles, Big Game, 10.3 miles, Sleeping Giant, 13.1 miles, Three Mile, 14.2 miles, and Pahaska, 15.3 miles from the trailhead.
Driving to the Trailhead: Follow U.S. 14/16/20 for 35.2 miles west from Cody or 15.6 miles east from the East Entrance to Yellowstone Park, to the prominently signed turnoff to Blackwater Creek Ranch and Blackwater Pond Picnic Ground, 200 yards north of the roadside Fire Memorial turnout.

Follow this dirt road east, reaching the turnoff to the picnic ground after 100 yards. Immediately beyond, the road bridges the North Fork. After crossing the bridge, avoid the left turn leading to Blackwater Creek Ranch, and proceed straight ahead; a sign points to BLACKWATER TRAIL.

Unless you are driving a high-clearance vehicle, either park just beyond the last junction, where there is ample space on the south side of the road; or continue ahead, cross the bridge spanning Blackwater Creek, and park on the south side of the road opposite the ranch's horse corrals, 0.2 mile off the highway. Hikers who park here will add 3.2 miles to the round-trip distance for this trail.

Drivers of high-clearance vehicles can continue up the unmaintained road, which is very narrow, and extremely rough and rocky beyond the horse corrals. You will reach the roadend and a small trailhead parking area 1.8 miles from the highway.

Introduction: This trail, the most scenic and rewarding dayhike in the North Fork area, features cool, peaceful forests, a vigorous mountain stream, and views of alpine plateaus, a large natural arch, and a vast expanse of rugged mountain wilderness. At the trip's end is a stone monument, erected in 1938, in honor of the firefighters who perished in a forest fire here in the summer of 1937.

The trail is easy to follow, the tread is smooth, and uphill grades are moderate.

Description: Hikers without the benefit of a high-clearance vehicle must walk 1.6 miles up the road from Blackwater Creek Ranch, at 6,200 feet, to the roadend and trailhead. The road follows moderate-to-steep grades as it passes through the lower, northern reaches of Blackwater Creek canyon.

From the roadend at 6,600 feet, the trail quickly leads down to a ford of Blackwater Creek, shin-deep and about 12 feet wide, with a gentle current. Beyond the ford, we gently ascend the canyon of Blackwater Creek, passing through a mixed forest of Engelmann spruce, subalpine fir, lodgepole pine, Rocky Mountain juniper, and Douglas-fir. Views from this forest are infrequent, but we do capture glimpses of the blocky tower of 10,874-foot Double Mountain to the southeast.

After walking 1.4 miles avoid a well-worn trail that branches right (uphill), and stay left. After another 100 yards, avoid a second right fork, and 50 yards beyond reach a signed junction. Bear left onto the signed CLAYTON MOUNTAIN TRAIL, and just past the junction reach a rockhop crossing of West Fork Blackwater Creek. Wind eastward for 100 yards to the main stem of Blackwater Creek, at another rockhop crossing.

From the crossing we ascend south up the canyon, at first passing beneath a shady canopy of mixed conifers. A few sun-burnished snags, remnants of trees consumed in the Blackwater Fire of 1937, jut above the shorter lodgepole pines.

At 2.5 miles we curve east and begin ascending a series of switchbacks. Soon dramatic views unfold, reaching south into the headwaters cirque of U-shaped Blackwater Creek valley. On the southeast skyline above the cirque are the lofty summits of Double Mountain and 11,096-foot Coxcomb Mountain. The broken cliffs that rim the alpine tableland of Sheep Mesa bound the cirque to the south and southwest. On the rim of the mesa, just south of Coxcomb Mountain, stands a huge natural arch—shown as Blackwater Natural Bridge on maps—featuring an opening some 200 feet high. In the broad valley below, young light-green lodgepole pines contrast with taller, darker green spruces and firs that escaped the 1937 blaze.

As we ascend the switchbacks, vistas continue to expand, reaching north and west across a landscape of rugged volcanic mountains. After 0.6 mile the switchbacks end and we traverse southeast toward a broad, steep bowl on the northwest flanks of 10,219-foot Clayton Mountain. After another 0.5 mile beyond the switchbacks, we bend into a minor draw—dubbed Clayton Gulch after one of the firefighters lost in the 1937 fire—and soon thereafter reach the Firefighter Monument, at 8,360 feet, 3.6 miles from the roadend.

This superbly crafted, octagonal stone monument features a large brass plaque bearing the names of the eight firefighters who "gave their last full measure of devotion" on August 21, 1937. These men, among the 15 firefighters who lost their lives in the

Blackwater Fire Memorial

1,254-acre fire, succumbed to smoke and flames on that windy August day in the draw just below the monument.

Tall gray snags surround the monument, joined by the renewed growth of smaller lodgepole pines, spruces, subalpine firs, and Douglas-firs. Vistas from this mountainside are breathtaking, encompassing a broad panorama of the Absaroka Range, including cliffs and "badlands," discontinuous forests, vast plateaus, and blocky alpine peaks. Prominent among the dozens of summits in our view are 10,914-foot Monument Mountain, and 11,193-foot Sleeping Giant Mountain, in the north and northwest, respectively. Far to the northwest is the bold crag of 10,267-foot Cody Peak, and beyond that peak, on the crest of the range at the boundary with Yellowstone National Park, is prominent Silvertip Peak, rising to 10,659 feet.

From the Firefighter Memorial, retrace your steps to the trailhead.

Trip 46

PAHASKA TEPEE TO SAM BERRY MEADOW

Distance: 7.2 miles, round trip.
Low/High Elevations: 6,720'/6,850'.
Difficulty: Moderately easy.
Use: Low.
Suited For: Dayhike.
Best Season: Mid-June through Sept.
Wildlife Viewing: Good.
Grizzly Bear Danger: Moderate.
Map/Trailhead: 36/42.
Nearest Campgrounds: Pahaska, 0.3 mile, Three Mile, 0.8 mile, Sleeping Giant, 1.9 miles, Eagle Creek, 4.9 miles, Newton Creek, 12.4 miles, Rex Hale, 13.8 miles, Clearwater, 18.4 miles, Elk Fork, 20.6 miles, Wapiti, 20.8 miles, and Big Game, 21.7 miles from the trailhead.
Driving to the Trailhead: Follow U.S. 14/16/20 for 48.4 miles west from Cody or 2.4 miles east from the East Entrance to Yellowstone

National Park, to the signed turnoff for Pahaska-Sunlight Trailhead. The turnoff is immediately east of the highway bridge spanning North Fork Shoshone River, and 0.2 mile east of Pahaska Tepee lodge.

Drive northwest down the dirt road 0.2 mile to the trailhead parking area next to the river. Two picnic tables, toilets, and a wilderness information sign are located at the trailhead.

Introduction: This fine dayhike follows the broad upper valley of North Fork Shoshone River. The trail involves minimal elevation gain, but is rocky in places as it traces the broad waters of the North Fork.

The forests in this valley were charred by the 319,575-acre Clover-Mist Fire in 1988. The fire, ignited by lightning strikes in Yellowstone National Park, consumed much of the forest cover in the North Absaroka Wilderness between North Fork Shoshone River and Clarks Fork Yellowstone River. As a result of the fire, all the rugged volcanic peaks surrounding the upper North Fork are in full view throughout much of the trip, no longer obscured by dense forest.

Description: From the information sign at the 6,720-foot trailhead proceed northwest on an old road, passing through an open forest of lodgepole pine and Douglas-fir. We amble beneath a power line to the top of a minor rise, where we enjoy a fine view of the wide North Fork meandering through the valley below. Giant Castle Mountain, rising to 10,161 feet, stands boldly on the northwest skyline, and will loom overhead through much of the trip.

Beyond that rise the tread narrows, and we traverse above the river's broad, clear waters. Continuing through the forest, the trail leads away from the river and follows an undulating course and soon enter a forest of charred snags. At 0.6 mile the signed CROW CREEK TRAIL branches left, but we stay right and continue up the valley. Shortly beyond that junction, we have a striking view west to the towering crag of 10,267-foot Cody Peak.

The remainder of the trip passes through a forest of black and gray snags. The entire valley's forests, save for the 9,000-foot ridge on the eastern skyline, were consumed in the 1988 blaze. Trailside slopes, their soil enriched by the fire and now exposed to full sun, support a dense mantle of greenery. Abundant shrubs are here, including wild rose, huckleberry, snowberry, Oregon grape, and a myriad of wildflowers deck the slopes, including wild hollyhock, groundsel, lupine, cinquefoil, sticky geranium, fireweed, blue harebell, and yarrow.

The mildly undulating trail ranges from the grassy banks of the river to the slopes above it. At times we pass above isolated groves of green conifers that somehow managed to escape the heat and flames of the large fire.

At 3.6 miles, just below the broad mouth of west-trending Jones Creek canyon, the oval grassland of Sam Berry Meadow opens up below (west of) the trail. A well-worn path branching left from the main trail here leads 150 yards down to a good packer campsite on the meadow's edge, just above the river.

Green Engelmann spruces and lodgepole pines border the riverbanks here, offering a pleasant terminus for our trip. Two bear-resistant food storage boxes are located in the meadow, but the campsites here are only infrequently used, mostly by hunters in late September and October.

Good views stretch north across the grassy spread to the rugged alpine peaks at the head of the valley. Prominent among the summits are pyramidal Peak 10676 and the red crag of 11,000-foot Grant Peak.

From Sam Berry Meadow, retrace your steps to the trailhead.

SUGGESTED READING

Flora

Arno, Stephen F., and Ramona P. Hammerly, *Timberline, Mountain and Arctic Forest Frontiers*. Seattle: The Mountaineers, 1984.

Craighead, John J., Frank C.Craighead, Jr., and Ray J. Davies, *A Field Guide to Rocky Mountain Wildflowers*. Boston: Houghton Mifflin, 1963.

Despain, Don G., *Yellowstone Vegetation*. Boulder, Colorado: Roberts Rinehart, 1990.

Duft, Joseph F., and Robert K. Moseley, *Alpine Wildflowers of the Rocky Mountains*. Missoula, Montana: Mountain Press, 1989.

Shaw, Richard J., *Plants of Yellowstone and Grand Teton National Parks*. Salt Lake City: Wheelwright Press, 1981.

Shaw, Richard J., *Wildflowers of Grand Teton and Yellowstone National Parks*. Salt Lake City: Wheelwright Press, 1992.

Taylor, Ronald J., *Rocky Mountain Wildflowers*. Seattle: The Mountaineers, 1982.

Taylor, Ronald J., *Sagebrush Country: A Wildflower Sanctuary*. Missoula, Montana: Mountain Press, 1992.

Wildlife

Herrero, Stephen, *Bear Attacks: Their Causes and Avoidance*. New York: Lyons and Burford, 1985.

McEneaney, Terry, *Birds of Yellowstone*. Boulder, Colorado: Roberts Rinehart, 1988.

Peterson, Roger Tory, *A Field Guide to Western Birds*. Boston: Houghton Mifflin, 1961.

Schullery, Paul, *The Bears of Yellowstone*. Worland, Wyoming: High Plains Publishing, 1992.

Geology

Alt, David D., and Donald W. Hyndman, *Roadside Geology of Idaho*. Missoula, Montana: Mountain Press, 1993.

Alt, David, and Donald W. Hyndman, *Roadside Geology of Montana*. Missoula, Montana: Mountain Press, 1986.

Campau, D. E., and H. W. Anisgard, editors, *Billings Geological Society Eleventh Annual Field Conference: West Yellowstone-Earthquake Area*. Billings, Montana: Billings Geological Society, 1960.

Fritz, William J., *Roadside Geology of the Yellowstone Country*. Missoula, Montana: Mountain Press, 1985.

Lageson, David R., and Darwin R. Spearing, *Roadside Geology of Wyoming*. Missoula, Montana: Mountain Press, 1988.

Love, J. D., and Jane M. Love, *Geologic Road Log of Part of the Gros Ventre River Valley Including the Lower Gros Ventre Slide*. Laramie, Wyoming: The Geological Survey of Wyoming, 1988.

History

Blevins, Winfred, *Roadside History Of Yellowstone Park*. Missoula, Montana: Mountain Press, 1989.

Janetski, Joel C., *Indians of Yellowstone Park*. Salt Lake City: Bonneville Books, 1987.

Moulton, Candy, *Roadside History of Wyoming*. Missoula, Montana: Mountain Press, 1995.

Urbanek, Mae, *Wyoming Place Names*. Missoula, Montana: Mountain Press, 1988.

General

Anderson, Bob, *Beartooth Country, Montana's Absaroka and Beartooth Mountains*. Helena, Montana: Montana Magazine, 1984.

Christopherson, Edmund, *The Night the Mountain Fell: The Story of the Montana-Yellowstone Earthquake*. West Yellowstone, Montana: Yellowstone Publications, 1962.

Glick, Dennis, and Mary Carr, Bert Harting, editors, *An Environmental Profile of the Greater Yellowstone Ecosystem*. Bozeman, Montana: Greater Yellowstone Coalition, 1991.

Keiter, Robert B., and Mark S. Boyce, editors, *The Greater Yellowstone Ecosystem: Redefining America's Wilderness Heritage*. New Haven: Yale University Press, 1991.

Moore, Rae Ellen, *Just West of Yellowstone*. Laclede, Idaho: Great Blue Graphics, 1987.

Reeses, Rick, *Greater Yellowstone: The National Park and Adjacent Wildlands*. Helena, Montana: American and World Geographic Publishing, 1991.

Simpson, Ross W., *The Fires of '88: Yellowstone Park and Montana in Flames*. Helena, Montana: American Geographic Publishing, 1989.

Wilkinson, Todd, *Greater Yellowstone National Forests*. Helena and Billings, Montana: Falcon Press, 1991.

Wuerthner, George, *Yellowstone: A Visitor's Companion*. Harrisburg, Pennsylvania: Stackpole Books, 1992.

Legend for Individual Maps

Paved roads	▬▬▬▬	▬▬ ▭ ▬
Improved dirt road		══════
Unimproved dirt road		======
Trail		▬▬▬▬
Cross-country route		· · · · · ·
Trail not covered in this book		– – – – – –
Trip number (large number)		**3**
Trailhead number (small number)		**3**
Campsite		Λ
Year-round stream		⌒
Seasonal stream		⌒
Spring		○~

Map 1

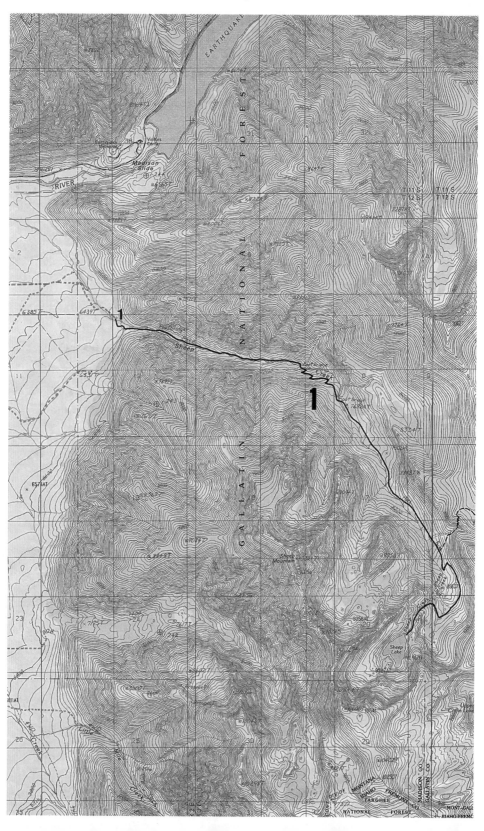

Map 2

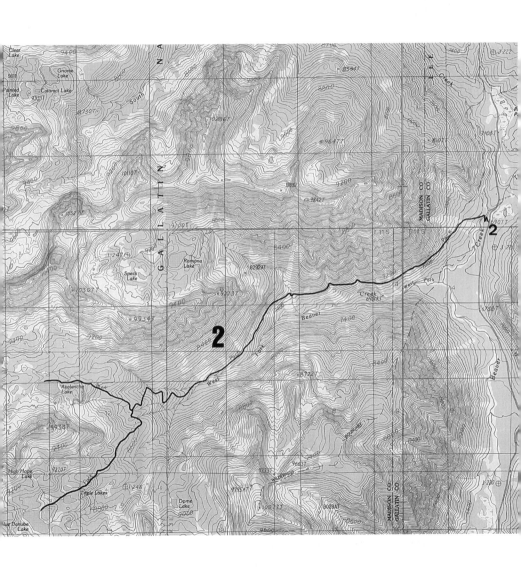

Map 3

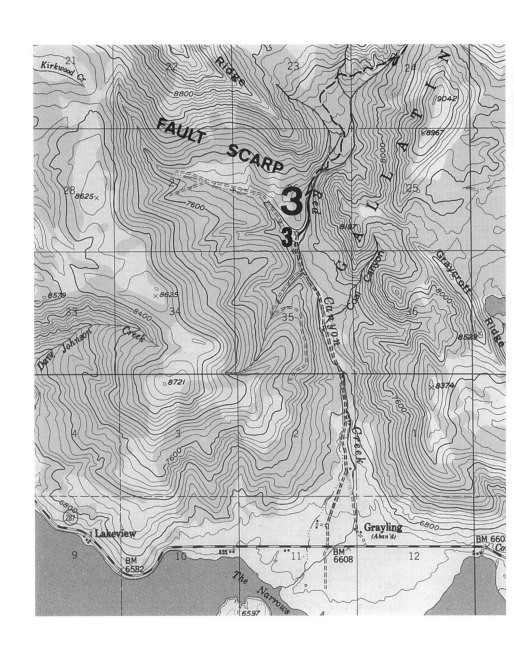

Map 4

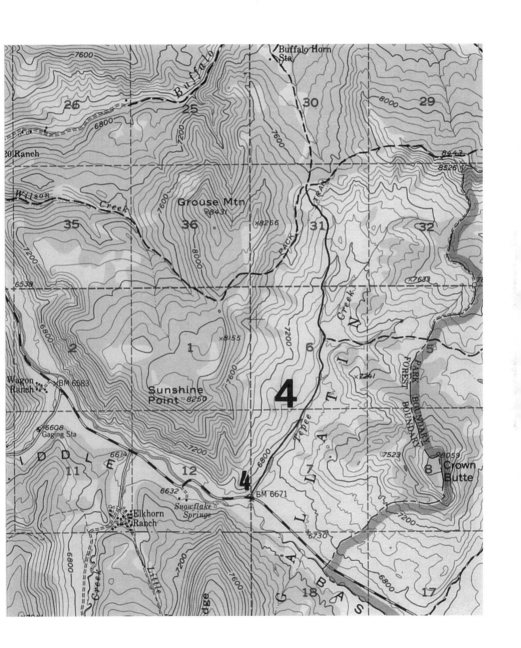

Map 5

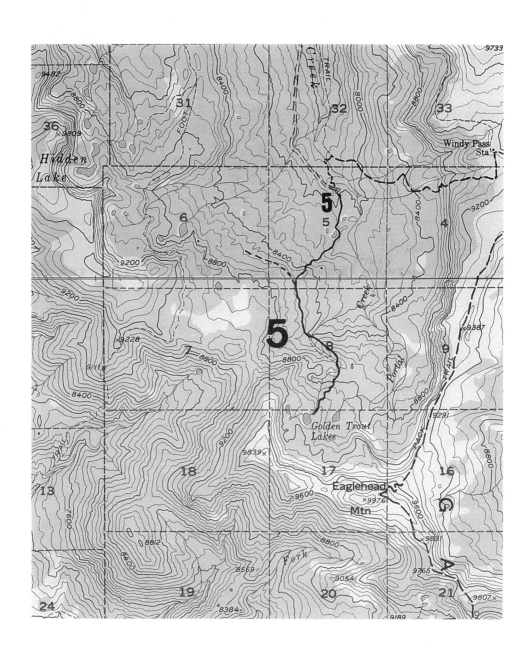

Map 6

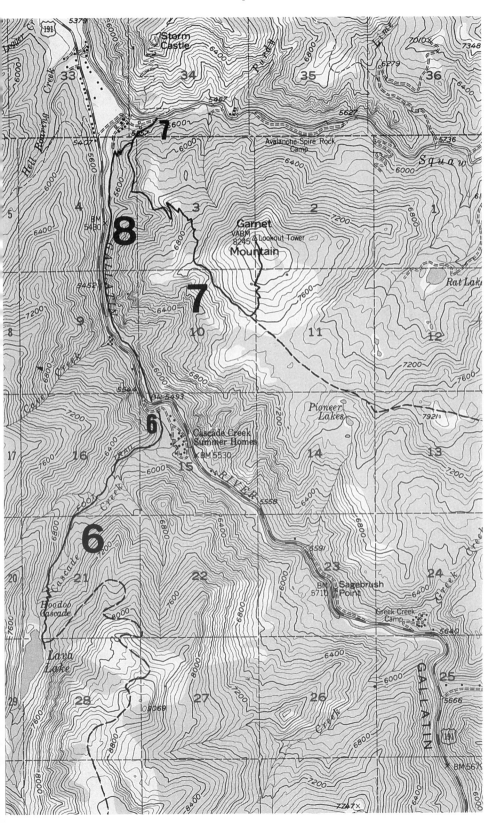

Map 7

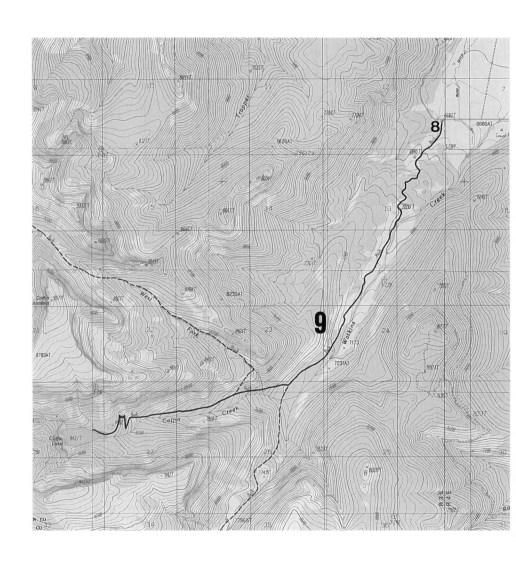

Map 8

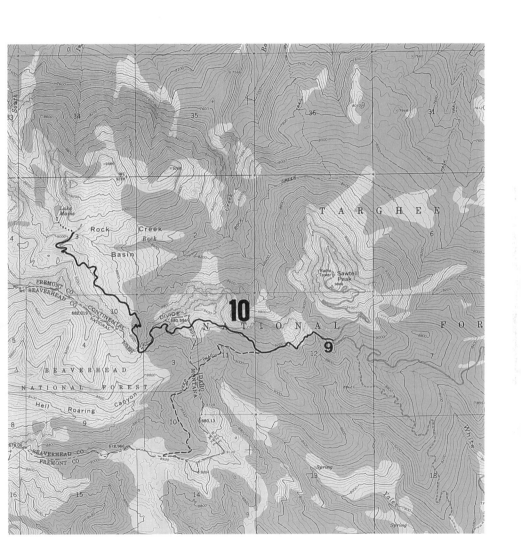

Map 9

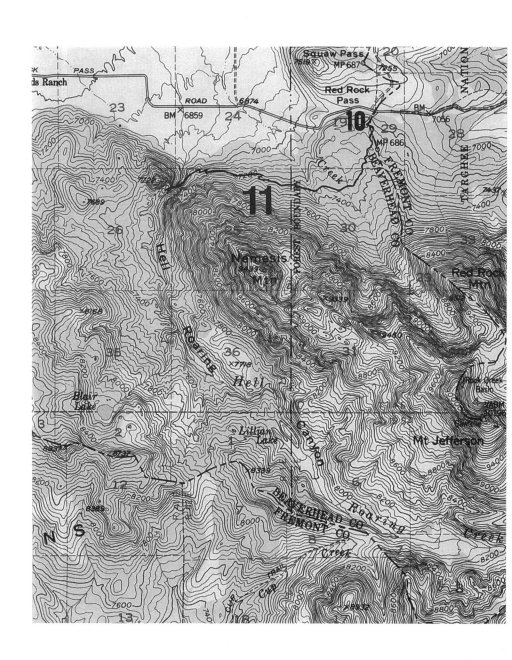

Map 10

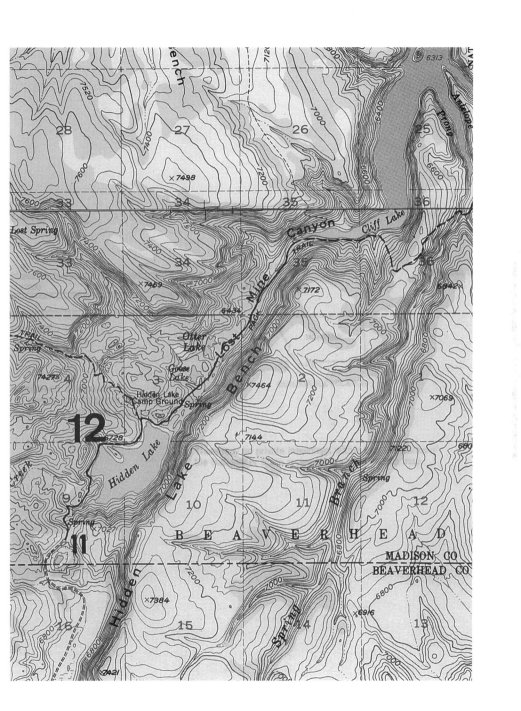

Map 11

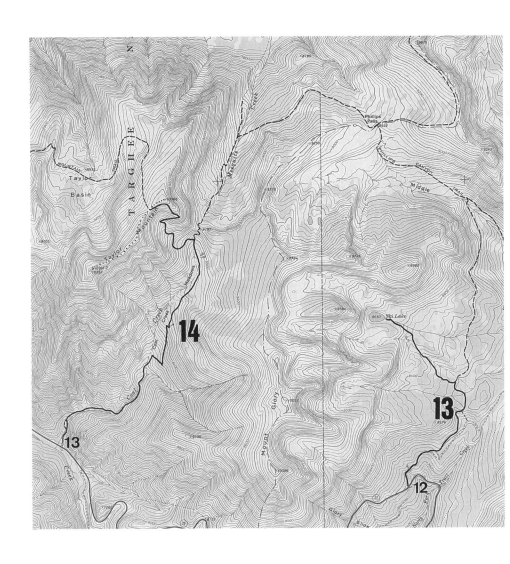

Map 12

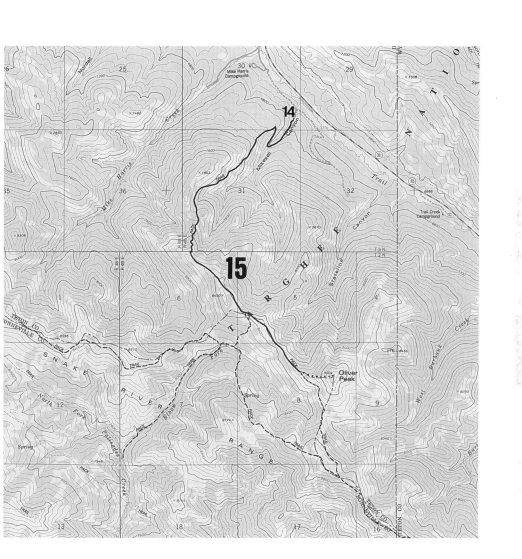

Map 13

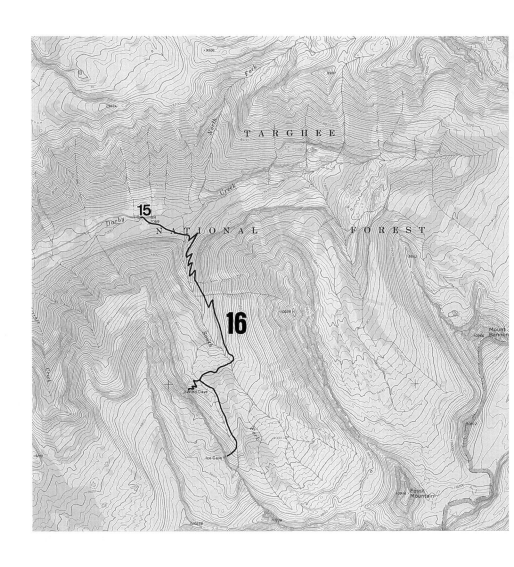

Map 14

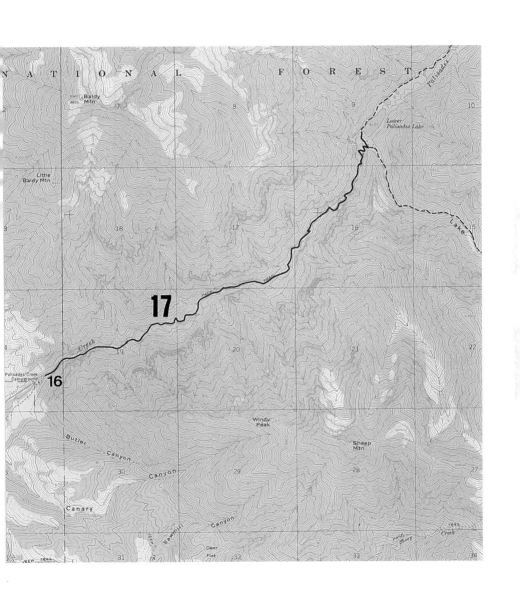

Map 15

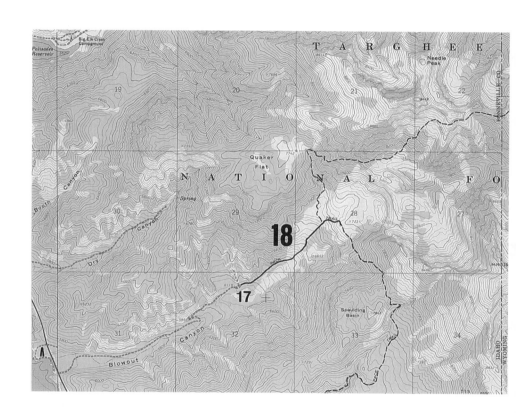

Map 16

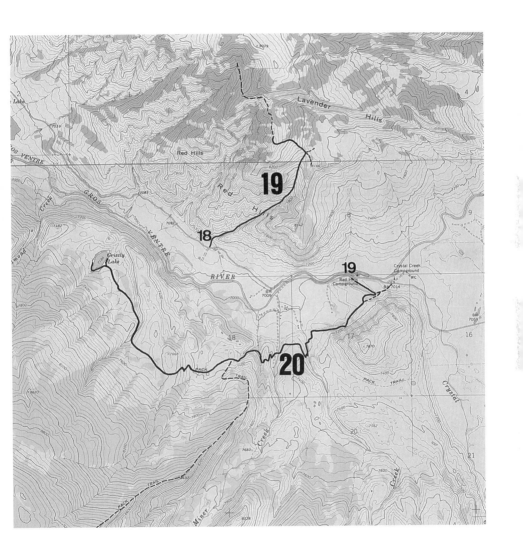

Map 17

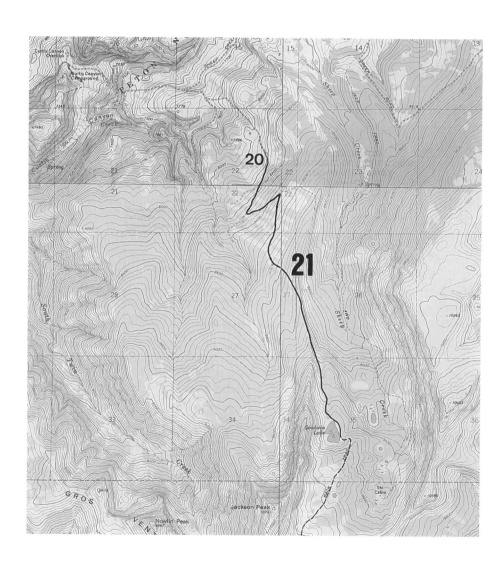

Map 18

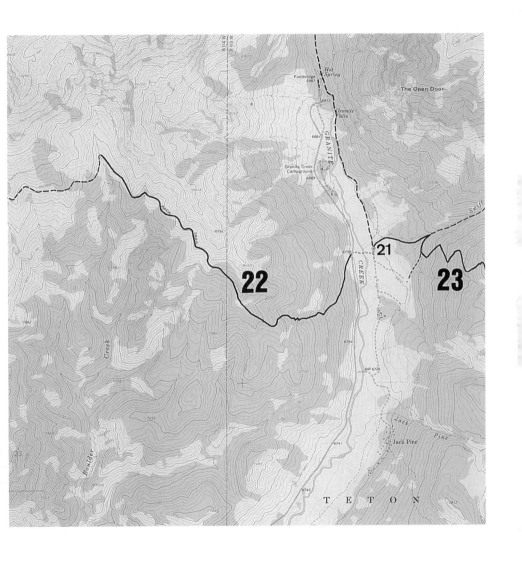

Map 19

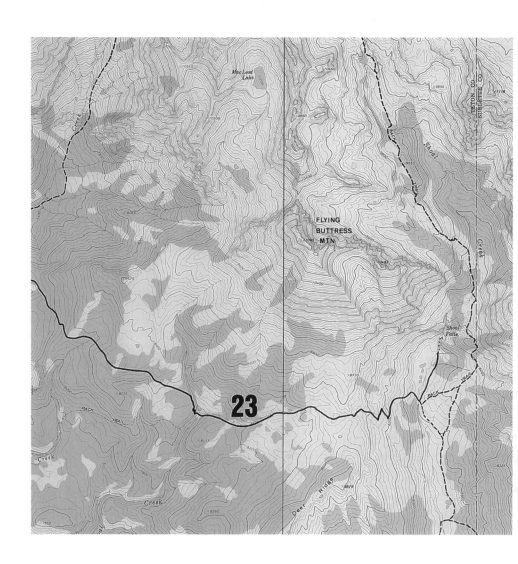

Map 20

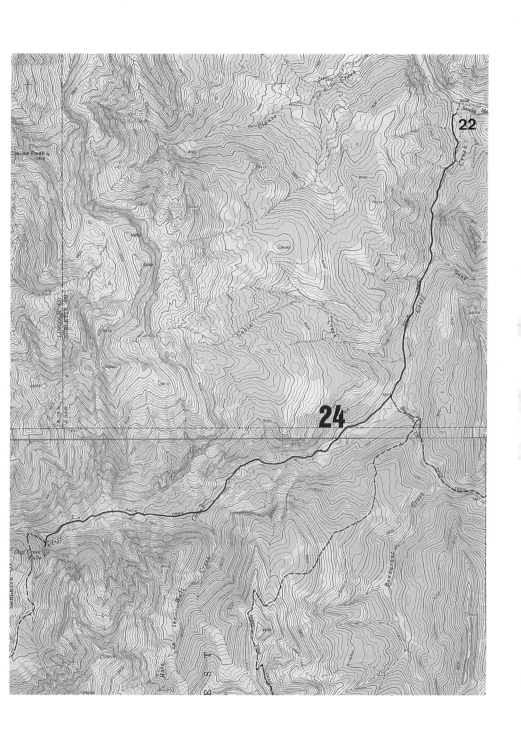

Map 21

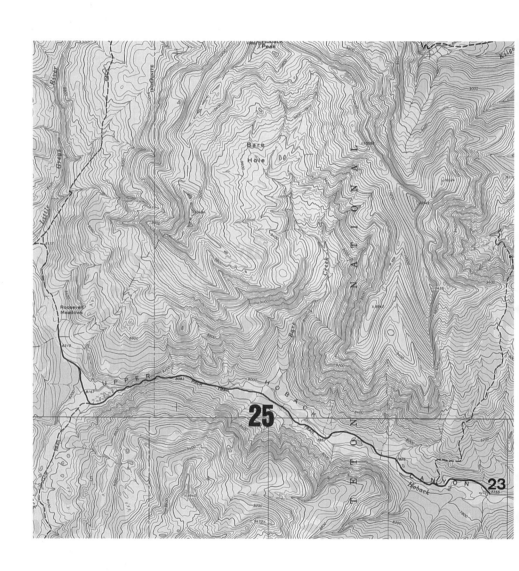

Map 22

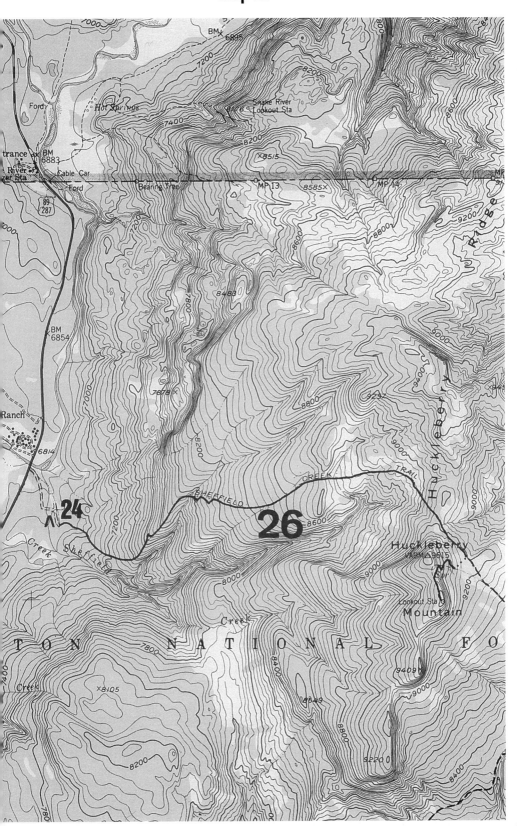

Map 23

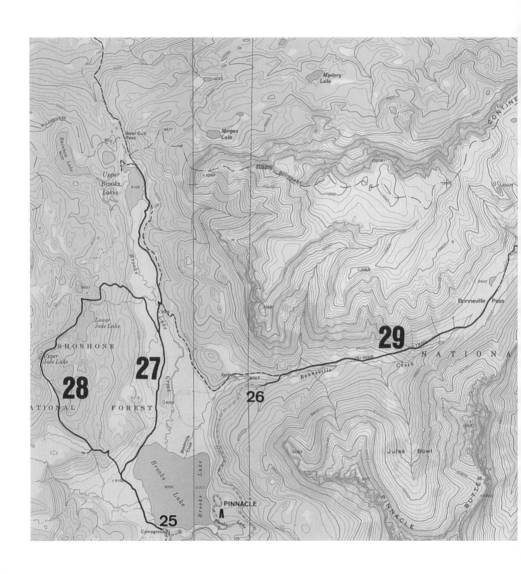

Map 24

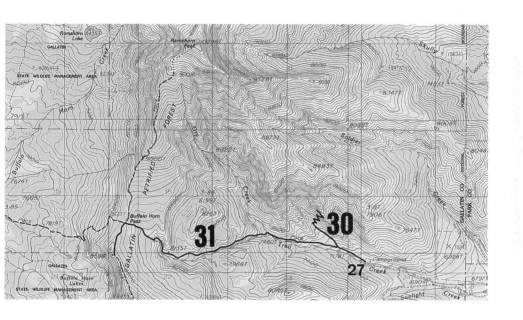

Map 25

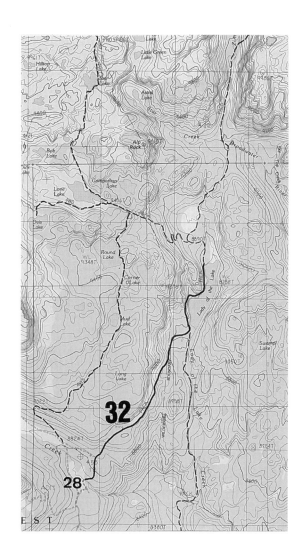

Map 26

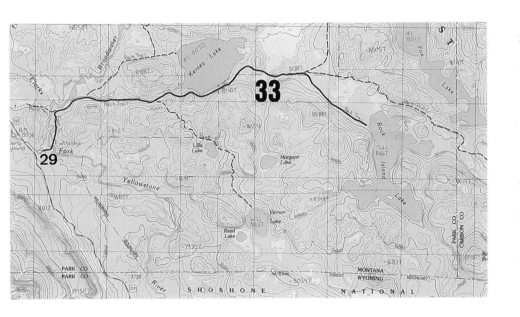

Map 27

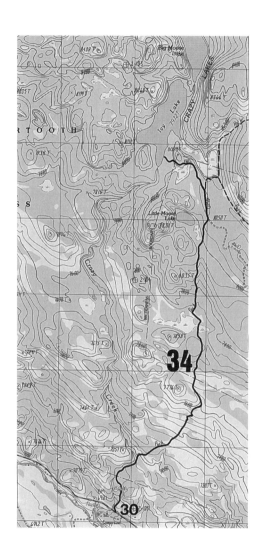

Map 28

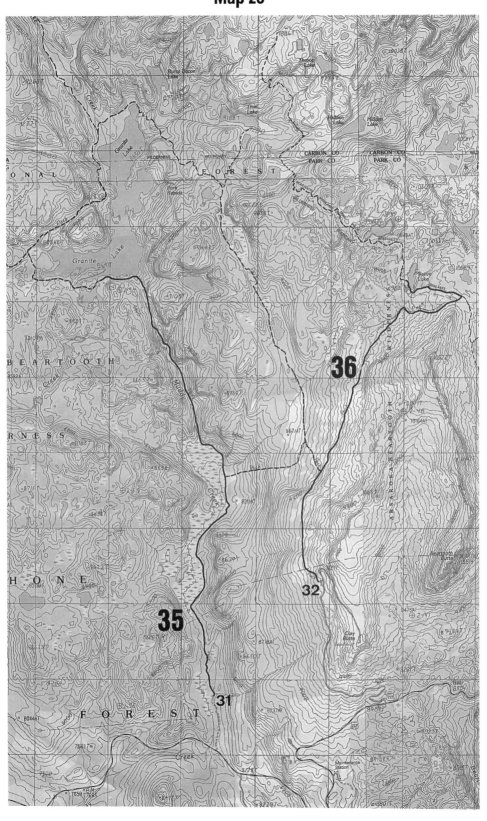

Map 29

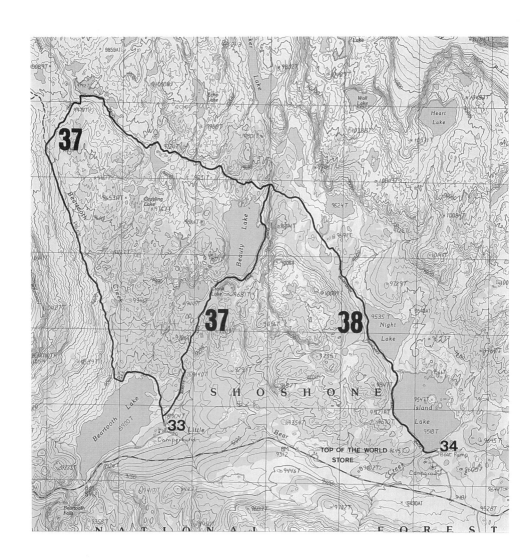

Map 30

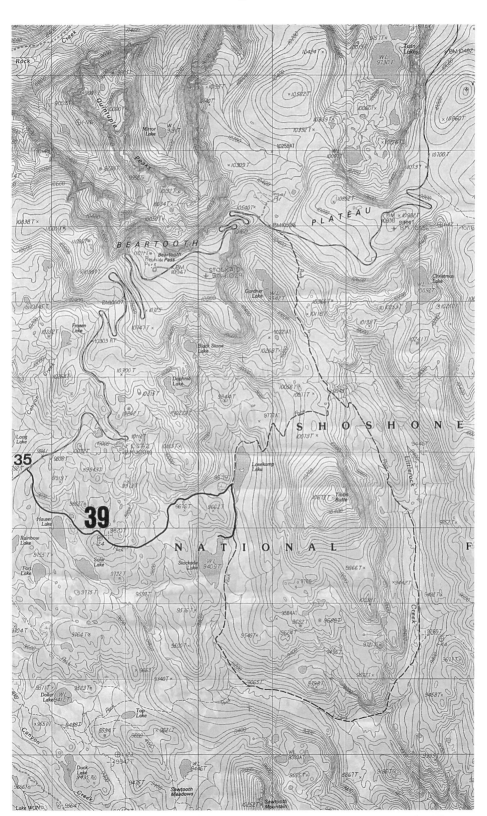

Map 31

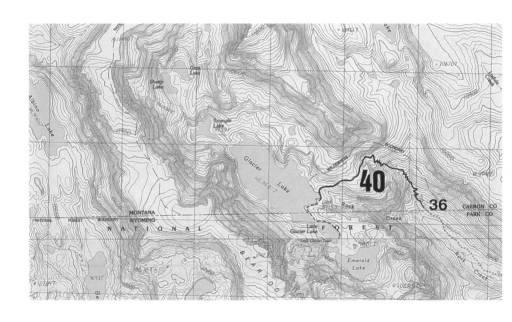

Map 32

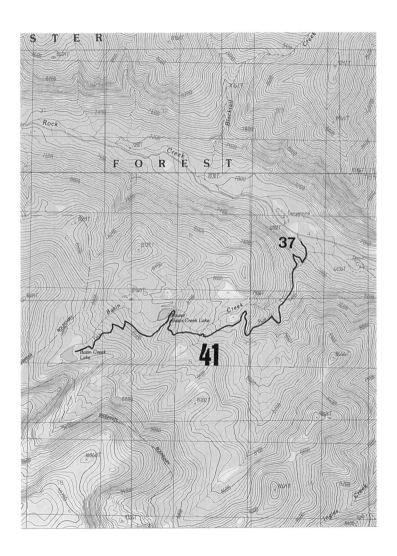

Map 33

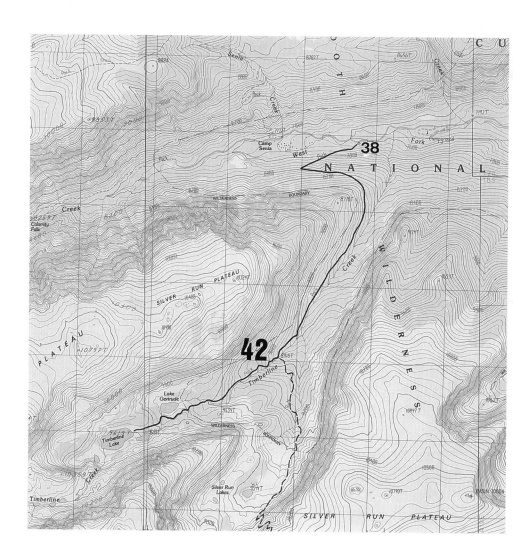

Map 34

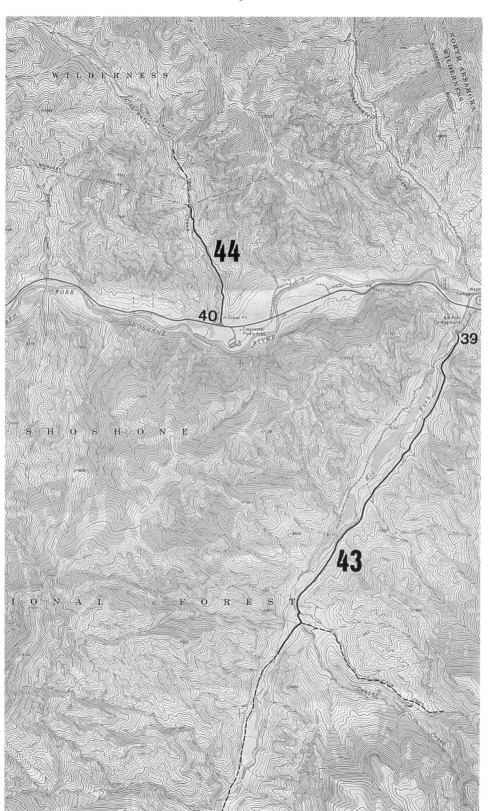

Map 35

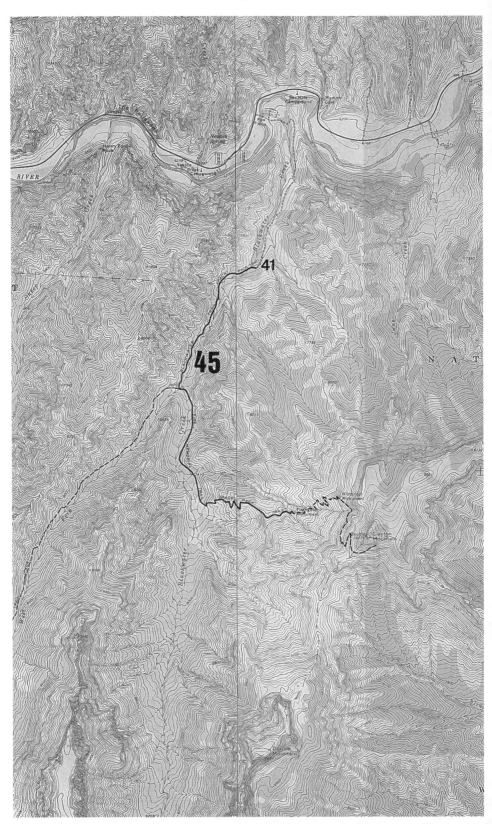

Map 36

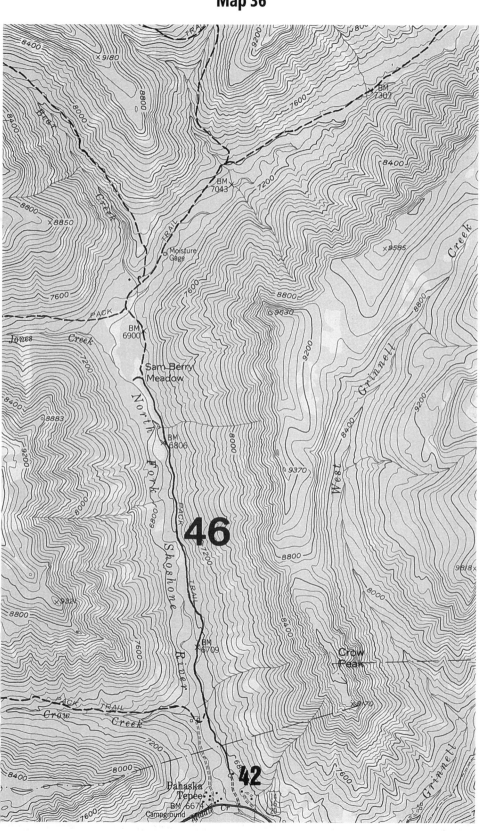

INDEX